The Pensive Image

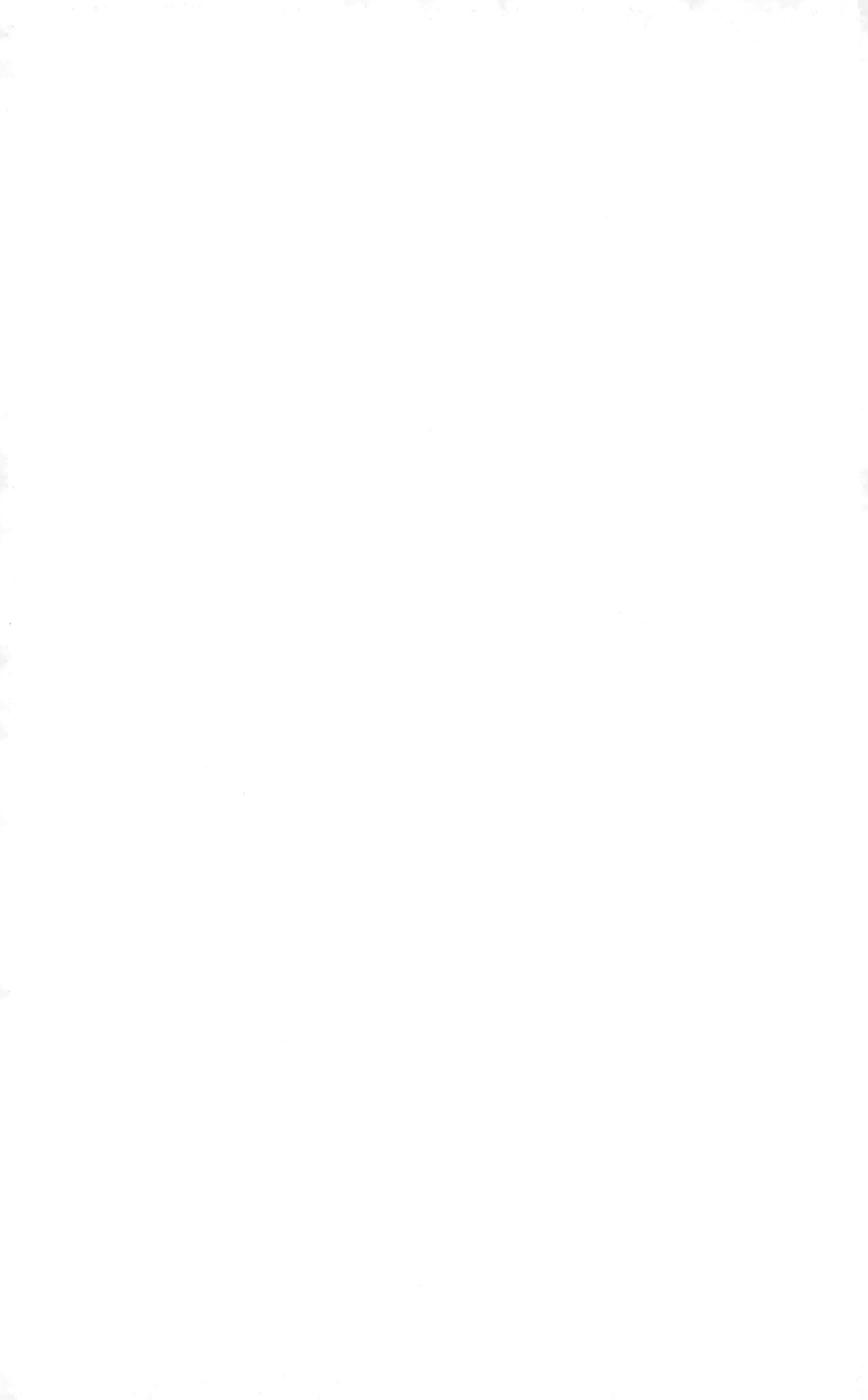

The Pensive Image
Art as a Form of Thinking

HANNEKE GROOTENBOER

THE UNIVERSITY OF CHICAGO PRESS · Chicago and London

The University of Chicago Press, Chicago 60637
The University of Chicago Press, Ltd., London

Published 2020
Paperback edition 2023
Printed in the United States of America

32 31 30 29 28 27 26 25 24 23   1 2 3 4 5

ISBN-13: 978-0-226-71795-1 (cloth)
ISBN-13: 978-0-226-82944-9 (paper)
ISBN-13: 978-0-226-71800-2 (e-book)
DOI: https://doi.org/10.7208/chicago/9780226718002.001.0001

Library of Congress Cataloging-in-Publication Data

Names: Grootenboer, Hanneke, author.
Title: The pensive image : art as a form of thinking / Hanneke Grootenboer.
Description: Chicago ; London : The University of Chicago Press, 2020. | Includes bibliographical references and index.
Identifiers: LCCN 2020030495 | ISBN 9780226717951 (cloth) | ISBN 9780226718002 (ebook)
Subjects: LCSH: Art—Philosophy. | Painting—Philosophy. | Art, Modern—History. | Painting, Modern—History.
Classification: LCC N66 .G76 2020 | DDC 700.1—dc23
LC record available at https://lccn.loc.gov/2020030495

♾ This paper meets the requirements of ANSI/NISO Z39.48-1992 (Permanence of Paper).

True painting, therefore, has not only surprises, but, as it were, calls to us; and has so powerful an effect, that we cannot help coming near it, as if it had something to tell us.

ROGER DE PILES, *THE PRINCIPLES OF PAINTING* (1708)

It is necessary to rid ourselves of the idea that the concept, the content of an artwork, is something already thought, as if it already existed in a prosaic form . . . art has the purpose of bringing a not yet conscious concept to consciousness.

G. W. F. HEGEL, *LECTURES ON AESTHETICS* (1820–1821)

Contents

Art as a Form of Thinking

Why speak of a painting, again? And why write about it? To say what in the end can never have been completely, exhaustively, said; to say just part of it, to retraverse a slice of time in which *that* painting came back like a haunting enigma, a problem, a question; to keep the "minutes" of that traversal, to stockpile the readings done, questioned, revisited, inexhaustible; to produce dazzling, sometimes patient, often inadequate traces of these readings.

LOUIS MARIN, *ON REPRESENTATION*

Thinking involves not only the flow of thoughts, but their arrest as well.

WALTER BENJAMIN

"To think is to see"[1]

In his lecture series *An Introduction to Metaphysics*, delivered in 1935, Martin Heidegger asks, "Why are there beings at all instead of nothing?" For the philosopher, this is the most *original* of questions—he uses the term *Ursprung*—because to raise it means in fact to make a leap (*Sprung*) from the very basis, or ground (*Ur*), of our existence. A thing is a being as it exists—it *is*, Heidegger insists, but where exactly does the Being of this thing lie, or in what does it consist? Are we able to "see" Being? Heidegger seems to suggest we can when he gives one of his typical, rather overburdened examples from the visual arts: "A painting by Van Gogh. A pair of rough peasant shoes, nothing else. Actually, the painting represents nothing. But as to what *is* in that picture, you are immediately alone with it as though you yourself were making your way wearily homeward with your hoe on an evening in late fall after the last potato fires have died down. What *is* there? The canvas? The brush strokes? The spots of color?"[2]

This passage is different than the one that inspired the famous debate involving Meyer Schapiro and Jacques Derrida, and in any case, I want to draw attention to something quite distinct. Heidegger suggests that what *is* in this painting—of what it exists as a painting—cannot be summed up by the canvas or the brushstrokes—or the image itself, for that matter. And yet Heidegger feels "immediately alone with it," connecting the apprehension of this painting's being with his own experience of being. We may not quite "see" Being, but we know where it is going. The painting, in fact, takes the lead. What *is* in this painting is *us* being alone with it, going somewhere with it, or more precisely, being driven by the questions it raises; the painting pushes us forward. In his writings, Heidegger often describes thinking as a pathway. What it means to think, he writes, is that we are underway; thinking gets us through in a movement toward a location that we apparently never seem to reach. To ask the question as to what this painting actually comprises is to philosophize, Heidegger claims. By putting these particular shoes there, this painting is in fact raising the question: Why are *these shoes* there rather than nothing? It also initiates a response by giving us a sense of direction through sending us homeward. Is this painting, in fact, "philosophizing" with us, by getting us through?

In this book, I argue that art is a form of thinking, and that painting is capable of offering us a thought, rather than a meaning or a narrative. That painting can give us a way "into" philosophical issues by offering us as viewers an entrance to its pictorial realm has been a recurring trope in the history of art. In his *Salon* of 1767, Denis Diderot described taking a long promenade through the landscape paintings of Claude-Joseph Vernet (1714–1784). This enthusiastic account of six distinctive "sites" records his excursions through fields and over hills and his experience of breathtaking vistas.[3] Diderot even mentions his small talk with the locals and enters into a Socratic dialogue with a tutor—only to reveal, at the end of his forty-three-page ramble, that all this time he has been standing in front of Vernet's pictures in the Louvre.

Diderot builds on a medieval tradition in which meditative images evoked forms of prayer comprising various mnemonic and affective processes that were meant to lead one away from bodily existence toward a more spiritual state so as to fashion oneself in Christ's image.[4] Landscapes as well as interior paintings, serving as essential aids for this sort of practice, provided meditative itineraries and spiritual maps by which viewers could shape their inner selves.[5] Not only were viewers instructed to emulate the actions of donors depicted in many of these paintings and join in their devotion, but they were invited "into" paintings to dwell in their interiors alongside, for instance, the Virgin Mary.

In Pieter Stevens's *Wooded Landscape* (1614; plate 1), created at the tail end of this tradition, we as viewers are situated "in" this vast landscape, as if plowing our way through it, just like the pilgrim in the foreground who strides on, staff in hand, toward higher regions marked by a makeshift shrine high on a rock. The landscape is so dense that our eyes need to adapt to the picture's darkness to behold the myriad pathways we can travel, encountering the ersatz shelters where we may pause on our journey. We almost get lost in this landscape, which is all the more surprising because the picture measures only 6.9 × 12.8 cm. Stevens painted this scene on one side of a playing card (the reverse shows a knight on horseback), which makes this a pocket-painting suitable to be carried along, for instance, within the pages of a prayer book. Serving as a visual aid for meditation on life's pilgrimage, this card may have traveled with its bearer and alternately may have accompanied long journeys of the mind and spirit.[6]

We might say that Van Gogh's painting represents Heidegger's philosophical alternative to such meditative religious imagery—after all, the philosopher saw Christianity and philosophy to be mutually exclusive enterprises. Following Heidegger to this extent, I argue that artworks are deeply engaged with philosophical issues, and as such operate at the intersection of philosophy, history, and theory—but not necessarily theology. Even though Christian theology permeated all aspects of early modern life, and much philosophy (and science for that matter) was imbued with Christian spirituality, my project, in contrast, is situated within the realm of secular visual thinking.

In her brilliant *The Art of Philosophy: Visual Thinking in Europe from the Late Renaissance to the Early Enlightenment*, Susanna Berger argues that visual representation became increasingly important for the explanation of philosophical ideas in the early modern period. Dealing with large, printed broadsides used for teaching Aristotelian thought, she convincingly demonstrates that definitions and concepts were often understood as being contained "in" those images. Diverging from studies on the role of imagery in early modern thought that have often concentrated on theology, Berger instead focuses on the links connecting image-making, knowing, and thinking in the (secular) tradition of Aristotelian education. The philosopher is known for his reliance on images; in *On Memory*, he claims that thinking is impossible without them.[7] He also likened the contrast between clear and cloudy (or aging) memory to stronger or weaker wax impressions, a metaphor positing that memory should literally be found "in" the image. This idea was ultimately taken up by Freud in his notion of the mind as a mystic writing pad.

With Berger, I contribute to a more fully worked out case for visual thinking and its impact on the history of art by offering the view that painting is exceptionally well suited to shape thought. As early as the sixteenth century, Giordano Bruno (1548–1600) declared that true painting was, in fact, philosophy, and the seventeenth-century artist and theorist Samuel van Hoogstraten (1627–1678) claimed as much when he stated that painting and philosophy are sister arts.[8] I have argued elsewhere that the seventeenth-century still life can be regarded as the most philosophical of pictorial genres; landscapes in devotional works, as we have seen, direct the mind toward introspection rather than interpretation, and portraits have been considered to represent theories of subjectivity. Nevertheless, the sense that art and thought are intertwined is a notion that was gradually disregarded after the seventeenth century, and by the nineteenth century, when aesthetics came under the dominion of philosophy, the gap between the two realms had stretched so wide that only a few bridges were left. One of the main questions that inspired this study is why aesthetics was annexed by philosophy and never found a real foothold within the history of art. The disciplines of art history and philosophy have largely neglected painting's capacity to offer up a thought. But artists themselves have never lost sight of their practice as a mode of thinking. I will give a few obvious examples by means of a brief history.

"Picture galleries house only thoughts"[9]

The history of the idea that painting and philosophy are comparable practices reaches all the way back to antiquity. Unsurprisingly, Nicolas Poussin (1594–1665) is one of the most prominent painter-philosophers in the history of art. This learned artist, who advised his viewers to "read the story and the picture," has inspired some of the best art-historical writing by Erwin Panofsky, Louis Marin, and T. J. Clark (which, I insist, testifies to the philosophical depth of Poussin's work). Poussin visualized much of his art theory in his practice; however, he also formulated many of his ideas in correspondence with his friend, art collector, and patron Paul Fréart de Chantelou (1609–1694), often mentioning that he was working on the "thought" (*la pensée*) of a particular painting. In 1647 he wrote, "I have found [my commissioner] the thought, that is to say the conception of the idea, and the work of the mind has been completed."[10] Reminiscent of the notion of the *pensiero* as well as Bernini's *concetto*, *la pensée* seems to be not an invention or idea as such but rather a forethought, which has led Thomas Puttfarken to argue that it may refer to an *aspect*, a particular mode of seeing.[11]

As a painter and a thinker, Poussin exerted a huge influence on the history of art. In late nineteenth-century French artistic circles, he was very much in vogue, celebrated by Van Gogh and others.[12] Of the artists who revered him at the time, Paul Cézanne was probably most spiritually akin to Poussin and sought to paint landscapes that would "re-do Poussin over again according to nature."[13] Cézanne liked doing "a little theory himself" as young writer Joachim Gasquet, visiting him in Aix-en-Provence, observed. Known for his enigmatic utterances, Cézanne remarked at one point that "the landscape thinks itself in me, and I am its consciousness."[14] Maurice Merleau-Ponty was quick to pick up on Cézanne's intriguing oeuvre and his provocative statements. Not only did Merleau-Ponty write about the artist's obsession with the view of Mont Sainte-Victoire from his studio window (of which hundreds of drawings, watercolors, and paintings survive), he also took some of Cézanne's paintings as a support for his groundbreaking phenomenology of perception. Differently formulated, Cézanne's paintings *were* the leading argument of his logic of sensation.[15] Moving ahead in time from Cézanne, Poussin played a significant role in the practice of Giorgio de Chirico as well, who produced a corpus of sometimes rather Poussinesque "metaphysical paintings," through which he established an aesthetics in pictorial terms.[16] Meanwhile, in Germany, Paul Klee intended to create a visual mode of thinking, in his pedagogical writings entitled *The Thinking Eye* (1922–1924) as well as in the rest of his works, which were to become the main source for Deleuze and Guattari's claim that art is a mode of thought.[17]

Adorno once wrote that "art stands in need of philosophy that interprets it in order to say that which it cannot say, whereas art is only able to say what it says by not saying it."[18] In this book I will take the opposite stance, arguing that it is *philosophy* that needs art to say what it cannot say. Philosophers—among them Descartes, Herder, and Merleau-Ponty—have implied that philosophy needs images in order to articulate complex constellations of ideas that cannot be formulated in words. Such thought-images contribute to thinking, or rather, they form an encounter that makes us think. Privileging thinking over philosophy, Heidegger asserts that raising this most original of questions—"Why there are beings instead of nothing?"—is an act, a *happening*. People often say that we cannot *do* anything with philosophy, he writes, but they have remained unaware that in the end it is *philosophy* that does something *to us*. Heidegger's example of Van Gogh indicates that philosophy can do something to us *through* a work of art: it makes us feel alone with it, poses questions to us, hits us, arrests us in our course, while driving us home.

This book argues that art indeed *does* something to us by generating such a happening, for instance, by raising questions, or by presenting us with a fundamental *encounter* that forces us to think rather than offering us something beautiful, expressive, or moralistic. I intend to make a case for a new category of artworks determined by their capacity to generate such "happenings," which I propose to call *pensive images*. I claim that due to their density and self-awareness, pensive images can—surprisingly—articulate complex ideas in visual terms, and as such they actively contribute to the ongoing creation of concepts.

I borrow the term "pensive" from Roland Barthes. In *Camera Lucida*, Barthes recounts the well-known story about André Kertész's clash with an editor of *Life* magazine in 1936 over a series of photographs. The editor rejected the series because Kertész's photographs "spoke too much," voicing a meaning that transcended any literal interpretation. Barthes concludes that Photography (with a capital P) is subversive "not when it frightens, repels, or even stigmatizes, but when it is *pensive*, when it thinks."[19] He further theorizes photography's capacity to be pensive by his juxtaposition between the much-discussed (and misused) notions of the *studium* and the *punctum*: while the *studium* is the punch line, the intended meaning "in" a photograph that we "get," the *punctum* is for Barthes something that *gets us*, that reaches out and touches us, that makes us *see* something that, although it is *in* the picture, is not explicitly part of the display. This is something that the viewer "adds" to a photograph, which is nonetheless already there. In an essay entitled "The Pensive Image," Jacques Rancière summarizes Barthes's explanation through a reading of Rineke Dijkstra's beach portraits and concludes that for Barthes the pensive image is an image of suspended activity.[20]

Whereas Barthes and Rancière reserve the term "pensive image" mostly for works of photography and literature, I apply it to a larger corpus of artwork. These works are united by the way they throw something at us as viewers that remains outside our known modes of interpretation, outside the fields of knowledge or history. For Barthes, this "something" stops us in our tracks and makes us ponder, and when it happens, *that* is the moment we start "adding" to an artwork. The gesture of "adding" to a picture happens in the time it takes to find in the movement of our gaze what has been hindering it, what has startled us. This arrest, apparently caused by some prickling detail, and the time we take lingering over what precisely caused it, that moment of wonder—that, for him, is where *pensiveness* can be found in an image.[21] Going beyond Barthes, I would define pensive images as those that confront us in such a way that our wondering *about* the work of art—its subject of meaning—is transformed into our thinking *according to it*. Just as Van Gogh's painting was for Heidegger a moment of solitude that enabled him to find a way home, pensive images stop us in our tracks so as to spin our thoughts in a different direction, leaving us slightly dazzled. We are not sure whether the thoughts we found are in our own heads or in the painting. Certain paintings can be full of thoughts, but it will be unclear who exactly is thinking them; even so, they will initiate a movement, not toward the things we do *not yet know* (that is where interpretation takes us) but rather toward the realm of the *not yet thought*. Along with being founded on the ideas of Heidegger, Barthes, and Rancière, the idea of the pensive image owes a debt to the closely related notion of *Denkbild* in the writings of Walter Benjamin. A literary miniature that we could call a prose poem, the *Denkbild* is meant to evoke a picture that provides us with theoretical insight—it can speak of that which one cannot speak.[22]

If we would be more open to an artwork's touch, if we would listen more carefully to what it has to say, we might perceive the glimmerings of a new methodology that would slowly pull us *away* from interpretation and toward a state of suspension where thinking can take place. One of my main objectives is to initiate a (re)discovery of art history's philosophical foundations that would enable the emergence of a "philosophical art history"—invoked by Panofsky, yet never systematically explored.

A Philosophical Art History

Over the past few decades, painting's philosophical potential has been touched on within art-historical discourse without being merged into a new, workable methodology. For instance, Yve-Alain Bois, in *Painting as Model*, explores whether painting can "think" in modernist art; Svetlana Alpers and Michael Baxandall's *Tiepolo and the Pictorial Intelligence* considers the intersection of thought in painting, as is evident from their book's title. In *Quoting Caravaggio: Contemporary Art, Preposterous History*, Mieke Bal claims that Caravaggio's paintings "think," and Ernst van Alphen makes an analogous argument about contemporary art in *Art in Mind: How Contemporary Images Shape Thought*. These works have been inspired to greater and lesser degrees by Hubert Damisch's unprecedented *The Origin of Perspective*, which argues that linear perspective provides artists with a pictorial grammar through which statements in painting can be made. Damisch raises the question of what is thinking in painting, and what would be the implications of such "thinking" for the history of thought.[23] This book is in part an answer to that question.

These and other pioneering works have caused a shift in art-historical writing characterized by a move beyond the understanding of early modern art as historical document or evidence of artistic self-expression. New approaches informed by (visual) anthropology and material culture studies redirected the focus of attention from an artwork's meaning to its function. Artworks no longer wait patiently to be interpreted by knowledgeable critics or scholars; they are now considered to be actively contributing to our experiences, anticipating our approaches or intervening in our actions. Caroline van Eck sees artworks as excessive objects operating as living presences, while Horst Bredekamp, who has coined the term *Bildakt*, credits them with agency and the ability to act. In *The Anthropology of Images: Picture, Medium, Body*, Hans Belting argues that we should separate art from the images that art-making produces. He claims that our bodies each serve as a medium onto which these images can be projected, and, as such, shapes our relations to self and world. In contrast to the approach of Belting and others, Matthew Hunter and Francesco Lucchini sought to reclaim art history as a discipline of objects rather than images. In an edited volume of *Art History* entitled *The Clever Object*, they introduce a new category of things that differ from more high-minded, "intelligent" artworks (they use Thomas Crow's *The Intelligence of Art* as their frame of reference). The editors successfully made this category all-inclusive to abolish distinctions among geographical areas or periods, and "clever object" is a winning term. However, the sheer diversity of objects under discussion somehow resist any clear definition of what clever objects are, what they are capable of, and what one is supposed to do with their label. The editors remain equally inclusive with regard to the clever object's possible predecessors but make no clear distinctions among theoretical, self-aware, knowing, excessive, visual, or material objects, which leaves this new category entirely unspecific and, as a result, difficult to apply.

Though their project is refreshing and stimulating, my approach will be different in that I intend to make a distinct case for a specific group of pensive images. My larger argument is that art is a form of thinking, but within the scope of this book, I focus on pensive *painting* or, more precisely, on a series of specific paintings that deeply engage with philosophical issues through their capacity to ask questions that possess a simplicity similar to Heidegger's "Why are there beings rather than nothing?" Even though I venture into areas like film studies and photography to radically distinguish the pensive image from other types of imagery, I consider my project to be a continuation of the legacy of scholars who have attempted to philosophize early modern painting, such as Christine Buci-Glucksmann, Daniel Arasse, Louis Marin, Eliane Escoubas, and Sarah Kofmann. My focus on pensive paintings gains new relevance in the context of the recent "revival" of contemporary painting as transitive and performative, or a kind of reenactment that reaches beyond its own limitations, as David Joselit claims in his influential essay "Painting Beside Itself." The Tate Modern exhibition *A Bigger Splash: Painting after Performance*, curated by Catherine Wood in 2012–2013, and the 2011 symposium "Thinking Through Painting: Reflexivity and Agency beyond the Canvas," organized by Isabelle Graw, Daniel Birnbaum, and Nikolaus Hirsch, further testify to contemporary painting's new direction.[24] Like these publications and events, I recognize in my close analysis of early modern artworks a kind of profundity, an interiority that differs from meaning, narrative, or critique, and through which these images become not so much clever or intelligent as *thoughtful*—one might even say, in a Hegelian way, self-conscious.

It is important to differentiate the notion of the pensive image from similar terms crediting painting with profundity, which have been fundamental in developing my thoughts. For instance, Victor Stoichita, in his modern classic *The Self-Aware Image: An Insight into Early Modern Meta-Painting*, considers pictorial self-awareness as a heightened sense of self-reflexivity. For Stoichita, painting is self-reflexive not because it merely plays with its limitations in an attempt to overcome them but because its very development as painting results from this continuous conflict with its boundaries. Through unremitting negotiations with its limits, painting permanently comments on its own nature as medium and status as representation. Stoichita's brilliant argument stands at the basis of my project, as it has inspired many ideas I pose here, and I wish to add to the direction of a theoretical or philosophical art history that he has initiated. However, I will further explore the subtle differences among various self-aware paintings in order to demonstrate that their concerns sometimes lie "beside themselves," as Joselit would have it, namely in the realm of philosophy. Even though some may be, not all pensive images are instances of meta-painting. On the contrary, a pensive image denotes not so much a self-referential commentary as a more indeterminate state of pondering in which the thought as such may largely remain unresolved. In contrast to "intelligent" images, pensive images are neither witty nor knowledgeable. Instead, they are filled with thought.

In his essay "The Boy in Bed: The Scene of Reading in N. C. Wyeth's *Wreck of the Covenant*," Alexander Nemerov describes a form of reading the image as a manifestation of the desire to show "what an image does that it does not know it is doing."[25] Compared to Stoichita's self-aware image in charge of its own commentaries, Nemerov's image can be said to be almost immature and in need of scholars to interpret it. In this light, my definition of pensive images takes Stoichita's insights to a new extreme by allowing painting to throw off the tutelage of art-historical modes of interpretation in order to start "thinking" for itself. Pensive images, I argue, prompt us to settle their indeterminacy and in doing so, they depart from the demanding or desiring pictures as explored by W. J. T. Mitchell in the tellingly entitled *What Do Pictures Want? The Lives and Loves of Images*. We are invited to settle things on the image's terms rather than our own.

The notion of the pensive image is also linked to the theoretical object, a term coined by Hubert Damisch and Louis Marin in the 1970s. For Damisch, perspective is a "theoretical object" that produces discourse around it, in the past as well as in the present; it was as fundamental a topic for Alberti as for Panofsky and remains the focus around which theories on vision or painting are spun. Marin seems to put forth a slightly narrower take by evoking it within an art-historical context and applying it to particularly enigmatic paintings such as Giorgione's *The Tempest* (c. 1504)[26] that raise tensions unable to be tempered or solved; as such, they have remained at the center of interpretive debates for generations. Other obvious examples of such text-producing paintings include Velázquez's *Las Meninas* (1656) and Jan van Eyck's *Arnolfini Portrait* (1434) and Annunciation paintings.[27] In her book on Doris Salcedo's political art, *Of What One Cannot Speak*, Mieke Bal translates the term to contemporary art by claiming that the artist as such will be her theoretical object. Like theoretical objects, pensive images raise philosophical issues but are, I suggest, more modest in operation. Whereas *Las Meninas* remains a dominant, awe-inspiring, and somehow very talkative artwork, pensive images are mostly quiet—shy, even—as they hide at the margins of art's history or in the corners of museum displays. They do not often find themselves at the center of art-historical debate but invite us to listen to them quietly. Only then might something be happening, a closing-in of the world when we feel alone with the work, when it becomes a touchstone for our thinking *about* our thinking; our encounter with it is an intensely private activity. Indeed, as we will see, one of the pensive image's main characteristics is stillness, a productive silence.

In addition, the continuing attraction of *The Tempest*, and for that matter Poussin's *Landscape with a Man Killed by a Snake* (1648), lies in the way they can revive our impulse to interpret, to talk about it, to produce text. Whereas a theoretical object is text producing, the pensive image does not exactly produce anything but rather sets something in motion. Its role is primarily enabling. It may make possible a journey or form a site where one can be alone with it, a quiet zone where certain ontological issues linger; it may establish the conditions for a surprise encounter by throwing something at us, much like Barthes's *punctum* does, or by offering us a direction that we are compelled to follow. The pensive image does not invite interpretation but defies it; instead of producing text, it articulates what goes beyond any textual response. It offers us a "happening" with no code to be cracked. As a result, it sets us on a course of thinking that starts not with us but with the image, and it remains undetermined and inexpressive. Once we are set on this course of thinking we wonder how we got there, and where we are going.

Instead of giving us grounding, it sends us floating. This is what the pensive image does. It puts us off guard.

Within the larger scope of this project, the pensive image serves as a vehicle through which we examine the ways that thinking is conflated with critique, theory, and philosophy by asking what role might painting, as a form of thinking, play in disentangling these overlapping undertakings.[28] Whereas Stoichita's self-aware image evokes criticism (in a Kantian way), and the theoretical object produces theory, the pensive image contributes to philosophy as (offering) a mode of thinking. Though clearly fitting into the larger picture of self-reflexive imagery, perhaps its closest relation is Benjamin's *Denkbild*, or thought-image, those short compositions mostly concerned with the mundane events of everyday life, that have their roots in seventeenth-century Dutch baroque art. It is partly for this reason that seventeenth-century Dutch painting provides the starting point of this study's explorations. Another reason is that Dutch painting celebrates everyday life at its most ordinary, as if repeatedly asking Heidegger's question why there are beings rather than nothing. Here is where my exploration starts.

The Case against Modernism

Seventeenth-century Dutch art is particularly suitable for my explorations because, as Mariët Westermann and more recently Thijs Weststeijn aptly observe, Dutch visual culture was utterly worldly in the sense that even its strong Calvinist ideology was often implemented in a pragmatic way.[29] The political system of the Low Countries was a republic, and the exuberant wealth resulting from its trade with the West and East Indies was bestowed on burghers (civilians), not members of an aristocracy or a preestablished elite. Various scholars have emphasized the often subdued role religion played in cultural expressions, as opposed to a more forceful secular or civil stance. Ed Snow also observes a strong secular undercurrent in Vermeer's *Woman Holding a Balance* (1664) that he presents as an exemplary instance of such a contrast between theology and worldliness. He reads the painting-within-the-painting of the *Last Judgment* not as a statement of the woman's vanity (as it commonly assumed) but as indicating the failure of the theological tradition to overcome her composed, worldly self-presence and her diminishment of otherworldly eschatologies. "Her serenity stands as a refutation not only of the polemics of an older theology but of the dualism of modern philosophy," writes Bryan Wolf in his discussion of Snow.[30]

Further examples of such triumphs over theology can be found in the hugely successful emblem books including those by Jacob Cats, who was nicknamed "father of the nation." Even though his morals are obviously Calvinist, his teachings on love, marriage, household affairs (including a remarkably large number of instructions on how to run an economical household), and mental and physical hygiene adopt a secular tone and are practical in nature. Combining word and image on one page, an emblem comprises a catchy epigram, a simple picture, and a short explanatory poem. Emblem books were meant to entice readers to think beyond what they read, and read beyond what is written, often on the basis of images of everyday objects or events. Images of emblem books by Cats or Roemer Visscher often feature kitchen utensils, cleaning tools, or children's toys. Along these lines, paintings, though sometimes vulgar, mostly depict seemingly insignificant moments in ordinary life. When we see women carrying out light household tasks like peeling apples or observe them involved in letter writing, we simultaneously witness a celebration of the material world that, while by no means perfect, exists in painting wholly in and of itself. The New School philosopher Jay Bernstein considers paintings by Pieter de Hooch to be "themselves a form of claiming, a way of rendering the sensible world of everyday experience such that it can be seen *as* sufficient and complete, hence fully worthy of our investment in it." What De Hooch offers, he continues, "is everydayness raised to the level of the monumental."[31] By creating the overriding impression of a sensual world that is irreducible to ideas about it, De Hooch is for Jay a forerunner of modernism.

The widespread idea that modernism has a privileged relation to philosophy is hugely problematic. I largely agree with Bernstein's first assertion on painting as form of philosophical argumentation. However, I do not define early modern art in terms of modernism's break from it but want to consider it in its own right. The initial stimulus of this project emerged from a dialogue not with modernism but with *contemporary* art practice and theory.

This book hopes to inspire artists as much as it has been inspired by them. This project began as a seminar series entitled *The Pensive Image*, under my direction from 2006 to 2008 at the Jan van Eyck Academy in Maastricht, the Netherlands, then a postgraduate institute for research in fine arts, design, and theory. The thought-provoking discussions among the members of my impressive audience—a mixture of artists, art historians, philosophers, graphic designers, critical theorists, and filmmakers—have shaped the project's basic conceptions and premises. The Jan van Eyck Academy—not related to a university or other educational institution—then occupied a unique position in the rapidly growing field of artistic research. Artistic (or practice-led) research takes as one of its starting points the idea that artistic practice is a mode of knowledge production. Such ideas may find roots in Jean-Luc Godard and Gilles Deleuze's claim that film is a way of thinking as well as in the medieval idea that thinking is a kind of craft (this was later picked up by Heidegger). Arjun Appadurai once said that "research is a systematic interrogation of the not-yet-known"; however, this is not to suggest that research-based art should have an instrumental pedagogical outcome.[32] On the contrary, artworks are often presented not as a "known factor," the result of research, but precisely as an object or installation whose thought process is ongoing, and begins not directly from ignorance but from not knowing. In their book *On Not Knowing: How Artists Think,* Elizabeth Fisher and Rebecca Fortnum collected artworks and essays that start not from a position of knowledge (or end with it) but from the unknown. Several contributions in this volume deal with notions of speculation, chance, and the unanticipated as impulses for art-making, and insist that learning to think involves an unlearning; a separate contribution investigates the (Heideggerian) notion of an artwork as the locus of the unknown. In another anthology, *Art as a Thinking Process: Visual Forms of Knowledge Production*, edited by Mara Ambrožič and Angela Vettese, the contributors emphasize the increasing understanding that an artwork is completed by the spectator, that it is not a "container" of thought but rather a thinking *process.*[33] These notions are based on the presumption that an artwork is not a result, not some end product of artistic research, but a mode of thinking that generates ideas. In fact, one of the dominant directions in artistic research encompasses a concept of art that reverses the more traditional assumption that artworks represent worked-out ideas, as we have seen with Poussin's *la pensée,* or as in Bernini's *concetto,* the concept or idea stands at the work's origin and finds its perfect, mature form in the work's physical completion. In contrast, in regarding art as a mode of thinking, the idea comes before *and* after the process of making, and all the while it is found *in* the work of art, which is to say produced by it, and "found" there by the viewer—like, we might say, a Benjaminian *Denkbild.* Unlike what is put forth on some of the writing on artistic research, for me, pensive images produce not knowledge, per se, but rather a theoretical insight (as Benjamin would have it) that leads us to the realm not of the unknown but of the unthought. As such, art practice is a powerful argument for the hypothesis that philosophy is not the exclusive property of philosophers; it is instead a practice that can be done in and through art, as long as this *happening* that Heidegger speaks of is taking place. Artistic research also reveals that theory is practice, just as much as practice is theoretical.

I take artistic research as one of my main sources influencing my definition of art as a form of thinking and to use its methodology to shape my own interrogation of early modern pensive images. One of this study's main premises is that art does not need philosophy to engage in reflection, as it is perfectly capable of doing so via its own means. Starting from the premise that philosophy's history is, in fact, a history of reflection, I see pensive images not as self-reflective but as philosophical reflections. In the introduction to *What Is Philosophy?*, Gilles Deleuze and Félix Guattari state that "no one needs philosophy to reflect on anything."[34] Though I could not agree more, I depart from their subsequent insistence that philosophy is neither contemplation nor communication nor reflection. Following Rodolphe Gasché's careful analysis of reflection in *The Tain of the Mirror*, I situate this project as part of the history of reflection that spans Aristotle's *noesis noeseos*, a thinking of thinking, Descartes's *Method*, Hegel's speculation, and Merleau-Ponty's hyperreflection and ultimately arrives at Derrida's deconstruction. More recently, François Laruelle has made the somewhat baffling statement that philosophy is an irreflexive practice, drawing a parallel with photography, where he observes a similar blind spot. For Laruelle, both philosophy and photography identify with a fixed subject-object position that cannot be critiqued from within their fields. He pleads for a position to rethink photography's and philosophy's respective identities *outside* their discourses to avoid falling into the trap of the fixed subject-object position that each of these practices have adopted as their system's foundation. Laruelle suggests finding a position to look at photography not from the outside but from within: through the finding of a new viewpoint in what he terms "non-photography." Laruelle is right to observe that within philosophical discourse art has been understood as a lesser form of philosophy. Fiercely arguing against this view, he claims that art and philosophy are complementary practices.[35]

If we understand philosophy as a history of reflection, seventeenth-century Dutch painting becomes particularly suitable for further exploration, as Hegel knew all too well. In his *Lectures on Aesthetics*, the philosopher observes a correspondence between philosophical reflection and the compelling reflective surfaces in Dutch painting. He finds himself particularly smitten by genre scenes by Gerard ter Borch and still lifes by Willem Kalf because of the way that both artists could paint the reflection of light on Venetian glasses or satin dresses. He was amazed at how the shine on these things was so bright and glittering that it seemed to bounce off the picture plane, all the while existing by dint of paint and canvas. The quality of this shine, its ability to suspend itself from its place of origin, provided Hegel with a metaphor, or rather, a conceptual structure, for art as such. Art occupies a middle position between sensible and ideal forms of thought, just like the shimmering of Ter Borch's satin dresses supersede the painted surface, floating halfway between materiality and pure reflection. Following Hegel to a certain extent, Wayne Martin argues that the trope of reflective self-portraits, for instance in golden goblets, makes seventeenth-century Dutch still lifes phenomenological studies "undertaken not in words but in oil" (Clara Peeters is a case in point here). He discusses a series of *vanitas* images and so-called breakfasts by Pieter Claesz and Willem Claesz. Heda in light of "rivalling Cartesian and anti-Cartesian traditions of self-consciousness."[36] Further exploring the correlation between physical and philosophical reflection, I argue that seventeenth-century still life painting philosophizes on the essential difference between appearance and being.

As such, this book is a defense of early modern art against the general assumption that art history has credited modernism with the exclusive potential to reflect in a self-conscious way, through strategies of autonomy, materiality, purposelessness, and an exposition of its own flatness. From the perspective of the contemporary idea of art as thinking, I will demonstrate that early modern art is as philosophically sophisticated as art historians have claimed modern art to be. The focus will be mostly on seventeenth-century Dutch painting but also will include other objects such as a dollhouse and certain prints. Each chapter will pair early modern works with late nineteenth- and twentieth-century art and theory in order to point to the similarities and the differences, in terms of continuity and complexity, in the conceptualization of certain philosophical issues.

This book comprises five chapters divided in two parts. The first part starts with the question of what a pensive image is, and identifies it by situating it in the larger context of the history of art. I argue that Barthes's pensive image is an amalgam of much older concepts that, once hotly debated, eventually were left hibernating in a corner of history. This project's aim is to historically ground the pensive image and revive its concept to prepare it for art historical application.

Primary means of such a preparation require tracing its history back to the early modern period, showing how it should be used in visual analysis, and situating it within the twentieth- and twenty-first-century discourses in which it has continued to resonate. The first chapter, "Theorizing Stillness," positions the pensive image vis-à-vis related concepts such as the eighteenth-century *punctum temporis* and Lessing's pregnant moment. The pensive image's most obvious characteristic—stillness—and its open form will be further explored in the context of Goethe's response to Lessing. The starting point of the discussion is the contemporary debate in film studies on stillness and the freeze-frame as the defining factor that distinguishes cinema from photography.

The second chapter, "Tracing the *Denkbild*," considers the notion of the thought-image, an important term for the Frankfurt school—particularly as a label for Walter Benjamin's prose poems first published in *Einbahnstrasse* in 1927—as the pensive image's closest relation. I will show that the *Denkbild* has its roots in the Dutch *denkbeeld*, which is intimately linked with seventeenth-century emblems as well as the more complex allegorical constellations that were called hieroglyphs. My journey tracing the *Denkbild* will lead me, via the so-called *merkbeelden* (thought-images) of the Dutch artist Romeyn de Hooghe (1645–1708) and Johann Gottfried Herder's writings on his hieroglyph of creation (*Schöpfungshieroglyph*), to Adorno's commentary on Benjamin's conception, calling it a foreign term, or *Fremdwort*, implying its Dutch roots. This chapter starts with one of art history's founding texts, Johann Joachim Winckelmann's essay on the *Belvedere Torso* in the Vatican's Museo Pio-Clementino, in which Winckelmann sees thoughts as if rippling under the marble skin of the sculpture's body. It is this unrest-at-rest that most profoundly defines the pensive image.

Comprising three chapters, part 2 discusses a series of pensive images, mostly taken from seventeenth-century Dutch art, to demonstrate how they, through engaging in philosophical reflection, contribute to the development of philosophical thought. The interaction between philosophy and art is reciprocal: art articulates ideas that philosophers pick up on (at a later stage), and philosophers look closely at art to find complicated structures that start to model their own systems of ideas. Two main strands frame my discussions in these three chapters. One is that the history of philosophy is a history of increasing self-consciousness, of thinking about thinking. Artworks have played a significant role in this growing awareness, by serving as vehicles that trigger thought (such as Stevens's card) or as locations where solitude and introspection can be found. But they are also surprisingly able to visualize major philosophical conundrums in ways that go significantly beyond the level of illustration; they are better considered to be "commentaries."

Chapter 3, "Room for Reflection: Interior and Interiority," focuses on the role of the house metaphor in philosophy and the visual arts in relation to what has been referred to as our state of philosophical "homelessness," the idea that thinking sets us on a trajectory that leads away from life's comforts toward bewilderment about our life, as such. One of my arguments is that painting might be the only means to provide us with a philosophical home, or at least a direction toward it, as suggested by my example of Heidegger's confrontation with Van Gogh's shoes. My discussion includes the role of interior painting in seventeenth-century ideology about the home and a consideration of an uncanny home in the shape of a dollhouse, likely an exact copy of the house that it housed.

Chapter 4, "The Profundity of Still Life" argues that still life painting is the genre *par excellence* for philosophizing. Its well-known penchant for raising ontological issues through *vanitas* images is only one aspect of its reflective qualities. Starting from a pearly dewdrop sliding off a petal in a flower piece by Jan van Huysum, I reveal that still life's investment in depicting physical reflection is linked to philosophical reflection on the finite and the infinite. Discussion of Pascal's thoughts on infinity, Alberti's theory of the point, and Damisch's early first essay on Paul Klee's *Equals Infinity* will enable me to compare early modern and modernist attempts at formulating visual thought, on infinity as much as on the limits of painting as such.

The last chapter, "Painting as a Space for Thought," further builds on the connection between painted and philosophical modes of reflection by focusing on shine. The focus is on Hegel's fascination with glimmer and glitter in seventeenth-century still lifes by Willem Kalf, an interest that ultimately results (I argue) in his theory on shine that lies at the heart of his aesthetics. In addition, the structure of some of Hegel's complicated concepts, among them *aufheben* and self-consciousness, was informed—one could say shaped—by pictorial shine. An extension of the discussion of shine will bring us into twentieth- and twenty-first-century realistic painting, in particular, the cityscapes of Richard Estes (b. 1932), through which I will show how painting, first in the wake of the invention of photography and then in the wake of modernism, has continued to grow increasingly and philosophically self-conscious through the use of extreme reflection.

In "Painting's Wonder," the conclusion, I speculate on the role of art (inside and outside *Wunderkammern*) to provoke wonder, which is, Plato claims through Socrates, the only possible beginning of philosophy.

PART I

Defining the Pensive Image

CHAPTER ONE

Theorizing Stillness

One of two things is usually lacking in the so-called Philosophy of Art: either philosophy or art.

FRIEDRICH SCHLEGEL

The Thought-Image

Around 1660 the Dutch painter Cornelis Bisschop (1630–1674) created a rather unusual blend of still life and interior painting (plate 2). We see a corner of what seems to be a typical seventeenth-century room, a boxlike space with a tile floor and wooden beam ceiling. Contemporaneous Dutch depictions of interiors (fig. 1) usually show people either absorbed in mundane household tasks or engaged in pleasant conversation within spaces that are warm and comfortable, exuding a sense of calm and restrained opulence. But here, despite the sumptuous still life dominating the wall, we find a desolate and drafty corner filled with evidence of haste. A fur-trimmed brown satin jacket has been thrown carelessly on the chair by a woman who, probably via the same motion, has stepped out of her satin slippers and dashed through the door. The jacket does not necessarily suggest urgency, merely neglect. Though wide open, the door allows for only a sliver of a view of the room behind it, where we see a streak of sunshine falling onto the wall and tabletop. These small patches of warm sunlight make the antechamber seem even chillier. Has the woman escaped into the more comfortable, sunlit front room? Why have we been left behind in this in-between space?

Bisschop has depicted a domestic corner that is usually overlooked in painting, a kind of hallway probably scarcely noticed even by a seventeenth-century person passing through it. At first sight, such a small and marginal picture demands very little from us, as viewers. There are no symbols to decipher, no clues given as to what exactly is depicted here. And yet this small, boxlike space is open to speculation. Something has left the scene that

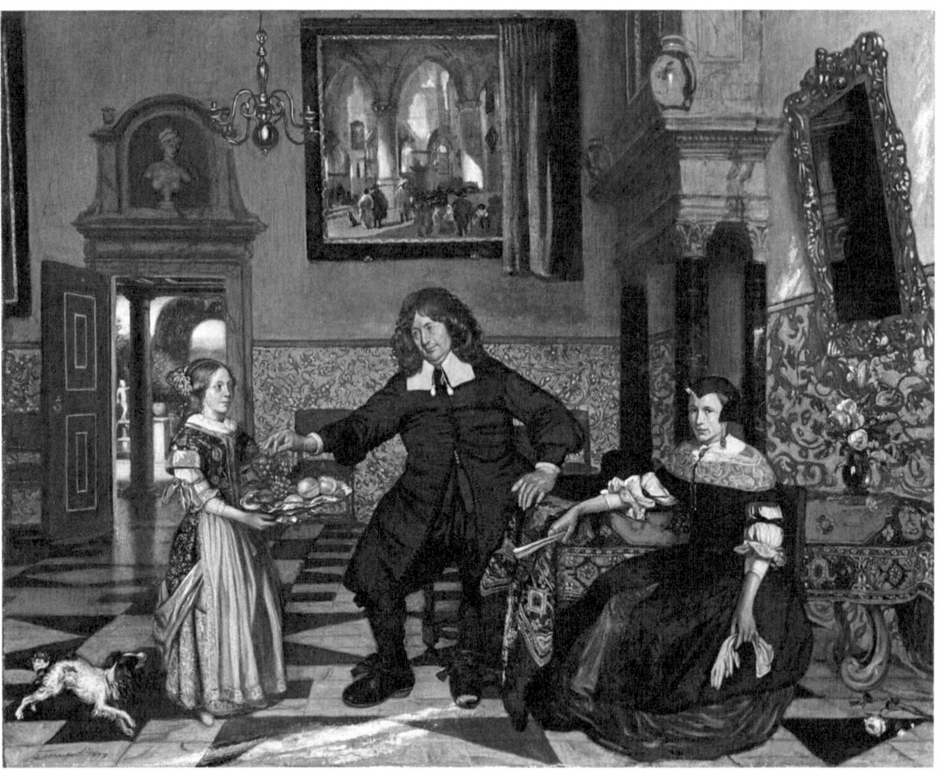

FIGURE 1 Emanuel de Witte, *Portrait of a Family in an Interior*, 1678. Oil on canvas; 69 × 87 cm. Munich, Bayerische Staatsgemäldesammlungen. Photo © bpk / Bayerische Staatsgemäldesammlungen.

we would like to retrieve. Looking closely at this image, we become less interested in what lies *behind* this plastered wall, its reality effect put forth through the inevitable nail in the upper left corner, and more in what is expressed by the very objects that are projected against it. In the stillness of this drafty little space, the things the passing figure has left behind command our attention; yet they do so without pushing us in any specific direction. We are asked not to decipher, but to muse. The composition of these few objects form a constellation of movement and time, which gives rise to thoughts about the temporality of a gesture, the fleetingness of a presence, or how such movements in time have passed without our noticing them; apparently, we have arrived too late at the scene and can perceive only remnants of a woman's rushed entrance. Is this what a space looks like after we have passed through it? We seem to have arrived at the end of a minute event or mini-narrative, yet the picture is one of suspense: the open door, the jacket's uneasy position, the suspended ribbons, the cut-off painting hanging over the doorway, indeed, the arbitrariness of the entire scene. Do we, as viewers, find ourselves pondering these things, or is the painting as such pensive, in the sense that it suggests an openness, a passive state filled with unease?

Bisschop's painting is an example *par excellence* of a pensive image—an image that neither tells a story nor conveys a specific meaning but rather articulates, through its form and materiality, a line of thinking. In Barthes's sense of the *punctum*, we have been touched by this work to the extent that we have started "adding" to it. It is not that we *get* this painting, but that the painting gets *us*. The gesture of adding to the picture, the time it takes to find the movement of one's gaze arrested by a prickling detail, and the period we keep wondering about it, pondering it, are where *pensiveness* in the image is found.[1] This pensiveness is exclusively generated by photography, because in film, Barthes explains, the viewer simply does not have enough time to add to the image. It is only in a still image that Barthes calls a photogram can a similar wounding occur.[2]

Though many critics have seen Barthes's *punctum* and *studium* as being opposites in kind, I suggest that we consider their relation in terms of figure and ground, whereby we can perceive a detail as a hole in textual fabric of its ground. We can better understand the relation between the notion of pensiveness and that which it stands out against by looking at Barthes's *S/Z* (published ten years before *Camera Lucida*), in which he touches on pensiveness for the first time. *S/Z* is Barthes's exhaustive treatment of Honoré de Balzac's short story *Sarrasine* (1830), whereby he explains in great detail five distinct narrative codes that he claims make up the fabric or texture of any narrative. One of his main arguments is that this weaving of multiple voices he observes in *Sarrasine* creates a plurality of meaning that never finds finality or ultimate determination. A significant instance of indeterminacy can be found in the story's last sentence: "And the Marquise remained pensive." Intrigued by this closing sentence, Barthes explains that there is, in fact, an infinite openness in Balzac's use of the notion of pensiveness, an illusion of polysemy, of multiple meanings unsaid and unexplored, or, as he writes, "the infinite openness of the pensive (and this is precisely its structural function) removes this final lexia from any classification."[3] Balzac's sentence, especially because it is a closing line of a story, functions for Barthes as the degree zero of meaning, an interruption between narrative and expression, escaping any closure or code—an opening, surely, where a form of pensiveness akin to that evoked by the *punctum* in photography can be discovered. Such an escape from any code or closure has been termed a thought-effect by Naomi Schor, and while this term, as such, might be very useful, it is precisely not an *effect* that Barthes observes in Balzac, but the very absence of any form of result.[4] Balzac's last sentence, as much as Bisschop's painting, demonstrates that, contrary to what has often been argued, pensiveness is not a state exclusive to photography. What Bisschop's painting, Balzac's concluding line, and Barthes's *punctum* share is that they all seem to "lift" a constellation of details, pricking holes, or narrative tensions from the texture in which they are embedded. Thus isolated, these figures express a brooding or mental restlessness regarding the absence of meaning. The touching or wounding quality of the *punctum* arrests the desire to see more; the raising of thought temporarily stops any urge to read further. Who or what, exactly, is pensive here?

My inquiry into the nature and meaning of pensiveness in art will not include famous icons of thinking, such as Albrecht Dürer's *Melencolia* (1514), Rodin's strong yet paralyzed male figure representing a thinker in action (1904), or his fragile female head emerging from a block of stone called *La Pensée* (*Thought*, 1901; conceived in 1895). Jean-Luc Nancy, who in an otherwise beautiful essay on Caravaggio's *The Death of the Virgin* (1605–1606) entitled "On the Threshold" deems the meditative figure of John the Evangelist standing aside on the right, hand propped under his chin, as the "thought" of the painting.[5] This would be thought expressed *in* an image, or *as* image. What I have in mind is pensiveness as a quality of the image that causes it to remain inexpressive.

In his discussion of Barthes's notion of pensiveness in *Sarrasine*, Jacques Rancière observes how it frustrates the sequence of narrative action. Balzac's sentence, in fact, ends the story in a frozen tableau in which the seated marquise does nothing but keep the entire narrative in a state of unrelieved suspense. Rancière argues that the depiction of the pensive marquise becomes a "painting" of pensiveness, an image not of something inexpressible but rather of inexpressiveness as such.[6] We can imagine this image to stand out as being the short story's last moment, cut off somehow from its narrative sequence as if it were a freeze-frame in a film. Rancière sees such narrative sequences dissolving into a still image not only in Balzac's story but also in Flaubert's *Madame Bovary* in small, visual, zoom-in scenes, as when a melting snowflake on Emma's umbrella marks one of her amorous encounters. Tailoring Barthes's notion to fit his own philosophy, Rancière declares pensiveness to be a sign of the modern rather than a classic text (as Barthes would have it), and hence proposes it as a figure that conjoins the two regimes of expression. In this Rancière's conception seem partly to run counter to Barthes's explicit point that pensiveness, in photography as much as literature, escapes any code or meaning.

Interestingly, though his ideas are inspired by film theory (about which he has written extensively), Rancière labels such visual moments in literature as *paintings*: "It is as if painting has taken the place of the texts' narrative sequence."[7] The question arises as to how we can understand this notion of pensiveness as a kind of frozen painting or *tableau vivant*, sharing with photography the motionless silence and the momentous arrest. Clearly, then, not a typically photographic state, Balzac's pensive image serves as an image of thought, or a thought-image. The passive state of pensiveness is therefore not a characteristic specifically of the marquise but of the frozen painting, whether literary, pictorial, or photographic. This frozenness is what generates a pensiveness that is, in the first place, a quality of the image, not of the character. As Rancière notes, the image may be full of thoughts, but this does not mean that the marquise is actually *thinking* them. And yet they are *in* the picture. How does a freeze-frame create pensiveness in an image? In what way does a temporal arrest, or a kind of motionlessness, as we have seen in Bisschop's painting, create a state of uneasy reflection? The issue as to the status of an arrested moment has been at the heart of the centuries-old *paragone* (debate) about the respective limits of poetry and painting, hotly contested, among other thinkers, by Gotthold Ephraim Lessing, Johann Joachim Winckelmann, and Denis Diderot in the mid-eighteenth century.

In recent years, the debate about the arrested moment has shifted from art history and aesthetics to film and new-media studies, where the significance of the freeze-frame, and more specifically the difference between the still and the moving image in terms of the opposition between cinema and photography, has been a recurrent topic of discussion, given the explosion of literature about these concerns over the past two decades. I take a fresh look at the old problem of stillness and motion as a means of separating the sister arts of painting, sculpture, and poetry by considering how scholars in film and media studies have explored the potential of the freeze-frame as a way of defining the position, or rather opposition, of photography vis-à-vis cinema. My premise is that pensiveness is a privilege not exclusively of photographs but also includes stilled images that seem to transcend media or genre limitations. Apart from a few exceptions, the debate in film theory continues to circle around the distinction between cinema and photography, but it has so far neglected to consider painting as sharing with photography features of arrest and stillness. For both arts, it can be argued that only *after* the invention of cinema did such stillness become pronounced. As we will see in the next chapter, because of their thoughtfulness, Balzac's frozen painting and Bisschop's, for that matter, are comparable to the type of literary miniature termed *Denkbild*, or thought-image, by Walter Benjamin and other

Frankfurt school thinkers. The concept of *Denkbild*, in many ways the precursor to Barthes's pensive photography, finds its origin in the hieroglyph, very popular in the seventeenth century when Bisschop painted his *Interior* and widely used in the next century as well. As I will discuss in the next chapter, the thought-image has traveled—largely unnoticed—through the work of the aestheticians Johann Joachim Winckelmann and Johann Gottfried Herder, working its way up to early twentieth-century European poetry and finally crystallizing in Benjamin's theory of the dialectical image. With this chapter I start my excavation of this image-concept by linking on the contemporary debate about film's ambivalent relation to the still with its early modern predecessor, the pensive image. Starting with a video work by Fiona Tan, *Island* (2008), a typical photofilmic image, I will retrace the idea of stillness, or more precisely, of stillness as motion, via Bellour's pensive spectator to Goethe's cinematographic perception of *Laocoön* leading him to distinguish between closed and open (or reflective) statues, to Lessing's pregnant moment that saves the visual arts from total mortification. As we will see, the pensive image does not stand alone but is embedded in a larger history, taking in a different shape and poetic form in different times, yet it is always characterized by a stillness that generates a passive, uneasy, and indeterminate state of openness that allows for the unthought to surface. This short history of stillness's intertwinement with thought will ultimately assist us in defining what exactly it is that moves (us) in Bisschop's *Interior*, which, as we will see, can be termed as a restlessness at rest.

The Still Image, the Freeze-Frame, and the Pensive Spectator

Fiona Tan's *Island* is a fourteen-minute black-and-white moving image consisting of long, unhurried shots of Gotland, a Swedish island in the Baltic Sea. We see the bare landscape of meadows near the sea populated with exposed trees and animated only by the incessantly blowing wind. A male voiceover slowly tells us about a woman who has come to the island to retreat. He tells us that the island is as a boat for her, which sails her through the hours, days, and weeks, enabling her to lose track of time so as to give her a space to think. In light of the fragmentary narrative, the landscape in front of us starts to mirror the inner mind of the protagonist whereby we see in the lonely trees, the heaving sea and the boundless horizon the shape of the hours and days floating by (fig. 2). The island becomes a map of her thoughts that she navigates; however, after having paced through it for too long, the

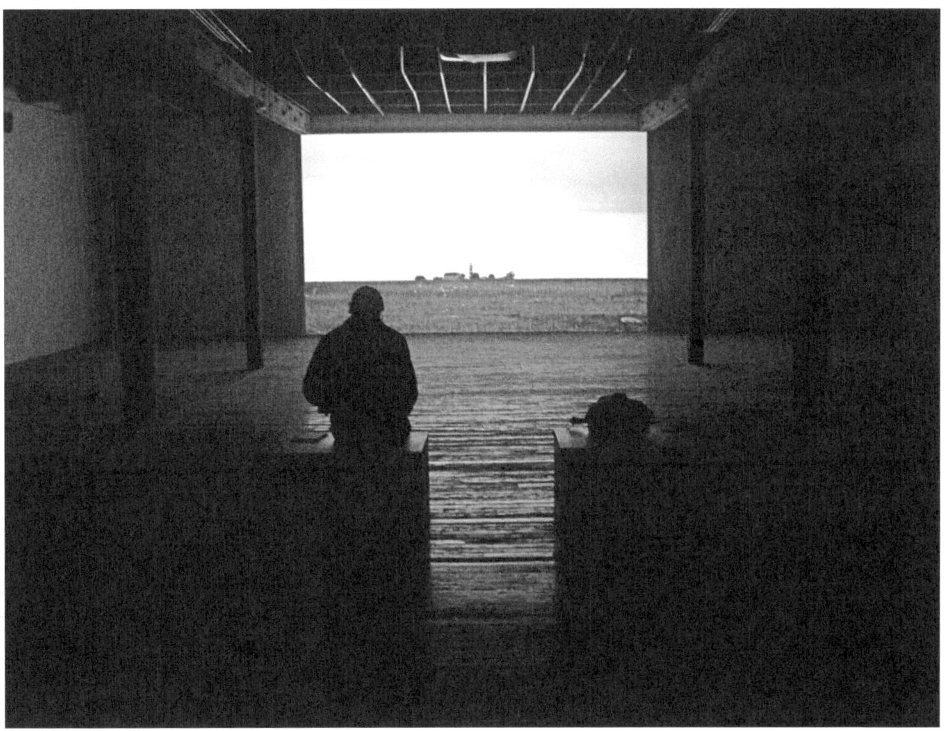

FIGURE 2 Fiona Tan, installation shot from *Island*, 2008. Video installation, black and white, 14 min. 20 sec., 5:1 surround, HD projector, media player, surround amplifier, surround speakers. Courtesy of the artist.

wide-open landscape becomes a prison, her growing restlessness accompanied by a tracking shot—the only one in the film—of grass rolling underneath us as if we are running over it. The film ends where it began, with a view of the lighthouse that marks of the outside world, a take that during the last ten seconds of the film transforms into a freeze-frame. Though barely visible, the stilling of movement within this very last frame raises the question of how we should define the kind of imagery that precedes it. Should we call Tan's work a "filmed photograph" or a "stilled film"? The black-and-white shots of silhouetted trees against white skies remind us of early photography, and in that light, Tan might be making the point, with André Bazin, that cinema is made of the stuff of photography, rather than standing in opposition to it. But she has animated photography here. In light of the rich history of landscape painting and its appeal to contemplation, the case can also be made that Tan has set a *painting* in motion.

Tan's work is typical of an increasing concern that has emerged among film makers in recent years with strategies of stilling and techniques of delay. This is particularly apparent in moving-image work made for art galleries. In addition to Tan we can name Tacita Dean, David Claerbout, and Harun Farocki, among others, who in their hybrid works—not quite film, not photography as we know it—have used a wide range of strategies for creating what has been referred to as "filmed photographs."[8] In his essay "Stop/Motion," Thomas Elsaesser wonders which dominant forces these artists dissent from. Is it photography's stasis that they seek to set in motion, or do they want to tame the rush and speed of the cinema, accelerated by quick montage? He blames the ongoing *musealization* of cinema and video art, where in the gallery's programmatic revered space the often self-referential work invites the viewer to engage with it as if it is making a special kind statement. Among other things, the emergence of time-based art in the gallery space has put the relation between stillness and movement, traditionally differentiating painting and photography from cinema and sound, in crisis. Whereas I largely agree with Elsaesser, I suggest that Tan's *Island* does not reflect a moment of crisis in the differentiation between the media but is an attempt to overcome their separate conditions. Within the course of the duration of each long, slow shot, some kind of montage is taking place, a blending of present and past, of the landscape and the mind, of picturing and mapping, of retreat and imprisonment. Does this work about a woman seeking refuge from reality also serve for the viewer as a site of refuge and contemplation, offering us the luxury of having time to think by way of losing track of it? The slightly trembling images may remain still, yet something is set in motion. With *Island*, Tan is not interested in the differentiation or clash between stillness and motion but in the extent to which their blending gives rise to a stillness in motion, a new modality that invites the viewer not to interpret but to think.

Similar to what Rancière noticed about Balzac's marquise, Tan's *Island* is full of thoughts, but it is unclear whether they all belong to the protagonist. The reflections on temporality and passing that are evoked seem to have been shaped by the trees' outline, the waving grass, the swelling waves, and the gushing wind rather than the words describing the course of her retreat. It is as if we see time flowing in an ongoing suspension of motion, where the landscape is waiting with us—or rather *for* us—all the while circumscribing the contours of time passing; indeed, we seem to sail through the minutes and the hours, all the while remaining there in the landscape, facing the sea. Before I will speculate about the relation between Tan's filmed photographs and hybrid images that predate the invention of cinema and photography, I will situate pensiveness in the context of cinema as a form of thinking.

The Pensive Spectator

The idea that cinema is a form of thinking has been brought forward most prominently by Jean-Luc Godard, Laura Mulvey, and Stanley Cavell. Closely following Eisenstein, Gilles Deleuze proposed that not just the *moving* image but *montage* generates a process of thinking, a sewing together of two irregular, seemingly unlinked images, that create a new, wholly unseen image that confronts us and makes us think. Mulvey and film critic Raymond Bellour find this "thinking power" in film in the emergence of the still, or the freeze-frame that arrests the flow of images to trigger reflection.

In "The Pensive Spectator," Bellour asks what would happen if the spectator of a film were suddenly confronted with a photographic still.[9] Clearly responding to Barthes's *Camera Lucida*, Bellour takes up Barthes's interest in the photogram, as it shares the quality of pensiveness with regular photography. Starting from Barthes's radical opposition between the moving, fleeting, and illusionary cinema that, in doubling life, seizes us as spectators, and the immobile, still photograph that, as it is touched by death, cannot be grasped, Bellour questions Barthes's observation that cinema cannot be "pensive" because movie images go by too fast for a viewer to "add" anything to them. Interested as he is in overlapping pictures and "in-between" images, Bellour makes a case for films that take photography as their subject—Michelangelo Antonioni's *Blow-Up* (1966) or François Truffaut's *L'Amour en fuite* (1979)—and where the film's narrative flow and image sequence is interrupted by still photographs. He argues that at the moment the flow of moving pictures is frozen and the viewer is presented with an arrested image, photography "bursts forth," stopping cinematographic time, or rather, blending the has-been-ness of the photograph with the now-ness of cinema. The arrest of the narrative and the flow of cinematographic frames exercises a profound effect on the viewer. Suddenly awakened from the mesmerizing filmic illusion of doubled life, the viewer becomes aware of his/her viewing position and starts "adding" to the frozen image her reflections on the medium thus evoked. What is being created at that moment, Bellour argues, is a "pensive spectator" for whom the merging of the two kinds of temporality results in an "uncoupling" of the spectator from the image. The photograph or photogram pulls the spectator out of the "pregnant force" of cinema, Bellour continues, and allows his/her reflections to emerge. Wittingly or unwittingly, Bellour refers in fact to Lessing's famous idea of "pregnant moment" in the visual arts, by which the essence of an entire narrative is summed up in a single frozen scene brought forth by the artist.[10]

Bellour's notion of the pensive spectator has had quite a resonance in the field of cinema studies. For instance, Garrett Stewart has proposed extending Bellour's argument, arguing that a most profound blending of time happens not in the appearance of a photograph but in the true freeze-frame of the photogram, whereby the motionless image is not just a still image but represents the actual stasis of the film reel as well. Only at this moment of self-negation, Stewart writes, can film start to image itself.[11] Taking a different orientation, Laura Mulvey has stated that the concept of the pensive spectator in fact anticipated the new technologies of the VCR and DVD (and, by extension, newer digital technologies), which now allow any spectator to easily stop filmic motion to study a stilled shot. The capacity now of any individual to freeze photograms of one's choice results in "a way of seeing into the screen's images, shifting them and stretching them into new dimensions of time and space," she writes.[12] The timing of an image can be caught for thought and reflection only when it is stilled, Mulvey asserts, giving the example of Dziga Vertov, who, at the beginning of cinema's history, was already keenly aware of the pensiveness of the still. Jumping in front of a slow-motion camera caused his head to be preserved as a blurry mess on film; yet, paradoxically, what was revealed, Vertov stated, were the "thoughts on his face."[13]

Though Bellour's notion of the pensive spectator is no doubt useful, its perspective comes at the cost of significantly weakening Barthes's insights—by following him at once too closely and not closely enough. In fact, Bellour reveals himself to be a rather conservative thinker when, in a double-folded gesture, he disregards Barthes's carefully laid out concept of photography and makes it a close relation of cinema again by robbing it, so to speak, of its pensiveness. No matter how accurately he describes the effect of the still image in cinema as being a wake-up call for his spectator, who then begins to reflect on what she or he is looking at, Bellour tries in fact to *restore* pensiveness as a *conscious* process by placing it firmly back within the suddenly awoken mind of a human spectator. He forgets, or wants to forget, that for Barthes, and Rancière for that matter, it is photography as such, and not its viewer, that is pensive. For both thinkers, their most radical stance is the understanding that pensiveness is a quality of the image rather than of the human mind. For them, the stilling of life and real time by a photograph sets something in motion, a process that receives merely a flat imitation in Bellour's understanding of the stopping of film. Whereas Barthes tries to analyze stillness as pensiveness by setting it off against cinema—which is less confrontational as a type of medium, as it closely resembles our experience of chronological time—Bellour overlooks this crucial difference by making the opposite argument, namely, that photography is ultimately the stuff of cinema. Bellour sides with Bazin, who famously called photography cinema's ghostly parent. Indeed, we could say, with Barthes, that the very thing that distinguishes photography from film *is* its pensiveness. And this is exactly what Tan's *Island* makes visible.

The main question here is, in fact, a classical point of contention. To grasp its essence, should a medium be defined exclusively on its own terms, or should it be understood in light of other media? The ongoing discussion about the interstices of still and motion images reveal how film's defining characteristics become more pronounced precisely at these interstices where the two media are at their most antagonistic (the ongoing debate around Chris Marker's *La Jetée* [1962] is a case in point).[14] The traditional question to raise is whether it is time or movement that defines cinema. Clearly for Bellour, not movement but time serves as film's determining aspect, while in contrast, Deleuze sees these elements as being endlessly intertwined. He argues that whereas in the prewar period, time in film was derived from movement, in the 1950s and '60s this "movement-image" was replaced by the "time-image," in which apparently unrelated pictures were connected by what seem to be irrational cuts. The opposition between time-images and movement-images intimates a break in the relation of the body to its own perception of motion in time and space. No longer is time *passing* as it did in the movement-image; instead it appears in its pure state through a false continuity, as seen in the work of Alain Resnais, or, one could argue, Tan. With the time-image, cinema no longer refers to an outside world or relies on a viewing subject but brings together disjointed images that give rise to "thought"; redirecting it toward a stillness *in* motion, a kind of productive collapse of their opposition.[15] Like Barthes and Rancière—but unlike Bellour—Deleuze sees "thought" as springing from the image. Likewise, following Bazin's idea of film as mummified change, Elsaesser argues that digital photography and film, intuitively understood as plucking stilled segments out of the flow of life, have allowed there to be an archive of what he calls the duration of the ephemeral, of fleeting feelings and transitory sensations that we are tasked with sustaining: "in memory, as intensities, *as the shape of a thought*, even as their perception exceeds the eye."[16]

The lively engagement with the theoretical consequences of the intertwining of the still and the moving image, by scholars as well as artists and filmmakers, centers on the centuries-old problem of defining a representational medium in terms of its particular distribution of space and time, a question that deeply concerned eighteenth-century thinkers like Diderot and Lessing. As we see with Elsaesser's and Deleuze's contributions, the final consequences ensuing from what happens within the interstices of space and time, and of motion and stillness—or rather, their moments of overlap and collapse—result in the rise of a thought or the contours of its shape. It is as if the *je ne sais quoi* of painting (such an important issue in eighteenth-century aesthetics) has been transposed, inhering now in the nature of stillness in photography and film as a moment of unease and uncertainty that can only be brooded over. The fidgetiness that it engenders is in fact a recognition, if not of the stillness of death, then of the ephemeral quality of all our sensations that force themselves onto us as thought, or rather, as thought's initial shaping by means of the freeze-frame. And this is what Barthes called the photograph's pensiveness.

Considering the persistence of this debate, the extent of its scope, and the complexity arising from the still/motion dichotomy, it is remarkable how few scholars recognize the connection with a much older debate, fully fleshed out by none other than Lessing, concerning the comparison between painting and poetry and the corresponding problems vis-à-vis their temporal and spatial aspects. A look into pre-cinematographic conceptions of space and time that deal with stillness and motion may provide some clarity here. As Bazin was among the first to theorize stillness, which he did (in 1945) in contrast to baroque painting, I will take his essay as my starting point.

Convulsive Catalepsy

Writing with the bravura he was known for, André Bazin declared in his celebrated essay "The Ontology of the Photographic" that film "delivers baroque art from its convulsive catalepsy."[17] Art had previously been embalming objects "in" images, but now the invention of cinema had made it possible to merge an image of the thing with the image of its duration. The result was that, for the first time, a medium was capable of "mummifying" temporal and spatial change. Unlike baroque painting, Bazin triumphantly writes, film is successful in its attempt to conquer time, and in its projected light, photography as well shrinks to become merely a "feeble technique" that can capture time only momentarily, and not wholly, as the moving reels of cinema do. Photography remains for Bazin the significant break with realistic art, that which invalidated painting's justification of itself as having the capacity to reproduce nature. Because of photography, painting lost its purpose as a mode of recording reality, and so turned away from the making of images and toward the fabrication of stilled objects, virtually dead, whose spasms remain visible when seen through a camera's lens.

Bazin describes baroque painting to be essentially a still medium, desperately trying to suggest life in the "tortured immobility" of its compositions.[18] But something rather different than just stilled scenes is implied by his phrase "convulsive catalepsy": a sequence of images seen as if under stroboscopic light, whereby figures' poses jerkily drag by, abruptly jumping from one frozen state into another. Blindly following his cinematographically shaped vision here, Bazin seems to consider the history of early modern painting not as a long sequence of tableaux which smoothly fade into one another but rather as a series of individually flickering scenes, as we see in very early cinema or failed animations. In differentiating film from painting, yet seeing the one medium through the lens of the other, Bazin is clearly struggling with the exact difference between the immutable and the mutable, and as a consequence with the distinct philosophical concepts of being and becoming.[19]

Admittedly, standing at the very beginning of what we now call film or cinema studies, Bazin developed his thoughts when cinema had just grown mature and found its proper voice via sound. However, his brushing aside of early modern painting as being irrelevant for further theorization about the definition of cinema as set against photography (and vice versa) has largely remained the practice in film studies ever since, while early modern scholars are reaching out to filmic procedures.[20] Bazin's gesture can easily be amended when we throw early modern art into the equation as a tool that can assist us in unraveling the complex entanglement of stillness and movement, and the philosophical concepts of being and becoming that they entail. After all, theorists and makers of early modern art have pondered the temporalities of the image for a much longer period than film scholars have. In the eighteenth century, the exchanges among theorists of art concentrated on the different expression of space and time in poetry and painting; the outpouring around the *Laocoön* sculpture among German aesthetics is the most prominent focus of these discussions. For we should realize that painting or sculpture was not seen as motionless, but on the contrary, was considered to be very much animated.

Motion Pictures

In 1798, Goethe published his "Observations on the Laocoon" in the first issue of his *Propyläen*. His essay would be the last significant contribution in a discussion on the sculpture—clearly an early modern theoretical object in Marin's sense of the term—that had been going on since it was unearthed in 1506 in Rome with Michelangelo as an onlooker (fig. 3). The scene is taken from a story that Virgil recounted in book 2 of the *Aeneid*, about Laocoön, a Trojan priest who warned his fellow citizens against bringing the wooden horse the Greeks had left behind within the city walls. Annoyed with Laocoön for interfering with her plans, Athena dispatched two giant sea serpents to

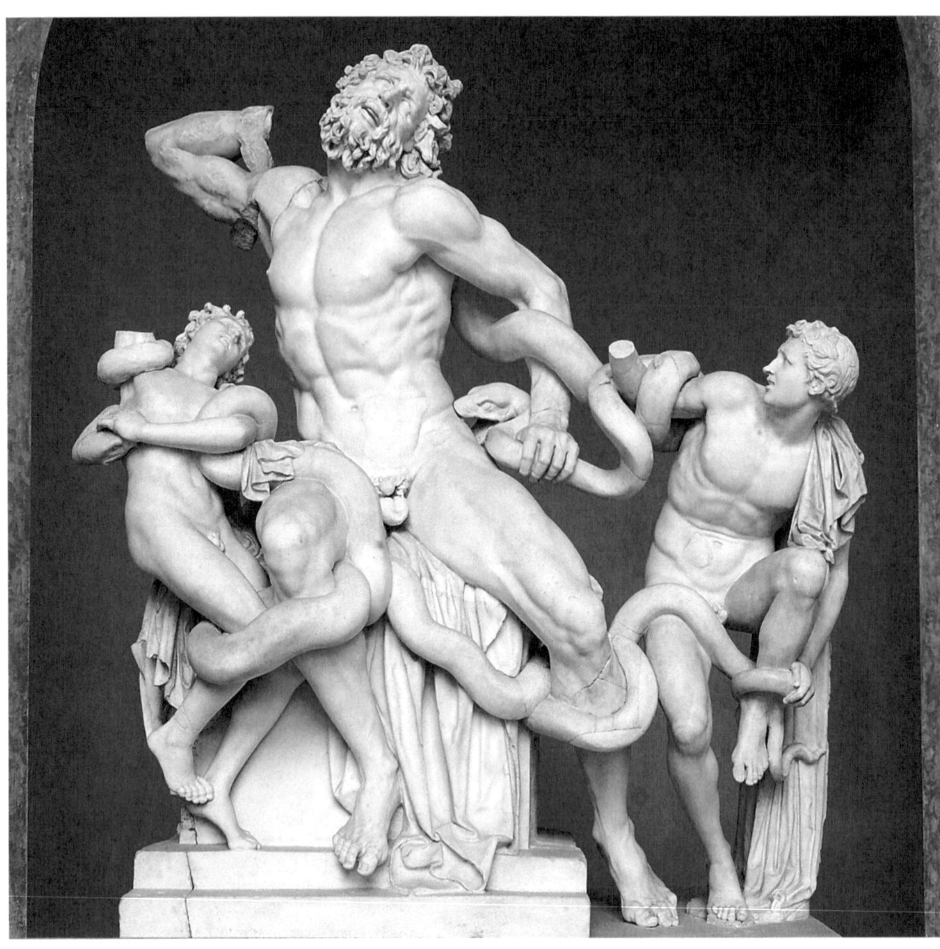

FIGURE 3 Hagesandros, Athenodoros, and Polydoros, *Laocoön and His Sons*. Marble, copy after a Hellenistic original from c. 200 BCE. Rome, Vatican Museum.

attack Laocoön's two young sons. Seeing the serpents wrapping themselves around the boys' bodies, Laocoön ran to their aid, only to become the third victim. While the serpents bit and squeezed the father and his sons to death, Laocoön sent horrendous cries into the air, likened by Virgil to the bellowing of a sacrificial ox that, escaping the altar, shakes off the axe embedded in its neck.

Although Goethe had seen the original sculpture in Rome on his Italian journey in 1786–1787, his observations published in *Propyläen* were based on a plaster copy that he had seen in Mannheim. Writing in response to Lessing's

Laocoön: An Essay on the Limits of Painting and Poetry, he takes Lessing's notion of the *fruchtbaren Moment* (pregnant moment) perhaps a bit too literally when he considers the monumental statue to be an almost living organism that, he argues, requires the active participation of the viewer.[21] Remarkably, he recommends that the best way to seize the attention of *Laocoön and His Sons* is to set it in motion.[22] Goethe suggests that we stand in front of the statue and shut our eyes: "let us open and shut them alternately and we shall see all the marble in motion; we shall be afraid to find the groupe changed when we open our eyes again. I would readily say, as the groupe is now exposed, it is a flash of lightning fixed, a wave petrified at the instant when it is approaching the shore."[23] The quick blinking of our eyes would set in motion a flashing play of light and shadow that would then make the group appear to be in dramatic animation. In hindsight, it is difficult to read this passage without associating Goethe's terms with photographic and cinematographic techniques. It is as if the writer intends to set in motion this most famous frozen moment by letting his eye act like the shutter of a camera, imitating the process of shooting an image in reverse. The flaring-up of light produced by quick-blinking eyes "fixes" the image as if in a camera flash, "petrifying" the upward motion of the bodies in pain as a wave about to break.

Goethe's physiological-optical approach toward viewing the sculpture is intriguing; however, it is not the stroboscopic perception alone that produces the its movement, but this in combination with the dramatic moment depicted: "When in fact a work ought to move before the eyes, a fugitive moment should be pitched upon."[24] The animation of the work, as such, derives from the fact that all elements of the action depicted should occupy the same ultrathin unit of time. "No part of the whole ought to be found before in this position," Goethe writes, while every part up to the smallest detail "should be obliged to quit that position."[25] He explains that all elements in a work of art should be pitched toward this next moment, when they would all move together toward the narrative's further unfolding. In *Laocoön and His Sons,* this moment has been perfected, giving the suspended moment a sense of independence and closure. This next moment, of course, never comes, and the unfolding remains in suspense.

Goethe distinguishes here three stages of constraint. Whereas the boy on the right is attempting to free himself, his father, though still struggling, has reached the moment when he will never be able to throw the murderous monster off his shoulders; he is on the verge of collapse. On the left, his other son also has no hope of escape, already defeated by the serpent's suffocating squeeze. The figure the least affected (the boy on the right), while trying to free his leg, thus not only witnesses his father's and brother's suffering, but also can anticipate his own imminent fate. As Goethe points out, the different levels of constraint come with different emotions. Not yet in pain himself, the young boy on the right cries out compassionately upon seeing the serpent bite his father deeply, while his brother is in total agony. Obviously, the father is doubly pained, as he can neither save himself nor his children. This direction toward closure is maintained as a principle of the compositional structure, and can also be seen as a development within the history of Greek art. Goethe sees an evolution in form from the open composition groups of figures in vase painting to the extremely animated, tight-knit assembly of *Laocoön and His Sons*.

The different roles played by the figures, the degree of variation in emotion they express, and the gradual process toward encircling leads Goethe to state that *Laocoön and His Sons* is an example *par excellence* of a "closed" (*Geschlossen*) work of art, entirely self-contained. The encircling of the serpents only reinforces the completeness of the various stages and double roles played by the characters. A masterful rhetorician, Goethe uses the terms "circle" and "circular" in quick succession to make his point. Even the process of viewing the sculpture group has been included within the serpents' firm grip, Goethe argues, as it is anticipated by the figure of the boy on the right, who is both a witness to the horrendous scene and an actor in it. Because of the tension between the implied exposition as seen by the boy as internal witness, and the complete group as seen by an outside viewer, the statue displays nothing but itself.[26] The internal viewing as doubled and complemented by that of the external viewer is what ultimately makes this statue independent and mature (*Selbständig*, literally "self-standing"), and above all, free.[27]

For Goethe, this sense of closure is fundamental to the successful interlinking of artwork and beholder. Other statues, for instance, "a Juno who reposes with majesty, a Minerva absorbed in reflection," Goethe writes, show subjects that have no relationship with the outside world.[28] Whereas they can be equally beautiful as *Laocoön and His Sons*, they lack the "fugitive" moment and, Goethe asserts with great assurance, "it is by this means that the work be always animated for millions of spectators."[29] The question is thus raised as to what kind of moment is depicted in such self-sufficient statues. A Minerva absorbed in reflection could very well be *Selbständig*, as *Laocoön and His Sons* is, but the sculpture cannot possibly be as closed and tight-knit, as there is no suggestion of temporal sequence. Closing one's eyes in front of this statue and opening them again in quick succession wouldn't produce the same sort of dramatic animated effect that Goethe described for *Laocoön and His Sons*; Minerva would not "move." The almost cinematographic perception that so fascinates Goethe would indeed be absent from a statue of Minerva lost in thought, who would remain frozen under any light condition. Could we, perhaps, call her pensive, like Balzac's marquise? Would her frozen stance, not prone to enclosure, thus be more open in its structure and production of meaning? Compared to the flickering, cinematographic appearance of *Laocoön and His Sons*, a reposing Minerva has indeed more affinity with a painting in Rancière's sense of the term. A rather passive image, such a statue possesses not the perfect closure so admired by Goethe but a rich openness. I suggest that we look into Lessing's conception of the "pregnant moment" to find a way of telling whether the pensive image is indeed its opposite.

Against Metaphorization

In *Discourse on Music, Painting and Poetry*, published in 1744, James Harris sets out to reject the famous *ut pictura poesis* doctrine stated by Horace in his *Ars Poetica* (18 BCE) and, before him, by the Greek poet Simonides (556–468 BCE). His title notwithstanding, Harris says little about music but argues at length for the superiority of painting over poetry. Each art's range of subject matter, Harris writes, is determined by its medium. Subjects most suitable for painting are objects, motions, and actions that can be represented in what he terms the *punctum temporis*, the single moment. Actions should be short enough to be pictured in an instant and intense enough to allow the viewer to apprehend the whole from this one part. It is unclear whether Barthes was aware of these writings, but the structural similarity of his *punctum* and Harris's *punctum temporis* is striking. Harris realizes that apprehending the whole from a part can be problematic when there is a lack of knowledge: "in a Story well known the Spectator's Memory will supply the previous and the subsequent. . . . [This] cannot be done where such Knowledge is wanting."[30] His uncle, the Earl of Shaftesbury, noted the same problem in his *Characteristicks*, yet he was not all too worried about it. He claimed that "That the Body . . . moves much slower than the Mind," meaning that a viewer would always easily "fill in" the gaps right before and right after the frozen figures to picture before his/her mind's eye how their action would unfold. "This different Operation may be distinguish'd by the names of *Anticipation* and *Repeal*," Shaftesbury claims.[31]

In his *Laocoön*, Lessing drives both points home when he takes the centrality of Harris's *punctum temporis* as his starting point for distinguishing poetry and painting on the basis of their mediums. Like Harris, he is less interested in what the two arts share in terms of effect and more in the strict borders of each medium's capacities, refuses to judge the one art in terms of the other. Yet Lessing's real problem with the *ut pictura poesis* doctrine is that critics have pushed the comparisons so far that they get bogged down in endless metaphorization; rather, they have started taking the metaphor "painting is as poetry" literally. In an attempt to stop the fabrication of false metaphors and inaccurate labels (particularly the expression "poetic painting" is for him a contradiction in terms), Lessing makes a strict point of taking the critics' expressions to the letter. Considering whether Laocoön screams once he is bitten by one of the serpents, as some suggested, Lessing claims the opposite. Whereas Virgil, as a poet, can have Laocoön bellow like a sacrificed ox, a statue simply is incapable of screaming, as the visual arts are, after all, mute. Therefore, the visual arts in general, Lessing suggests, should concentrate on a moment of stillness *before* the narrative's denouement. Rather than depicting the story's climax by letting out screams of pain, the sculpted figure of the priest *anticipates* this moment to come. Shaftesbury made a similar point when he wrote, in sentimental terms that Lessing would not dare using, that "the Artist has power to leave still in his Subject the Traces of Footsteps of its Predecessor . . . when the plain Traces of Tears new fallen . . . remain still in a Person newly transported with Joy. . . . By the same means, which are employ'd to call to mind *The Past* we may anticipate *the Future*."[32] Both Lessing and Shaftesbury agree that the *punctum temporis* is fruitful, suggestive of change to come. In that sense, they both remain close to Aristotle's notion of *peripeteia* as a dramatic reversal in a play, its most powerful moment, when the unfolding of the narrative suddenly turns into its opposite, when fortune reverts to tragedy, or tears turn into joy. Lessing implies that the pregnant moment or *punctum temporis* is, strictly speaking, not a well-defined moment but the interval before it, an in-between instance in which Laocoön silently draws in his breath before the anticipated scream. Goethe similarly suggests the fruitful moment to be a kind of interval, a visual anacrusis when he gives the example of a wave that temporarily stands still before crashing and rolling down. This visual anacrusis, therefore, can be neither transitory nor climactic. Even though we as viewers should recognize the represented story in the "blink of an eye" (*Augenblick*), Lessing insists that a painting is meant for lengthy and repeated contemplation: "it is evident that the single moment [*Augenblick*] and the single viewpoint from which it is seen, cannot be fruitful enough. Such moment can only be called fruitful when it gives free rein to the imagination. The more we see, the more we are able to think. The more we think about what we see, the more we are able to believe what we see. . . . Thus when Laocoön sighs the imagination can hear him shout. . . ."[33] Earlier, in 1678, the Dutch art theorist Samuel van Hoogstraten wrote in similar terms about a kind of movement encapsulated by an artist in a singular moment in painting that should be apprehended in a blink of an eye, which he termed "eye-blinking movement" (*oogenblikkige beweeging*): "It is not enough for a picture to be beautiful, it must have in it a certain moving quality that has power over those who see it . . . and so it is with Artists, they do not stir the mind if they omit this movement."[34]

In a reverse gesture, we have seen that Goethe takes Lessing's blink-of-an-eye moment, using it not to designate arrested time but to set the sculpture group in motion, fighting the philosopher with his own tools. Lessing seeks to demonstrate how the space of the visual arts is in fact always resistant to being taken up by a moment as it is frozen and can be lifted from this moment to turn into a narrative. The fruitful moment is what can *override* the restrictions of the material, enabling the viewer to see not merely the stone sculpture but everything that is suggested but not actually there. We could argue, with David Wellbery, that Lessing's theory is dangerously close to suppose a complete mortification of the visual arts.[35] Whereas poetry's mode of expression, the sound of the voice, is immaterial and as such is proximate to thought and the imagination, the material signs of the visual arts curtail the imagination as much as activate it. For Lessing, the pregnant moment just barely saves the visual arts from being utterly static and petrified. The traditional film studies debate has for a long time been stuck in a similar impasse by holding on to opposite concept pairs of stillness/mortification and movement/life. Even Barthes could not find a proper way out when he writes, slightly hesitantly, "When we define the Photograph as a motionless image, this does not mean only that the figures it represents do not move; it means that they do not *emerge*, do not *leave*: they are anesthetized and fastened down, like butterflies."[36] However, painting, as Van Hoogstraten claimed as well, holds on to the viewer's attention only if it manages to animate its composition, bringing it to life. Exactly how such animation may differ from Lessing's pregnant moment will be shown in a comparison between an early modern action painting and a very animated still life.

Possessing Movement

Around 1621, Cornelis Claesz. van Wieringen painted *Battle of Gibraltar in 1607*, depicting a clash between the Dutch and the Spanish (fig. 4). On April 25, 1607, the Dutch fleet carried out a surprise attack on the Spanish fleet anchored at the Bay of Gibraltar. The Spanish admiral, observing from one of the ten galleons under his command, was so amazed at the sight of the twenty-six rather smallish warships approaching that he asked his second-in-command if the Dutch were really going to attack. The reply was that they most certainly would. Though the Spaniards quickly tried to maneuver their

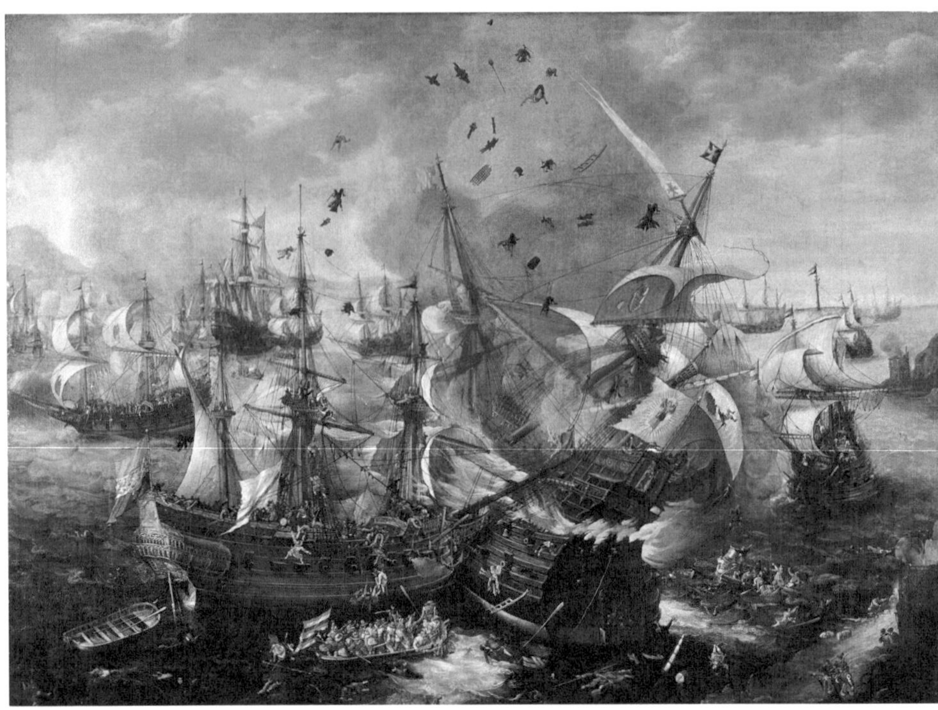

FIGURE 4 Cornelis Claesz. van Wieringen, *Battle of Gibraltar in 1607*, c. 1621. Oil on canvas; 136.8 × 187 cm. Amsterdam, Rijksmuseum.

ships, they were trapped like rats. In less than four hours, the Dutch captured the flagship, destroyed the other galleons, and killed some four thousand sailors who vainly tried to swim ashore. The victory was great, and the number of Dutch victims small, although Admiral Jacob van Heemskerk died early in the battle and was later buried in the Netherlands with great fanfare.

To appropriately commemorate the victory, Van Wieringen carefully selected the precise moment of reversal during battle: the explosion of one of the Spanish galleons due to a lucky (if well-fired) shot that landed directly in its powder magazine. This kaboom moment is painted as it would never have been seen in reality by the naked eye. This is a genuine *peripeteia*: while flames shoot out of the belly of the ship, the upper part is ripped off and for a split second hangs in midair, while the masts snap like matchsticks and the sails bellow and catch fire. The pressure of the explosion causes men and things to be thrown into the air as if they are mere leaves on a stormy autumn afternoon; one figure is still holding a sword while tumbling through the sky, a barrel is losing its hoops, baskets turn summersaults. Van Wieringen clearly attempted to "stretch out" the moment of the explosion by spreading it out on the canvas. One of the strategies he employed was to work with pairs of objects that he placed at different heights: cannon pushers, barrels, and ripped-off parts of rail are placed up in the sky and down below in the water, so that we can imagine the various projectiles' pathways shooting upward and tumbling down. There is even a pair of bleeding legs floating in the air, torn apart from a torso, which, hat still on its head, can be found in between two flagged masts.

If there is such a thing as an early modern action painting, here we have one of its finest examples. Lessing would have been satisfied: there is no danger for stasis or mortification. When he claimed that the depicted moment could not be fruitful enough, Van Wieringen's *Battle of Gibraltar* could have served as his example. We imagine way more than we see when we virtually follow the upward and downward tracks of objects and figures, parts and wholes. It seems as if Van Wieringen activated gravity as one of his most effective rhetorical tools. While the figures and objects fall, the exploded ship will slowly capsize, waves will break against the sides of the smaller boats, men will fall splashing into the sea, and everything up to the tiniest detail will be pitched toward total collapse—akin to what happens (on a smaller scale) to the wave in Goethe's description and to what Lessing speculates will be Laocoön's fate.

Nothing could be further from this spectacular early modern action painting than Adriaen Coorte's *Still Life with Hazelnuts* (1696; plate 3). On a cracked stone ledge lie a handful of hazelnuts, neatly blanketed in their husks against a dark, black background. A leafy twig attached to one of the husks sticks out as a miniature parasol. That is all there is. The little picture is utterly unassuming, even more so when we consider its historical position at the tail end of the monumental tradition of splendor and sensual celebration in seventeenth-century Dutch still life. Compared to the fracas of the sea battle, Coorte's picture gives us hardly anything to see. It is devoid of visual extravagance; there are no bright screaming colors, no shimmer or shine, and in particular, no action. Through its understated dimensions (it is smaller than a sheet of notebook paper) and its muted color palette, the painting seems almost apologetic about how little it has to offer. The fact that this simplistic scene is painted on cheap paper glued to cardboard rather than on canvas or panel only adds to its humbleness. Compared to Van Wieringen's exuberant and boisterous composition, full of noise and movement, Coorte's piece is simple, small, and somehow very silent. To Lessing, this would be an instance of petrified nature, an example of a spatiality that resists incorporation into the temporal movement of the imagination.[37] He in fact wanted the visual arts to effect a transformation from the materiality of the thing to the immateriality of the imagination. By emphasizing how time is prolonged within the compact space of the tabletop, Coorte's small picture is the opposite of a pregnant moment. The hazelnuts' frozen state is not incorporated into a temporal sequence but resists being aligned with any such sequence. Following Lessing for a moment, would this painting, therefore, *arrest* the movement of the imagination?

Reading Lessing closely, we see that his focus on the "moment" in painting, which he called *Augenblick* (the blink of an eye), is in fact not an actual moment but a *perception* of this brief span of time. Space in the visual arts is defined to the extent to which it can be perceived and thus is reduced to what is visible within it. As such, it is, always, subordinated to time. In *Laocoön*, despite the distinction between poetry as a temporal and painting as a spatial art, space never gets conceptualized on its own terms. If we would follow Lessing closely, Coorte's piece should be dismissed as not being proper art. It would allow for no lengthy contemplation, nor free rein of the imagination, nor a transformation of the material into the immaterial. There is no movement that could be translated into a temporal moment, there is no suggestion of a next moment, no pitching toward what comes next.

Yet it is characteristic of pensive images in that it is in this indeterminate moment that this tiny tableau comes to life as if it were a pictorial kind of "it-narrative" (*avant la lettre*).[38] The hazelnuts seem to slowly awaken from a deep sleep, trying to stretch the ends of their husks, as if they are repressing the impulse to yawn. The longer we look, the more we see that each hazelnut starts to take on individual traits which turn it into a character, playing its role in a dimmed, pale light on this minimalist stage as directed by Coorte. Indeed, they are not merely lying there but seem to be heading in a certain direction. While the central hazelnut steals the show, proudly presenting its wormhole as a mark of its excellence, two kernels on the right seem to be having a kind of intimate moment, rubbing shoulders as if to greet one another after a long absence. On the left, one hazelnut is turning away, about to leave the scene. Is it being called back by the other lone hazelnut that approaches it from behind? Can we hear them? Are they *whispering* to one another?

Coorte's painting is an excellent example of an animated still life in the eyes of French art critic Theophile Thoré-Bürger. He argued in the 1860s that the term *nature morte* did not do justice to the things on display because they were not dead: they respired, they still *lived*. Thoré-Bürger insisted that there was animation in immobility, and life in death, and for him these polarities bounced off one another in still life painting; yet they also seem to merge, in paint, without losing any of their extremeness. In the same vain, in his wonderful essay of the 1930s on Dutch art, the poet and diplomat Paul Claudel wrote about objects in Dutch still life painting as looking off balance, and as though they were about to fall: "There is a napkin or a rug on the point of unrolling, the handle of a knife ready to become detached, a little loaf of bread falling into slices as if of its own volition, and overturned cup, all sorts of vases or fruits tumbled in a head, and overhanging plates. . . . Dutch still life is an arrangement in imminent danger of disintegration; it is something at the mercy of time."[39] Here, Claudel is trying to push Lessing's theory of the pregnant moment to the extreme when finding a peripatetic arrangement even in such immobile, timeless images as we find in still lifes. And yet, when we start looking at such images as things at the mercy of time, these apparent motionless pictures start to vibrate. Following Claudel in this respect, we find a series of small and modest instances of such imminent dangers everywhere, even in a simple display of a bowl of wild strawberries by Jan Jansz. van de Velde III (1658; fig. 5). While the glass of white wine stands solid like a temple's pillar, the bowl is placed on two of the cherries, whose chubby flesh gives way as it is pressed by bowl's rim. The twig of cherries on the right is also in a quite precarious position, two of its three fruits dangling dangerously over the table's edge. They are indeed at the mercy of time; the third cherry, dragged by the weight of the other two, will soon tip over, pulling with it the carefully placed spoon in its fall, and the pits—already pushed to the very edge of the table—will follow suit. Van de Velde deploys gravity in this small scene with as much effectiveness as Van Wieringen did in his *Battle of Gibraltar*, yet with completely different result. Whereas Van Wieringen is successful in pursuing a painting with a closed form, despite the explosion, Coorte manages with minimal means to break through patterns of expectation to confront us with a scene that is entirely without action. Even such common tropes in flower still lifes as a fallen petal or a crawling insect suggesting activity have been left out. And yet, Coorte's hazelnuts seem to breathe or vibrate. Coorte demonstrates that action and activity are not the same as movement, and that paintings like these can offer unpitched instances of stillness.

Restless Rest

In his *Disconnected Thoughts on Painting, Sculpture and Poetry* (1781), Denis Diderot wrote that "the life and the action of a figure are two very different things. Life is represented in a figure at rest. Artist have given the word *movement* a particular meaning. They say of a figure at rest that it possesses *movement*, that is, it is about to move."[40] Unlike Lessing, for whom the moment of stillness anticipated a climax, the figures (and objects, we may say)

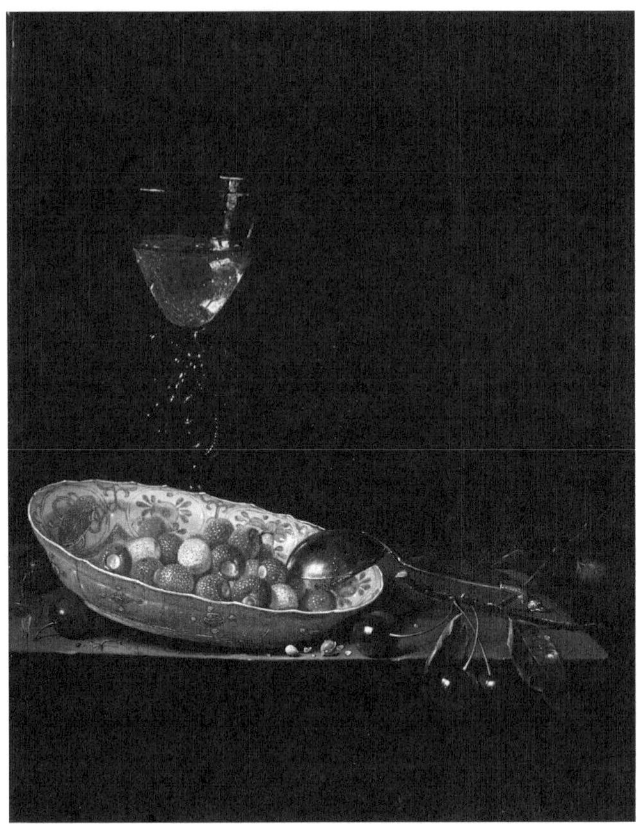

FIGURE 5 Jan Jansz. van de Velde III, *Still Life with Strawberries and Cherries*, 1658. Oil on panel; 38 × 30 cm. Oxford, Ashmolean Museum. Photo © Ashmolean Museum, University of Oxford.

at rest that Diderot and Goethe refer to "possess" movement yet express no inclination as to its aim or direction. Goethe's Juno and Minerva are shown as they are *about* to move, but they are still holding off. While it remains unclear what their next gesture will be, they do possess the potential. They are unpitched, as it were, and in a state of *possessing* movement rather than anticipating it.

We see a similar divide in Bisschop's painting, where reflections on temporality and passing evoked in us as viewers seem to be shaped by the constellation of motionless objects in the image. It is as if we see time arrested at the moment the female figure has left the hallway, a frozen moment in an ongoing suspension of action where the objects are waiting with us, all the while circumscribing the contours of an irretrievable moment, of which only the remnants are visible to us. As we have seen, painting, unlike photography (especially in Barthes's definition of the medium), has the capacity to add movement or animation to seemingly motionless objects, to make them possess movement-to-come, *in rest*. This sense of motion is something of a blending of different layers of time that are superimposed like two transparent sheets. Painting, unlike cinema, cannot show this kind of montage of past and future. However, pensive images such as Bisschop's do precisely that: two kinds of temporality seem to fuse when the drafty corner representing the moment right after the woman's rushed passing merges with the current of air that remains hanging there in suspense, frozen forever. There is something moving in this scene, restless: thought as such, of course.[41]

In Bisschop's painting we see, in fact, a constellation of objects arrested in time that picture a line of thought. I consider this *Interior* and other paintings like it, as literal thought-images (German, *Denkbilder*: *Denk*, "thought"; *Bilder*, "images") (Dutch, *denkbeelden*), in which not only are philosophy and art united, but through their stillness they arrest our flow of thought to show us a particular constellation, a thought process at a standstill. What paintings by Bisschop and other apparently inexpressive images like the work by Jacob Vrel (active 1654–1665) show is an almost banal formal language of household things that has been given a sense of brooding, of being absorbed in something through which something abstract is articulated that remains, however, partly impenetrable.[42] These images are not allegories or emblems that can be deciphered but thought-images that remain open, incomplete, and, to a certain extent, frustrating. The unthought is somehow *in* the image through objects and bodies that, though at rest, all the while possess movement. Such images do not bring the sort of closure that Goethe found so remarkable about *Laocoön and His Sons*. Instead what they have opened up are ways toward theoretical reflection. I will look further into the way in which movement can be captured in rest as a way of setting out a line of thought that is somehow moving through the sculptured body. And no one was better aware of thoughts moving through sculpted bodies at rest than Johann Joachim Winckelmann, whose work we will look at in the next chapter.

CHAPTER TWO

Tracing the *Denkbild*

The senses and passions speak and understand nothing but images. The entire store of human knowledge and happiness consists in images.

JOHANN GEORG HAMANN, *AESTHETICS IN NUCE*

Painterly Stillness

Even before Johann Joachim Winckelmann settled in Rome and could see *Laocoön and His Sons* in the flesh, so to speak, he had written on the sculptural group in his first book, *Thoughts on the Imitation of the Greeks in Painting and Sculpture* (1755). In this essay, having already seen a plaster copy, Winckelmann identified *Laocoön and His Sons* as the embodiment of his concept "*edele Einfalt und stille Grösse*" (noble simplicity and calm grandeur), the chief characteristic of the great works of Greek art. Though *stille Grösse* has usually been translated into English as "calm grandeur," Winckelmann actually meant "still" or "quiet."[1] "The more tranquil the state of the body the more capable it is of painting [*schildern*] the true character of the soul," he declared.[2] Winckelmann did not mean that tranquility as such would guarantee grandeur, and he would have agreed with the later remark of Johann Gottfried Herder, in his notes on Winckelmann's text, that "Repose by itself is lethargy, and a sort of . . . death."[3] Yet the complete absence of any kind of tranquility in the representation of the violated body would result in Laocoön's suffering being inadequately—that is, excessively and indecorously—portrayed (Winckelmann uses the rhetorical term *parenthyrsos*, exorbitant and unsuitable pathos). Therefore, a certain kind of tranquility was needed to represent suffering, appropriately yet in a grand style. As such, Laocoön's stillness is one *in spite of* the convulsive spasms of the body, which we see, for instance, in the hollowed-out abdomen—a result of the deep breath Laocoön draws in—that, Winckelmann writes, at the same time "expos[es] to our view the movement of his entrails, as it were."[4] Indeed, the stillness in *Laocoön and*

His Sons is meant to be expressive of a state of resistance or contradiction to the intense pain indicated by the priest's swollen muscles and rising chest. This sculpture is for him a paradigm of Greek art, because it presents a perfect balance of conflicting tensions. The artists were masters in selecting that one particular action that stood in closest possible proximity to a state of tranquility found somewhere within Laocoön's experience of pain. Grandeur is thus found in a conflict of forces when tranquility becomes expressive of intense pain. It is through this conflict, Winckelmann insists, that the true soul is "painted."

As Hegel indicated in his *Lectures on Aesthetics*, given in Heidelberg and Berlin and posthumously published eighty years after Winckelmann's *Thoughts on the Imitation of the Greeks*, Winckelmann had been looking for a new sense by which to contemplate art, a "whole new way of looking at things" that aimed to discover the true idea in both the artwork and the history of art.[5] One of his discoveries was precisely the conflict of tensions between Laocoön's "moving" entrails and the stillness resulting from his deep breath; or rather, how art's true soul was "painted" even though he was dealing here with sculpture.[6] Evidently, he seemed to imply that painting as a medium possesses a greater sense of tranquility than sculpture does. I will compare Winkelmann's tranquility to the "painterly" stillness, which Rancière observed in Balzac's pensive marquise and Bisschop was able to capture in his *Interior*. In this chapter, I will further explore this notion of stillness in the work of Winckelmann as a figure of thought. Such stillness, I argue, always encompasses a moment of great anticipation, of something to come, to become, to swell even, like the breast of Laocoön when he draws his breath or Goethe's wave at the moment before breaking. The kind of stillness that we thus find in art was explored at great length by Winckelmann, who characterized it as a creative, thought-bearing force in what is probably his most famous text: the ekphrasis of the *Belvedere Torso*. As we will see, Herder was deeply impressed by Winckelmann's close reading of the *Belvedere Torso* as being reflective of thought processes, and Herder would further extend Winckelmann's ideas, channeling them toward the full-blown notion of what he calls a *Denkbild*.

I will trace the journey of the notion of the *Denkbild* from its early manifestations in seventeenth-century art theory to its philosophical conceptualization in the work of Herder and Winckelmann, finally to the writings of the Frankfurt school, in particular, of Walter Benjamin, who labeled his collection of short, literary miniatures *Denkbilder*. Within the scope of this chapter, I cannot explore the various links that may exist between *Denkbilder* and other cultural expressions such as emblemata, but I will discuss the so-called

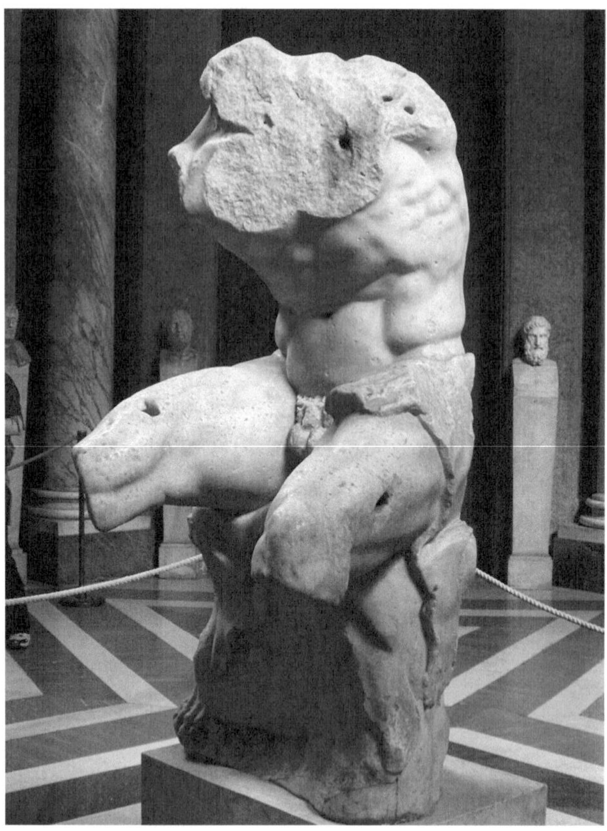

FIGURE 6 *Belvedere Torso*, 1st century CE. Rome, Museo Pio-Clementino.

hieroglyphs of Dutch print maker and scholar Romeyn de Hooghe, who likely was a source of inspiration to Herder, who in his turn was an influence on Benjamin's thought. As we will see, Herder had quite a liberal understanding of an image, building philosophical constellations that he referred to as images, even creating an image of text by his idiosyncratic use of typography.

Rippling through the Body

Winckelmann's "Description of the Torso in the Belvedere in Rome" (1759) is a document that is as mutilated as the object it discusses (fig. 6). From the outset, the writer explains how he had initially wanted to discuss the most perfect statues of antiquity—*Laocoön and His Sons*, the *Apollo Belvedere*, the *Belvedere Torso*, and the *Antinous*—in a threefold presentation: namely, as engraving, as ideal description, and as artistic description. In this way he could depict them in the most complete way. But then, in a gesture of reticence, Winkelmann declares that he has given up on this overly ambitious plan, admitting that even the present (ideal) description of the torso running merely a handful of pages is still in need of some finishing touches. Rather than being a completed text, this piece of writing is a test, Winckelmann declares, "of what there is to think and say about such a perfect work of art, and as an example of the inquiry into art."[7] As an example of "doing" art history, even as it is declared from the start that this exercise was bound to be a failed ekphrasis, this is a most crucial text in Winckelmann's oeuvre. The challenge for the aspiring art historian in this inquiry is how to let this apparently perfect work of art emerge out of a far from perfect form: this statue, or what is left of it, is stripped of its main features, including its head, arms, and most of the legs. Essentially, it is a mere chunk of stone. How to make sense of a fragment like this?

Winckelmann's tour de force is breathtaking. Unlike Goethe, who advised viewers to bring *Laocoön and His Sons* to life by blinking rapidly in front of it, Winckelmann promises that "if you consider this work with a calm eye," the chunk of stone will initiate you into the secrets of art.[8] Subjected to this calm, contemplative eye, the mutilated body of the *Belvedere Torso* will slowly transform itself into the great hero Hercules, Winckelmann insists, who we envision here at rest in between two of his labors. In the course of his discussion, despite his insistence on keeping calm, as his eye scrutinizes the surface of Hercules's body, he becomes gradually more excited about the wonderfully articulated action and reaction of its muscles, the mass of the swelling chest, the swelling cure of its vault, or the force of its tights. Time and again, his enthusiastic eye rest on curves that, he implies, articulate the contrast between the quiet and peaceful poses of the figure, and the motions visible in the muscles under its skin. As with *Laocoön and His Sons*, but in a much more sophisticated fashion, Winckelmann considers the torso to be the perfect match between muscle tension and lofty spirit. In this case, the contrast between the perfect and noble form and the immortal spirit that it stands for, in fact, is greater than in *Laocoön and His Sons*, as Hercules possesses, after all, a far from proper "form."

His own words notwithstanding, Winckelmann is less interested in revealing the artwork's secret and more in initiating a particular kind of restoration project. The real test lies not in describing the torso in the full glory of the complete body it once had, but to prove how a close observation of the currently mutilated figure reveals the very potential of mastery. His adoring writing demonstrates how we can "think" of this figure's perfect beauty, not as it *was*, but as a way of *becoming*, as if it were rising in front of our eyes. The bare stillness of this chunk of stone is filled with the signs of bodily strain resulting from heavy physical exertion. Hercules's body is actively heroic, yet passively contented, as Alex Potts so aptly phrases it.[9] The essence of this mutilated figure's beauty lies in this repose, in the self-possessed activity of the resting body. "Stillness is the state that is the most proper to beauty, as it is to the sea," Winckelmann later wrote in his *History of the Art of Antiquity*.[10] Yet just as the depths of the sea may be filled with strong currents that can be made evident by a slight surge over its calm surface, the chest of Hercules swells, his body becomes a landscape filled with sunken valleys, the rising hills of musculature, and meandering rivers. Water, as a kind of language of beauty of its own, is employed by Winckelmann as a central metaphor that enables him to not only to argue for the torso's beauty but to get lost in his own contemplations, as if carried away by a wave: "As in a rising motion of the sea the previously still surface swells into a lovely tumult with playful waves, where one is swallowed by the other and is again rolled out from the very same wave, here, just as softly swollen and drawn in suspension, one muscle flows into the other, and a third, which raises itself between them and seems to strengthen their motion, loses itself in the latter, and our glance is, as it were, likewise swallowed."[11]

The image of a muscle that resembles a wave raising itself in between two others, thereby reinforcing its swelling while swallowing your intense gaze, is an effective metaphor for the loss of self, and Winckelmann is all too willing to let himself be rocked away, as if sprawled upon the hero's heavily breathing chest. Much has been said about the homoeroticism of his writings, in particular of his enthusiasm for the flanks of sculpted male figures, and this text, brimming with desire, is no different. However, we should recall that the description of the *Belvedere Torso* is for Winckelmann a test. It is the only description he published as an independent essay before he incorporated it into his *History of the Art of Antiquity* (1764), and later included as a model of an allegorical reading of ancient art in *An Attempt at Allegory* (1766). Published in three different texts, it occupies a fundamental place in his oeuvre as a model or paradigm of art history. His project is not so much to make sense of what he considers to be one of the most beautiful surviving fragments of antiquity but to restore it—yet not as the perfect work of art it once was, but what it will become, once this damaged object is included in art's history, or rather in its system, as Winckelmann would have it. As a fragment, it is no longer "actively" participating in the full course of its monumental history, but it is "at rest," so to speak, as part of art's system. Yet before our calm eyes, we see how the object ripples with tension and swells to proportions it may never have had even in optimal state of production. It is this very dynamic, involving this object's historicity and its becoming in which Winckelmann is interested. No matter how erotically invested his indulging gaze is, the torso is a model of beauty that is embodied yet mutilated, historicized yet immortal. It is a concrete idea, so to speak. "What a conception [*Begriff*] develops here at the same time out of the hips," he writes, approaching body parts as if they were philosophical concepts.[12] Characteristic of Winckelmann's style, and on display quite a bit in this essay, is his complete merging of description and theory, looking and thinking. For instance, when he is musing about the figure's thighs and how they must have carried the hero to far lands, his mind suddenly "was recalled by means of a glimpse at his back."[13] Typically, Winckelmann oscillates between the spectacular sights of this stone body and the wanderings of his thoughts, a rocking back and forth that effectively becomes a creative force in the sense that thought seems to become embodied in stone, just as the figure's posture and other physical characteristics become indicative of concepts. This creative force is apparently so transformative that it even allows for the reappearance of Hercules's vanished limbs: "the remaining missing limbs begin to form in my thoughts, flowing forth and together from what is present and effecting, as if it were, as sudden restoration."[14] Not much like Michelangelo, who proved an excellent "reader" of Laocoön's muscles, correctly perceiving that the priest's missing arm would have been bent behind his neck (confirmed when a fragment of the arm was found in a builder's yard in Rome in 1906), Winckelmann reads the torso's flowing curves as if he were following them with his finger so as to keep track of his thoughts. Or more precisely, he traces the muscles' contours by caressing the sculpture with his gaze, following his line of thought through every curve and ripple of the marble. He searches for moments of tension apparent in the figure's muscle tissue, where stasis is about to break so that the figure's conception begins growing, *becoming* something, rather than merely *being there*. "If it seems incomprehensible to locate a thinking power in some part of the body besides the head," Winckelmann explains, "then one learns here how the hand of a creative master is capable of animating matter."[15] And this is exactly what he has tried to demonstrate in this short description: how matter, in this instance stone, can be animated, how there is motion in stillness, if not of muscles swelling or water surging then of thoughts rising. Indeed, the description of the *Belvedere Torso* is Winckelmann's clearest attempt to show how stone curves can generate "thinking power." Ultimately, what has been animated here is thought.

In this light, it comes as no surprise that the "Description of the Torso in the Belvedere in Rome" was inserted into *An Attempt at an Allegory*,

Particularly for Art (1767) as a model for the allegorical reading of an ancient artwork. Winckelmann defines allegory to be a "suggestion of concepts by images" that are "saying something that is different from what one wishes to refer to," or saying something that takes a direction other than what the expression would suggest.[16] In the same breath, he sees the allegorical as encompassing "everything that is indicated by pictures and signs," which does not mean that all art is allegorical, but rather that the mind is constantly translating objects into images, images into concepts, a process illustrated in his essay. In fact, he moves away from the idea that art's main aim is to imitate nature.

Winckelmann's suggestion that the sculpture of antiquity is satiated with thought could not have been further from the views of Lessing, who objected that the visual arts contain elements fundamentally alien to thought, blocking rather than stimulating the imagination. In his review of Lessing's *Laocoön*, published in 1769, the popular philosopher and translator Christian Garve (1742–1798) summarized a generally shared assumption about such a process: "Thoughts are determined to some degree by their signs and that which would have seemed doubtful or even incorrect to us, if expressed simply or plainly, strikes us in the more appropriate and illuminating designation we have given it as true and evident. In this way, the soul is often blinded by its own light."[17] As we have seen, Lessing argues for purity of medium, and hence fiercely opposes a deliberate mix of natural and arbitrary signs in the visual arts, which is precisely what happens in allegory. Compared to Lessing, for whom the artwork is an aesthetic object serving no other function than to present itself as an autonomous vessel for intrinsic beauty, Winckelmann's *Torso* can be labeled as a thought-image, a *Denkbild*, a form that *shapes* rather than contains its abstract meaning. The *Belvedere Torso* embodies thought as much as thought runs through it, directing it to a beyond that the statue itself cannot reach.

In fact, Winckelmann's ambition is to move away from mimesis as art's aim and toward an allegorical approach to art in general. Transgressing the notion of mere allegory, the *Torso* as thought-image is an organizing instrument, purveying a mini-system in which opposing forces are laid bare yet appear to be swelling, like an indrawn breath, into something larger than itself, expectant yet in suspension. For now, I suggest we call this conception a line of thought. This line of thought is not a single concept or idea, but as we have seen with Winckelmann's water metaphor, it comprises a larger network of associations and interactions that allow disparate elements to coexist when they turn into a creative force. To fully understand the extent to which an artwork such as the *Belvedere Torso* can be understood as a *Denkbild*, we should turn to the great theorist of *Denkbilder* in the eighteenth century, a man who, not coincidentally, provided some of the best commentary on Winckelmann's writings: Johann Gottfried Herder.

Typographic Thoughts

In *Critical Forests: First Grove* (1769), Herder, a fervent reader of basically everything, takes up a defense of Winckelmann against Lessing's attacks in *Laocoön*. On page after page, Herder fulminates against Lessing's conservatism and his lack of refinement, claiming that the he "does not present a finished train of thought but . . . thinks out loud." In contrast, he celebrates the perfection of Winckelmann's writing, which is likened to "an ancient work of art. Formed in all its parts, each thought obtrudes and stands there, noble, simple, sublime, complete: it *is*."[18] Herder's attention to the two scholars' style is particularly fitting within his conception of philosophy as a whole, as he assigns a specific task to the use of philosophical language. He parts ways with influential eighteenth-century thinkers such as Christian Wolff (1679–1754) who rejected any dressing up of words—a philosopher should write pragmatically and not like an orator or poet (detesting poetic philosophy, Lessing could not have agreed more). Herder, in contrast, considered language to be a most powerful and complex cultural tool that not only mediates or articulates but actually triggers the process of thinking.[19] Unlike anyone before him, Herder places language at the heart of a philosophy of knowledge, for which he has been called the "father" of the philosophy of language that gained such prominence in the twentieth century. In his writing he breaks with the basic rule in philosophical argumentation never to appeal to the reader's emotions. He writes as if speaking directly to his audience in the combined role of orator, poet, and thinker. His aim is to motivate and stimulate his audience's thoughts as much as to seek their understanding of his ideas and reasoning; but most of all he intends to appeal to their emotions. Herder is convinced that there is no such thing as a universal language or even general concepts, as words always fall short of expressing distinctly the individuality of one human being. As long as expressions are intended mere generally, they lack singularity and liveliness, Herder argues, and as a result, we as readers are simply words as empty phrases without truly understanding them. A word needs character or some distinctive trait to enable it to express something abstract, that is, something more than its literal signification. One way of breaking with the supremacy of a universal language and consequently with philosophy's corresponding principle to write in naked language is to make words more expressive. Herder wishes to distinguish particular moments in a given text by adding feeling, for instance, through exclamation marks or by giving specific passages a sense of temperament through the use of a particular typeface. Over the course of his career, the philosopher developed a wide range of modes for dressing up naked words, by placing them in varied, quickly alternating sentence structures, using plenty of punctuation marks, and isolating particular words and phrases via brief and effective interjections. It was clearly important for him to emphasize words typographically, evident from his use of *Sperrdruck* (adding spaces between the letters of a word) in certain instances rather than the more prevalent usage of italics.[20] The result is typographically stunning: a wild patchwork of irregular sentences, intensive use of italics and letter spacing, and one-word interjections speckled with exclamation marks seem to jump off every page of Herder's immense philosophical oeuvre. These textual devices were rhetorically effective, because the look of the page communicated a distinct "image" of immediacy, frankness, passion, and restlessness, more than a little reminiscent of concrete poetry. Herder scholar Hans Adler has suggested that we, as readers, should look at his texts not only from above, but also from the side, so as to see the italicized words standing out from the page. Emerging under our awry glance is a kind of textual image that appears as an imprint of Herder's deeply emotional mode of thinking. Instead of naked text, we see, as Hans Adler so aptly phrases it, a "rippled" surface with "outstanding elements" connected intentionally through typographic emphasis, creating an almost tactile effect.[21] Can we say that we can "read" Herder's thinking as it ripples through his typography, just as Winckelmann was reading thoughts as they were rippling through the muscles of the *Belvedere Torso*?

Herder's typographic idiosyncrasy brings out his abiding interest in the materiality of the arbitrary sign. Usually, in other (philosophical) writing, awareness of lettering and typography disappears while the reader becomes absorbed in the text and attends to the meaning of words and phrases, which, it is presumed, are bound to no particular typographic expression. But Herder lets the image of the word surface in his writing, so that what emerges via his typography is a *Denkungsart*, a manner of thinking. For him, the method of his thinking is—literally—*in* his text. "If words are not just signs," he writes, "but instead so to speak the shells in which we see thoughts, I look at an entire language as a great range of thoughts become visible, as an immeasurable country of concepts."[22] According to Herder, within an immeasurable country of concepts (*ein unermäßlich Land von Begriffen*; what he sometimes also calls a "field of thoughts," *Feld von Gedanken*), certain constellations of concepts and ideas start to stand out, emerging from this field not unlike the way the emphasized words stand out from Herder's published page. These kinds of constellations are what Herder calls *Denkbilder*, or conceptual images, customarily translated into English as thought-images. *Denkbilder* are organizing principles that keep the jumble of words and thoughts in check. They structure the chaos of words and thoughts according to underlying patterns and channel them into recognizable, visible networks. While serving as a functional construction, they play a crucial role in Herder's thinking; he even refers to them as being pure forms of humanity (*reiner Formen der Menschheit*).[23]

Herder's *Denkbilder*

In 1786, Herder published *Nemesis: Ein lehrendes Sinnbild*, in which he invokes the personification of Nemesis.[24] Relying heavily on Winckelmann's essay on allegory, to which he frequently refers, Herder traces Nemesis's roots in word and image back to antiquity. He may have been familiar with Albrecht Dürer's print *Nemesis* (c. 1500; also sometimes referred to as *Das große Glück*; fig. 7), in which we see a winged female figure hovering over a mountainous landscape where, nested in a valley, a small village is visible near a riverbank. The figure holds up a golden goblet symbolizing fortune in one hand while squeezing under her arm a bridle, a symbol of control and moderation, one of its ribbons dangling behind her as if leaving its trace. Her pedestal is a sphere that stands for the fragile balance of our destiny, which Dürer depicts here as pressing a cleavage into the layers of clouds covering the valley, indicating the strength of her impact. As carrier of both fortune and restraint, this is Nemesis as Herder would like to see her—not as she is commonly known, as the goddess of revenge, but rather as a more complex protectress against excess and a distributor of fortune. Reviving the image from oblivion as a means of rescuing her reputation, modifying or rather extending its meaning in the process, he insists on understanding Nemesis not as a bringer of doom but as a principle of moderation, to be loved rather than feared. She is the embodiment of balance, standing for the force leading toward it, as she represents for Herder the world's tendency toward equilibrium in nature and human history alike. Capable of looking right into people's hearts, Nemesis is able to weigh an individual's responsibility against the fortunes of the world, and in the course of time she harmonizes these extremes. She unites not only history with nature but also subjective experience with the unfolding of history at large. Transforming his iconographic discussion of a forgotten motif into a didactic tale, Herder stresses that his depiction of Nemesis is a

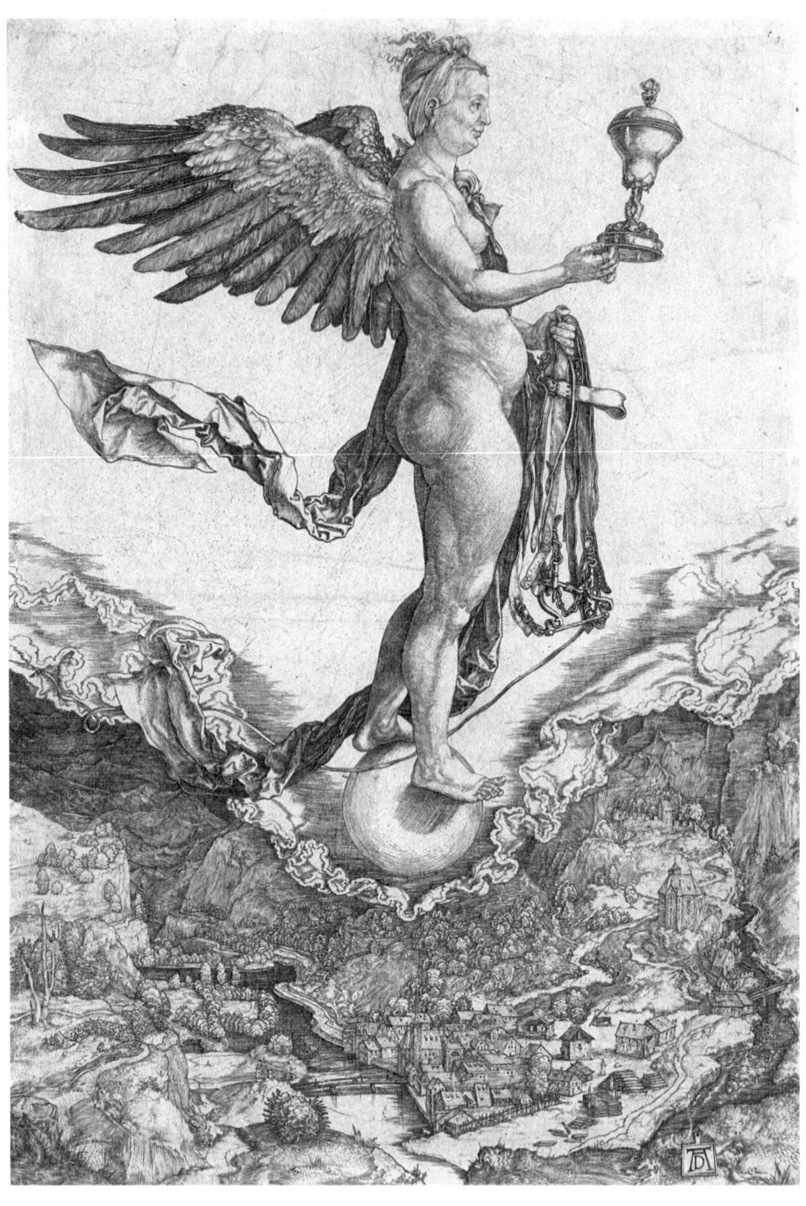

FIGURE 7 Albrecht Dürer, *Nemesis* (*The Great Fortune*), 1501–1502. Engraving; 33.3 × 23.1 cm. New York, Metropolitan Museum of Art.

"teaching" image for us, as it speaks to our "inner Nemesis," reminding people blessed by fortune of the danger of hubris: "he must learn to bridle himself, even if Hope puts wings to his steps."[25]

Ultimately, for Herder, this *Denkbild*, in all its contradictions and complexities, serves as a framework for his concept of humanity.[26] As no theory could, the very image of Nemesis makes history meaningful as a process resulting from dialectical forces, where the universal touches the individual, thereby providing insight into the greater scheme of things. Herder's overall conception is based on his idea that images can better express ideas than words or abstract concepts ever could: "One can express in pictures what is never or only weakly and miserably expressed through stark-naked abstractions,"[27] he writes in "Über der Wirkung der Dichtkunst auf die Sitten der Völker" (1778). As he refrains from referring to specific depictions of the goddess, the question arises as to what kind of picture he had in mind when he composed his *Denkbild*. He must have been acutely aware of the lack of complexity in the basic iconographical pictures of Nemesis, for instance, in Andrea Alciati's widely known *Emblematum libellus* (1542) where we see personifications such as Nemesis alongside Hope, but each has been placed on a separate pedestal. Alciati's emblems emphasize the antagonism between two motifs in the iconographic tradition, a tension that Herder understood not as separate strands but as part of one larger dynamic. He seems to respond directly to Alciati's emblem when he declares, by quoting an epigram, "I worship Nemesis and Hope on one altar."[28] His carefully composed image of Nemesis goes beyond the largely unambiguous personifications of Renaissance or baroque allegories in that he makes it multifaceted, a merging of precisely those tensions that cannot quite be unified but keep each other in check. Our interpretation and understanding of Nemesis as *Sinnbild*, Herder argues, can save us from being dragged down by the vices of our human nature and assist us in rising toward a more beautiful—harmonized—form of humanity characterized by the fundamental contradictions that she embodies.[29] Whereas some commentators have named the baroque emblem as a possible inspiration for Herder's *Denkbild*, the structure of his Nemesis image and others like it is far more complex than what is suggested by the emblem's clear-cut tripartite of motto, picture, and explanation. Moreover, emblems are largely straightforward moral life lessons, scripted in the kind of word-image puzzle that its intended popular audience never found too difficult to decipher, hence the enormous success of such emblems. Herder's *Denkbilder*, however, are much more sophisticated in meaning and in structure and are aimed at an intellectual readership. I suggest that his *Denkbilder* may have links to the baroque emblem, but they are more attuned with another kind of picture-puzzle that circulated in intellectual rather than popular circles and attracted the attention of many philosophers, painters, and writers: the hieroglyph.

Thought's Embodiment

Before Egyptian hieroglyphs were properly deciphered in 1822, the term "hieroglyph" referred not only to actual Egyptian inscriptions but also to the more general idea that there had been a primordial language of pictographs predating the separation of word and image. Archaeological fragments gave evidence of such pictographs, which were thought to embody ancient knowledge whose code had yet to be broken by contemporary scholars. Such obscure pictographs were seen as ciphers, clues to a lost past, and they initiated wild speculation about the kind of universal language spoken on earth before the fall of the Tower of Babel. They also sparked a series of linguistic and philosophical arguments about the primacy of images over text, the origins of language. Interest in the interplay between word and image, and natural and arbitrary signs, was gradually rising. Collectors of curiosities and naturalia started to draw parallels between taxonomy and language, which in turn fostered the didactic view that "the sciences find easier entrance through the eyes than through the ears."[30] Students and scholars were encouraged to "read" the book of nature in pictures—and to read things *as* pictures—a process that, according to Aristotle, left a more lasting impression on the mind than did perceiving things merely as things. Comenius (1592–1670) had great faith in the potential of pictographs and Chinese characters to reveal the secret of the development of a universal language, and he called on scholars to devote themselves "to the discovery not only of a language but of thought."[31]

Whereas earlier, scholars had been suspicious of enigmatic imagery and conceived emblems to be perversely obscure and possibly bordering on the superstitious—the Earl of Shaftesbury denounced them as "enigmatical, preposterous, disproportional, gouty and lame forms"—toward the mid-eighteenth century the tide started to change.[32] Giambattista Vico was a strong advocate for studying hieroglyphs as a way of approaching the earliest instances of the use of language, and complained bitterly in *La scienza nuova* (1725) that "[s]cholars have failed to understand how the first nations thought in poetic characters, spoke in fables, and wrote in hieroglyphs."[33] But soon philosophers, writers, and painters became more seriously interested in the hieroglyph, not only as the basis of ancient Egyptian writing but as a hyper-flexible figure, a kind of vehicle to shape thought. Surprisingly, this figure was applicable to multiple media: poetry could be defined as hieroglyphic, but so could allegorical images, knots of intricate philosophical concepts, or epistemological conundrums. The figure of the hieroglyph was thus equally adaptable to the art of poetry and painting as it was to philosophy or theology, and hence it was used to indicate enigmatic or idiosyncratic elements within a given poem, picture, or argument. Conceived as a perfect blend of symbol and allegory—or arbitrary and natural signs—and calling for a hermeneutic approach, the hieroglyph was said to reside at the very foundation of human thought and so came to stand for a particular material concept of language: as thought's *embodiment*, rather than its vehicle. Diderot certainly understood it that way; in his *Salons*, he offered his readers highly detailed descriptions of artworks he had seen at the biennial Louvre exhibition, often running to several pages and punctuated with intensely emotional responses. These descriptions, which he named hieroglyphs, were meant to evoke in his readers' minds tableaux of the artworks Diderot had seen. Such tableaux were intended to serve as immaterial, nonverbal substitutes for his verbal descriptions, which in turn were surrogates for the concrete works of art. Intended to efface itself once the connection between concrete artwork and mental image was made, Diderot's hieroglyph was actually a phase of transmission, a mode of writing akin to a channel that enabled the image to travel, via its verbal description, to the reader's mind.[34] In addition to being a self-effacing form of ekphrasis, a hieroglyph thus denoted an ambiguous and enigmatic form of writing that required complete involvement of the reader for it to emerge visually. For Diderot, all poetry was fundamentally emblematic, not as an *expression* of an idea but as a tissue of superimposed hieroglyphs *picturing* it. Far from veiling meaning, the hieroglyph produces—performs—meaning.[35] In pictorial discourse, the term "hieroglyph" was used as a synonym for complicated emblems and could refer to actual prints as well as a deliberately complicated mode of painting, close to allegory. Samuel van Hoogstraten went even further when he claimed that all painting is hieroglyphic. In his influential *Introduction to the High Academy of Painting* (1678) he declares it simply wrong to call painting "mute poetry," because evidently "Pictura speaks abundantly, in a hieroglyphic manner."[36] Prior to Van Hoogstraten, Gerardus Vossius (1577–1649) argued in his posthumously published treatise on painting entitled "De Graphice" (1650) that the Greek verb for painting meant "writing," which supported his larger claim that the two practices were closely linked.[37]

In the course of the eighteenth century, the hieroglyph increasingly became, in the hands of artists and scholars, a kind of mold by which thought processes could be shaped, an interstice between word and image, language and thought, sign and meaning. We could go as far as to state that the hieroglyph became a chameleon-like figure, capable of taking a verbal, mental, or pictorial form while remaining the embodiment of thought. Herder's reinvention of *Denkbild*, and its obvious appeal for depicting, or indeed shaping, philosophical concepts, was not a general response to the discourse on hieroglyphs; it had a concrete—pictorial—equivalent, namely, the unique series of engraved hieroglyphs, called *merkbeelden* or *denkbeelden* (thought-images) developed by one of the most prolific Dutch book illustrators of his time, Romeyn de Hooghe. As we will see, Herder was inspired by De Hooghe's work and appropriated from him his specific method of construction and analysis, as well as his terminology: the term *Denkbild* was directly taken from the translation of the Dutch *merkbeeld*.

Romeyn de Hooghe's *Hieroglyphica*

Romeyn de Hooghe's monumental work *Hieroglyphica of merkbeelden der oude volkeren* (*Hieroglyphica or Emblems of Ancient People*) was published in 1735, almost thirty years after the death of its author. Apparently considered too radical to be brought out when it was written, the work gained momentum when Enlightenment thinking became more mainstream, resulting, along with much else, in a rising interest in the hieroglyph. Thus, belatedly, De Hooghe's book found an eager audience. A German translation by S. J. Baumgarten followed suit in 1744 under the title *Denkbilder der alten Völken*. Though there is no direct reference to De Hooghe's work in Herder's oeuvre, he may indeed have known it well, voracious reader that he was, or perhaps he heard about it through his fellow philosophers Lessing and Johann Georg Hamann, who acknowledged it in their work.[38]

De Hooghe's lengthy study consists of sixty-three full-page etchings and four hundred pages of accompanying text, discussing highly sophisticated ideas on past and present world religions. A learned artist who possessed a doctoral degree in law, De Hooghe was an exceptional illustrator and was deeply involved in debates about the arts and sciences, in particular astronomy, physics, and materialist philosophy. The engravings in *Hieroglyphica* are not mere illustrations of the text; the intricate compositions, assembling mythological figures, pictorial motifs, antique symbols, and a wide range of well-known personifications, *are* De Hooghe's complicated theological arguments about the origins and meaning of Christianity, Islam, and the various fractures within the Church. The text plays a subordinate role, as entries keyed to the various numbered elements in the pictures.

De Hooghe's work is not intended to be a history but rather a genealogy of world religion. In plates such as *Of Islamic Beginnings* or *Reformation*,

De Hooghe extrapolates the changes in the function of religion caused by the scientific revolution, offering a critique of the corruption of religious institutions and an explanation of their steady decline across the ages. Neither a libertine nor an atheist, he was a true follower of Spinoza. His agenda is clear: his monumental and deeply intellectual study does not so much argue for individual freedom of inquiry as encourage it—and he does so, precisely, via his enigmatic hieroglyphs. The minutely detailed engravings spelling out his complex religious views are introduced by the first two plates, intended to illustrate the method of his hieroglyphic argumentation. Like many thinkers of his time, De Hooghe assumed that the Chinese and the Egyptians wrote in hieroglyphs (*zinnebeelden* in Dutch), and that painting essentially developed from these pictographs. The format of hieroglyph was therefore particularly fitting to think through the origins of world religions and the profound interconnections of their doctrines and sacred texts. In his "Introduction to the Reader" De Hooghe explains that the union of foreign and familiar elements in an argument requires a pictorial rather than a verbal description in order to make it universally understandable. He further supports his claim by suggesting that there are, in fact, two forces of imagination effective in the creation of such pictures. First, the dynamic runs from interior to exterior, as the concept in the brain has been translated as an image by the philosopher or artist; and second, it goes from exterior to interior, when the viewer acquaints him or herself with the picture's content. This discussion shows right from the outset that *Hieroglyphica* is not to be an easy read aimed at a general audience. De Hooghe has high expectations that not only will his learned readers follow his meandering, intellectual reflections, but they will also add to the image, complement it to a certain extent, with their own thought processes.

An additional reason for the use of hieroglyphs is that its format enables De Hooghe to unite past and present elements and to juxtapose foreign and familiar things. After all, Europeans, De Hooghe writes, prefer crystal-clear images that would be transparent enough to serve as a shop sign through which the viewer can see all available merchandise on display for sale. One image should thus be able to encompass an entire collection of interconnected things and thoughts, past and present, familiar and unfamiliar, clear and obscure. To match word with deed, De Hooghe presents his reader the first plate (fig. 8), displaying the origin and progress of Egyptian hieroglyphs, to clarify the reading method required for his illustrations. His main point in this first engraving is to explain how the art of making hieroglyphs relates to the scholarship needed to understand them. Both practices are represented here. The enthroned female figure on the left embodies the art of speaking in hieroglyphs. Her bright eyes are radiant as she carves, in great majesty, an

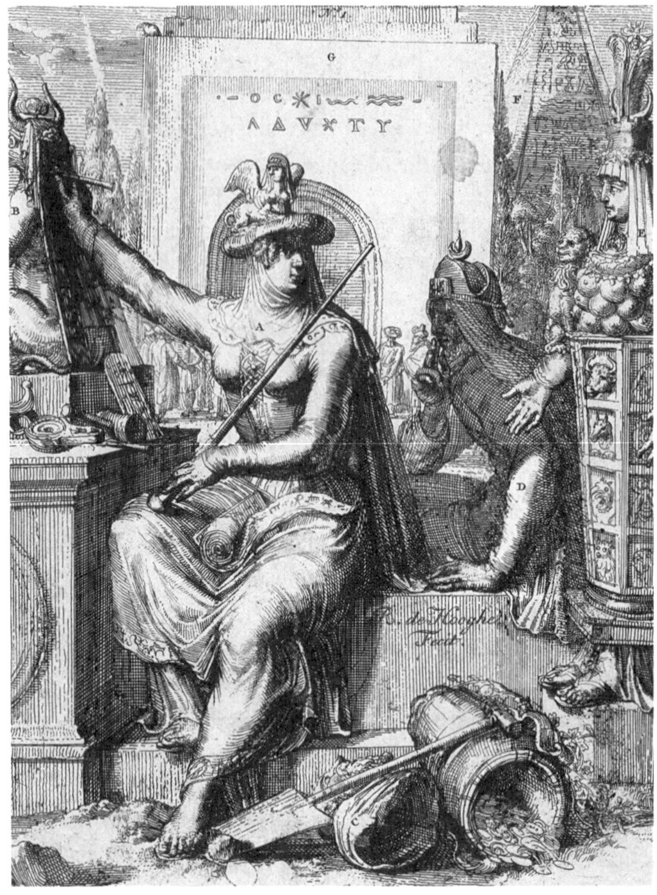

FIGURE 8 Romeyn de Hooghe, *Hieroglyphica of merkbeelden der oude volkeren*, 1744. Frontispiece. Photo: Rijksmuseum, Amsterdam.

inscription on the stone tablet that for us remains obscure. She is approached from behind by a sphinxlike figure who is overshadowed by her: this is the personification of the art of interpretation, who scrutinizes her back without hope of ever getting more than a partial view. He holds a finger to his lips to indicate that even for those initiated in the art, this knowledge is insufficient to wholly decipher the enigma of the hieroglyph because its pictogrammatic meaning is infinite. Indeed, in his exposition De Hooghe stresses that the art of hieroglyphica is ultimately unfathomable. The incomprehensibility of the enigmatic pictures represented in hieroglyphic compositions is one of his

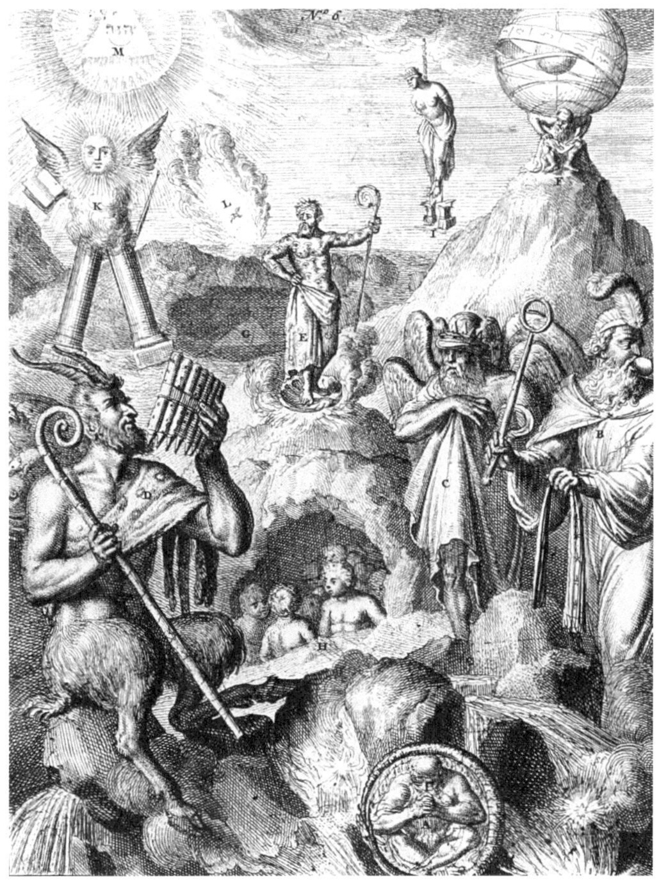

FIGURE 9 Romeyn de Hooghe, *Hieroglyphica of merkbeelden der oude volkeren*, 1744. Illustration from chapter 6, "About the Separation of the Chaos." Photo: Rijksmuseum, Amsterdam.

recurring themes. For instance, in chapter 6, "About the Separation of the Chaos" (fig. 9), the notion of impenetrability has been depicted by contrasting a dark abyss with the break of dawn. With this hieroglyph, De Hooghe tries to think through the mystery of the creation and the origin of humanity, whose legacy has come down to us only in conceptual images, because language did not yet exist for the first humans. Stumbling over a theory about how letters were invented, he gets stuck in his own intricate web of figurative language and finds himself confronted with the paradox that if language had not yet been invented, how could God's speech in the Book of Genesis—"And God said, 'Let there be light'"—be recorded for posterity? Even to the great master himself, hieroglyphs always retain a shadow side that remains at least partially unfathomable.

Herder must have been inspired by De Hooghe's creative use of visual language and his impressive erudition as much as by the challenge the hieroglyphs posed for him. Becoming De Hooghe's ideal reader, he complements the hieroglyphs by bringing in his own set of fascinations and subsequently creates his own *Denkbilder* according to De Hooghe's recipe. His best-known *Denkbild*, the so-called *Schöpfungshieroglyph* (hieroglyph of creation), draws on the entire project, and particularly on chapter 6.[39] The *Schöpfungshieroglyph* is a seven-tier pictograph based on Genesis, in which Herder, very much a man of his time, intends to bind together time and space, as well as the origins of both humanity and language, in what Hugh Nisbet has termed his usual procedure "to try to interpret the same phenomena both teleologically and naturalistically."[40] As he writes in *Aelteste Urkunde*, the dominant image of this pictograph is of dawn, or *Morgenröte*, which builds on several juxtapositions in De Hooghe's book, most clearly the abyss/dawn opposition in plate 6, and serves as a metaphor for the beginning of creation as well as of enlightenment. It is an image through which we can understand that Genesis 1:3, "And God said, 'Let there be light'" (Herder explains, going beyond De Hooghe's struggle with the same verse), unites the origin of language and creation. Through a mixture of word and image, his own ideas and those borrowed from De Hooghe, Herder's image of *Morgenröte* stands not just for a day rising but for a world *becoming*, humanity emerging, and language materializing. The overall idea of dawn as successfully joining the mythical origin of life and language with eighteenth-century progress in the sciences further guides us toward accepting Herder's idea that the age of reason—in the capacity of dawn—was God's *revelation* rather than his downfall, as other enlightened philosophers have claimed. As such, this hieroglyph of creation provides a unified viewpoint from which to see, through the chaos of the earth, an emergent humankind. Rejected by theologians in Herder's own time yet picked up on by Romantic poets and painters such as Philipp Otto Runge (1777–1810), the *Schöpfungshieroglyph* was Herder's alternative to received ideas of progress cast as a linear process, with the present age at the apex of mankind's evolution, which was crucial for the development of (German) landscape painting around 1800 (fig. 10).[41]

"The thought-image was so to speak the whole characteristic, historical, philosophical and poetic language of the Creation,"[42] Herder declares, typically summing up too much to be comprehended at once and putting in too much for one sentence to contain. Yet such shortcomings in language are

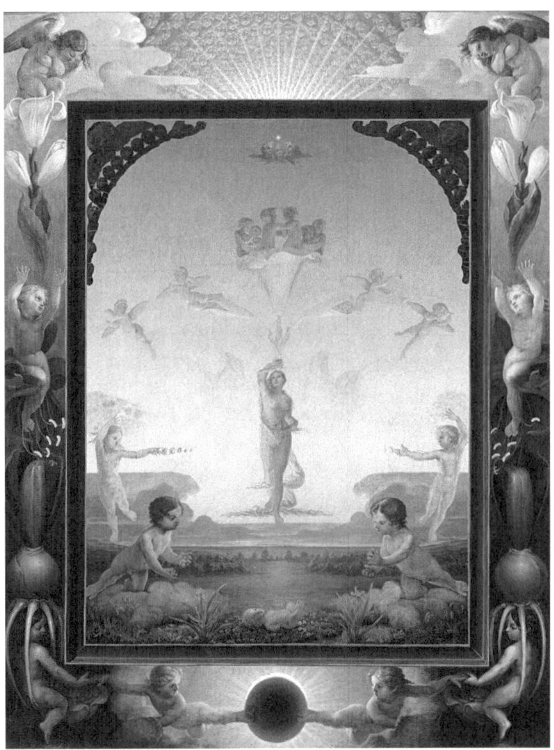

FIGURE 10 Philipp Otto Runge, *Dawn*, 1809–1810. Oil on canvas; 109 × 86 cm. Hamburg, Kunsthalle. Photo © bpk / Hamburger Kunsthalle / Elke Walford.

precisely what the *Denkbild* could overcome: in an image, one could actually summarize a complex assemblage of philosophy, theology, history, and poetry and demonstrate more clearly than words ever could the extent to which they were intertwined. As we have seen, to depict philosophical or historical conundrums as *images*, Herder borrowed freely from the rich tradition of iconography, and other motifs are taken from mythology, fables, and the Bible. Herder's *Denkbilder* thus demonstrate a poetization of philosophy, whereby philosophical thought is represented through borrowed fictional images that are placed in allegorical structures to extend beyond their traditional and often fixed meaning.[43] Like his exceptional use of italics and *Sperrdruck* bring fresh meaning to arbitrary signs, Herder draws new outlines around ancient molds of personifications and places them in unorthodox settings, thus giving them new significance. Such gestures are in agreement with his claim that the whole of life is encompassed by poetics, to the extent that "we do not see images but rather create them. . . . Hence it follows *that our soul, like our language, allegorizes constantly*."[44]

Just as we create images while looking at them, redrawing outlines and adding to them, we see constellations of concepts rising from Herder's typeface, and in both instances there is rest in movement, a moment of arrest during the flow that transpires while we read a text or our eyes scan images, when thoughts are added and concepts become visible. Much later, Walter Benjamin would similarly describe his idea of the literary *Denkbild* as a dialectics at a standstill, a constellation of thought arrested. For Benjamin, both movement and arrest take part in the process of thinking, as he famously wrote in one of his *Theses on the Philosophy of History*.[45] A *Denkbild* results from this process as an arrest of a thought so as to make its course visible within a constellation of things.

Denkbeeld/*Denkbild*: A *Hollandismus*

Isn't your thought-image [*denkbeeld*] always more beautiful than your painting?

CAREL VOSMAER, *AMAZONE*

In his *Notes to Literature*, Theodor W. Adorno comments on his friend Benjamin's *One-Way Street* (1928), a collection of sometimes very short prose sketches or aphorisms presented as *Denkbilder*. Adorno defines the term *Denkbild*, taken from the Dutch (*ein Hollandismus*), as Benjamin's particular term for his "scribbled picture-puzzles": "parabolic evocations of something that cannot be said in words. They do not want to stop conceptual thought so much as to shock through their enigmatic form and thereby get thought moving, because thought in its traditional conceptual form seems rigid, conventional, and outmoded."[46]

Like Herder, Benjamin was searching for a style or figure by which that what cannot quite be put in words could nonetheless be communicated through language, and likewise he was attempting to compose an image in words that does not *contain* thought or *mean* thinking, but would arrest it as a kind of a snapshot of something that cannot be said but can be *thought*. For that reason, *Denkbilder* cannot be paraphrased. Their content is synonymous with their form in the sense that the method of thinking is *in* the writing. In a more pronounced way than Herder's, where the passionate use of typography stops the flow of reading, Benjamin's *Denkbild* is a hindrance, a stumbling block of words that intends to give a picture of the way language resists fully expressing ideas; or rather, of the impossibility that it could do so. "Caution: Steps" is literally such a stumbling block. Reading the short sections of *One-Way Street* is like seeing Benjamin wandering around the streets of Berlin being struck by sign posts, traffic signs, or posters on walls, and learning, as if by surprise and in an almost involuntary, Proustian way, something about the course of history, even as he is acutely aware all the while that within the larger urban sphere of the past, life is an experience akin to being directed through an one-way street. Being stopped occasionally in his tracks, Benjamin finds himself reflecting on the process of writing, or the concept of history as such. "Caution: Steps" contains only one sentence on the writing of prose: "Work on good prose has three steps: a musical stage when it is composed, an architectonic one when it is built, and a textile one when it is woven," he states, seeing in writing an overlapping process similar to what Diderot found in hieroglyphic poetry.[47]

In "Construction Site," probably among the most telling pieces, Benjamin sees children playing with debris at a building site, creating a world of their own within the actual world, in which worthless thrown-away objects obtain new value and interconnect with other things. Children do not need specifically produced toys, Benjamin writes, as they are themselves much better equipped to select the materials they need. Yet "Construction Site" is not just a reflection on the children's world within a grown-up one, but also, as Gerhard Richter reminds us, the image of history as such as a site where the historical materialist is the naive garbage collector of history, a figure who wants not to push aside the debris, but to place it in a new configuration.[48] Vital for the understanding of Benjamin's *Denkbilder* is his use of poetic montage. His prose pieces are examples of a philosophical poetics, the kind of poetical philosophy Herder was so passionate about creating.

Adorno explains how the term *Denkbild* was first employed by the poet Stephan George (1868–1933), who occasionally used it in his work. For instance, in a cycle of poems entitled *Siebente Ring* (1907), a gesture of gratitude toward the French after a visit to Paris, he glorifies his fellow poets Verlaine and Mallarmé, exclaiming at the end of the third stanza: "And bleeding for his thought-image: MALLARME!" indicating this poet's suffering for the vision expressed in his poems. Contemporary commentators heavily criticized George for his predilection to insert foreign terms (*Fremdwörter*) in his work. In particular, his fellow poet Rudolf Borchardt wrote an absolutely devastating critique in 1909 in which he fulminated that the German language had very little use for stultifying Dutch barbarisms like the *Denkbild* apparently so treasured by George. In reference to *Der Siebente Ring*, Borchardt contemptuously wails that George—as was clearly revealed by Mallarmé as well—may have everything to do with images (*Bilder*), but surely nothing with thinking (*Denken*). After this tirade, German literati were not particularly keen on using the term, and it somehow fits very well with Benjamin's historical-materialist views that he, much like the children he saw playing in "Construction Site," picked up the discarded term, recognized its potential through the joining of *denk* and *bild,* and transformed it into the structure for his reflective miniatures. In doing so, he invented a new literary category. Assuming that the term was a mere synonym for "idea" in a platonic sense of (mental) image, Borchardt located its origin in the baroque. What the harsh critic did not realize was that George had not picked this up from seventeenth-century texts but had "found" the word in the poems of his Dutch friend Albert Verwey (1865–1937), whose work he had translated on occasion.[49] For instance, in Verwey's poetry cycle *Origins* (of which George had translated the first two sections), a series of reflections on the essence of life, we find:

> Pray that it lives. For only that it can
> Not find itself, the life, that suddenly exists
> As dampness and warmth, which is what it finds
> In the dark soil—, the light of heaven
> The seed, that can live, let grow—
> Each seed: a little plant, a thought-image [*denkbeeld*], and a child.[50]

It is interesting to note that the *denkbeeld* stands at the essence of life as encapsulated by a little seed, as well as for what it will become. It denotes in this context the promise of growth and the completion it might achieve over time. In the work of Verwey, as well as Benjamin and Adorno (but less so in George's), the thought-image never *is* but always has an open, slightly uneasy, and almost malleable form that, like the hieroglyph, is as cryptic as it is infinite. George and his friend Karl Wolfskehl were apparently fascinated with the term and asked Verwey for its etymology. Clearly delighted with his little commission, the academically inclined Verwey (who would later become Professor of Dutch Literature at Leiden University) started research and discovered the roots of the term in seventeenth-century scholarly work, in particular, translations into Dutch from Latin of philosophers such as Spinoza and the then well-known Willem 's Gravesande (1688–1742). Verwey refers to *denkbeeld* as a typically scholarly term (*geleerdenterm*), yet neither George nor Verwey seem to have been aware of the existing etymology of the German translation, which had in fact circulated in intellectual circles. In addition to Herder, Winckelmann uses it as a derogatory term in his *History of the Art of Antiquity*, and much later the portrait painter Joseph Karl Stieler

(1781–1858) brings it into play in his description of the portrait gallery of Ludwig I, where he uses *Denkbild* alternatively with *Gedenkbild* or monument and *Mnemosynum* in its double meaning of memorial and souvenir.[51] We see how this collision of different yet related meanings continues to resonate in Benjamin's utilization of *Denkbild* as an image of thought and a thoughtful image. It generates a mode and monument of remembering the past as passing through cast-away objects or street signs which somehow bear witness to a lost world and therefore stop us in our tracks—to find ourselves as being caught in some kind of spatio-temporal interval with our head suddenly filled with "superimposed tissue," as Diderot would have it, picturing an idea of something that cannot be otherwise said.

The Dialectical Image

In 1670, the Dutch bookseller and writer Willem Goeree (1635–1711) published his *Introduction to the Practice of Universal Painting*, a little-known treatise outlining his theory of art. Not an artist himself, Goeree preferred the training of the mind over the practice of the hand, and he recommended that before even touching the brush artists should obtain knowledge of the visible world, of history, anatomy, and natural philosophy. Though he was not a philosopher, Goeree's text does reveal traces of the philosophy of the time, particularly the writings of Descartes and Spinoza, especially those concerning the imagination and various theories about the formation of mental images. Explaining the importance of the art of painting on the formation of our imagination, Goeree found a way to present pictures as forms of cognition. Writing not in Latin but in Dutch, he coined the term *denkbeeld*. He must have found it an apt and useful term. In early editions of his treatise, it is spelled hyphenated, *denk-beeld*, to stress its composite structure and perhaps to maintain some of its initial novelty. His section on painting as form of knowledge reveals that Goeree had a rather sophisticated sense of the term's meaning, questioning the distinction between "*denk-beelden* that we read or make up from something ourselves, and between images that we observe in a painting"—which, he admitted, are transferred to the mind in a manner that remains unclear.[52] In fact, Goeree reflected on the difference between concrete and mental images, a doublesidedness we have seen was essential for Diderot's deployment of hieroglyph, and, for that matter, Benjamin's development of his *Denkbilder*. Indeed, like these later thinkers, Goeree ultimately implied that an actual distinction cannot be made: we might say that for him the *denkbeeld* remains a composite of sorts. However, in Goeree's case, the *denkbeeld* serves as mode of transition not from word to image, but between concrete elements in a painting, and the image in the mind we make of it. Goeree showed us that from the very beginning, *denkbeelden* have been invented or employed to denote an overlapping tissue spanning the material and the immaterial, a kind of channeling of concrete imagery toward the mental image of abstract concepts, and vice versa. From its very origin, the thought-image emerges from the interstices, not only of image and mind, but of those between various media, describing a process of metamorphosis from a textual shape into another, from pictorial into mental form. More precisely formulated, the thought-image *is* this transformation: it stands for the unfathomable "rising" of an image from a text, or of a thought from a street sign.

In this light, it is no coincidence that Goeree's paragraph on the imagination is immediately followed by a section discussing what was an apparently pressing issue at the time: whether painting could depict lifeless objects in motion. Goeree is surprisingly outspoken on the topic, arguing with verve that painting is capable of depicting virtually anything: "no one will contradict that art follows nature in everything, in particular that which can be seen over a period of time and with contemplation [*na-denken*]."[53] Wittingly or not, Goeree sees a direct correlation between thought-images and the art of duration, which provokes thought as a result of picturing stillness in motion. We are back where we have started. Bisschop's *Interior* seems to sum up Goeree's argument, as it is the very image of motion achieved via stillness, which I have proposed to call pensive. Before Herder and Winckelmann, and even before De Hooghe's learned work, Goeree described how still images of motionless things in particular arrest viewers and provoke them to think.

We could say that thought-image—*Denkbild* or *denkbeeld*—is a word that does not know its proper place, that it is a concept that is essentially transgressive regarding boundaries between different media and is constantly trespassing different discourses. It has experienced an evolution via translation, from Dutch to German to Dutch again, and it is telling, I feel, that it has to a certain extent remained untranslatable in English, or in French for that matter, where it is usually translated as *image de pensée*. In all these languages, therefore, the term remains a kind of *Fremdwort*, an amalgamation of foreign and familiar elements. As we have seen, for Herder, and also for De Hooghe to a certain extent, it has been precisely that dialectic movement from the known to the unknown, from the recognizable to the unthought, that was introduced to them by the *Denkbild*. It would not go too far to state that the thought-image is, essentially, never a complete entity but is always involved in a process of translation. It seems to emerge precisely from a fusion of sorts, revealing its capacity and significance only *in passing*, in the passage from one language into another, from one medium into another, from poetry to prose to a philosophy of history and back again. Herder once said that history and philosophy are united in a poetic form, and Winckelmann and Benjamin would likely have concurred.

Perhaps less a traveling concept, migrating across disciplines in Mieke Bal's sense of the term, the thought-image should be considered as a predisciplinary blueprint, a construct that adapts itself easily as a malleable composite uniting various modes of expression. As such, it ultimately serves as a stumbling block—not unlike Herder's typographical emphasis or Benjamin's "Caution: Steps"—that arrests us in our course.[54] Mediating between action and rest, and stillness in motion, this blueprint has an open yet impenetrable structure that, like the "painting" of Balzac's marquise, does not itself think but lets itself be filled with thought. As we have seen, a thought-image is a literary, philosophical, and artistic figure that operates on the overlapping fields of different media, precisely where borderlines get vague and blurry so that something else stands out, like Herder's *Sperrdruck* on his page, the surfacing of the "unthought." In that sense, the thought-image is an instrument *par excellence* with which new concepts could be made, which is ultimately, according to Deleuze and Guattari, the task of philosophy. In the next chapter, we will continue considering thought-images as resulting from a kind of passage—through streets, through texts—when raising the question, with Heidegger, whether thinking is a kind of dwelling, and if painting can provide a space, a kind of shelter where thinking can take place.

PART II

Painting as Philosophical Reflection

CHAPTER THREE

Room for Reflection
Interior and Interiority

Something in the world forces us to think. This something is an object not of recognition but of a fundamental *encounter*. What is encountered may be Socrates, a temple or a demon. It may be grasped in a range of affective tones: wonder, love, hatred, suffering. In whichever tone, its primary characteristic is that it can only be sensed. In this sense it is opposed to recognition.

GILLES DELEUZE, *DIFFERENCE AND REPETITION*

Thought about thought, an entire tradition wider than philosophy, has taught us that thought leads us to the deepest interiority.

MICHEL FOUCAULT, "THE THOUGHT OF THE OUTSIDE"

The Back Room

In the 1660s, the Dutch master of church interiors, Emanuel de Witte (1617–1692), painted one of the very few domestic scenes that he created during his career (plate 4). We see a spacious room and glimpse two rooms behind it in a seventeenth-century Dutch bourgeois house. It seems to be a particularly beautiful day: sunlight bursts in through the high windows, leaving large bright patches on the smooth, immaculate tiled floor. The fold in the long orange curtains on the right suggests a summer breeze, imparting a sensuality that only adds to the quiet comfort of these rooms, apparently filled with domestic bliss. Though relatively modest in size, the picture evokes spacious openness—the two shining, well-polished chandeliers emphasize the height of the ceilings. It is as if we are able to look around in the painting, a quality also typical as well of De Witte's church interiors, which frequently seem to encompass more space than, strictly speaking, the picture can contain or our perception take in. The more we look, the more we realize that there is actually very little going on in this painting. Compared to other so-called *seeing-throughs* or *doorsiens* characteristic of seventeenth-century Dutch art

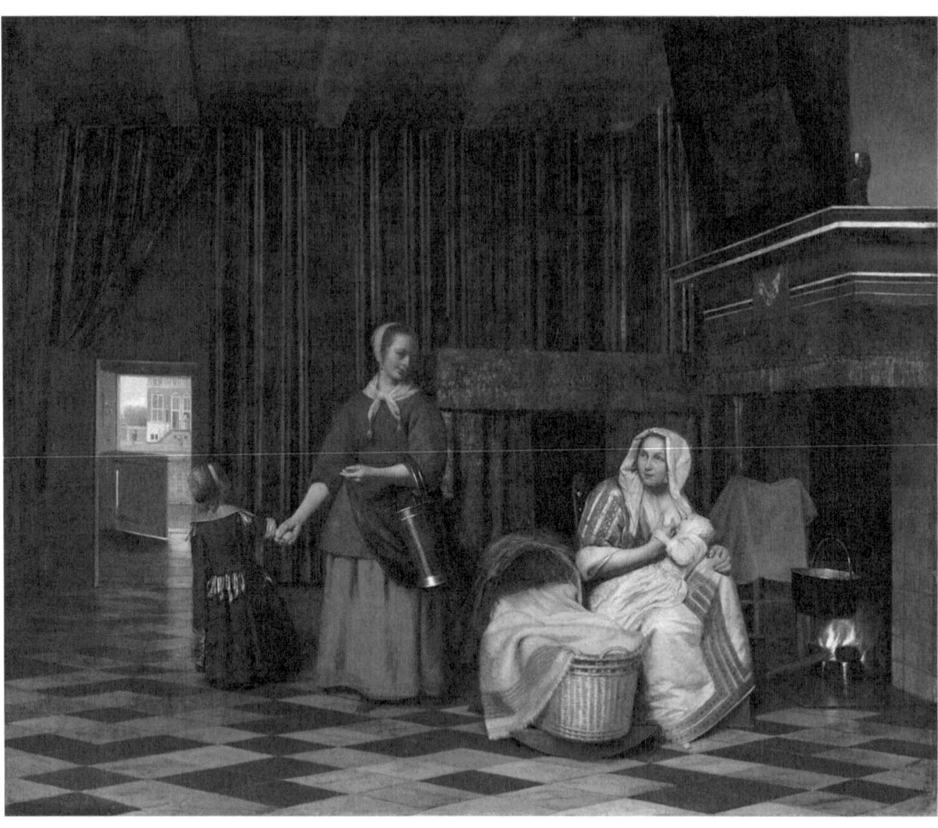

FIGURE 11 Pieter de Hooch, *Woman with Child and Serving Maid*, 1663. Oil on canvas; 64 × 76 cm. Vienna, Kunsthistorisches Museum. Photo: KHM-Museumsverband.

in which the beholder is made an accomplice in the act of spying on a hidden scene, there is little excitement. Oblivious to our gaze, a woman seen from the back is fully absorbed in playing the virginal in the front room. Her partial reflection in the mirror above the instrument, showing only her bonnet and forehead, cuts off most of her face, reinforcing the sense that she is unaware of a beholder. Her music-making at leisure is contrasted by the dutiful female servant in the back room, who is absorbed in wiping the floor. A suggestion of narrative may be found in the barely visible head peeping through the bed curtains, which, along with the sword on the chair nearby, discloses a mostly hidden male figure that further pulls us in. De Witte's success in fully drawing us in as viewers may be further measured when we compare his work with a similar interior by fellow Dutch painter Pieter de Hooch from the same decade (fig. 11). Though De Hooch allows for a *seeing-through*—we can even see another house on what seems to be the opposite side of a canal—he has also carefully arranged his figures and props: the woman nursing her baby, the empty cradle beside them, and the servant holding hands with an older child have a theatricality that places us firmly on the other side of this scene. We, as onlookers, remain outside this pictorial space. The staging of the figures invites us to look at the display, but the room lacks the invitation of De Witte's interior that encourages us to move at will within it. Our eyes, plunging deep into this domestic space, "plow" through it in the direction of the doorways; we zoom around the water pump in the second room, pass the busy maid, and end up at the open window in the back, which most likely overlooks a garden.[1] Fully immersed in the capacious pictorial space, perhaps we actually feel a desire to stay there, to retire to the back room to look out the window and ponder. Indeed, the painting as a whole reveals a kind of openness that does not necessarily ask to be "filled" with meaning. Instead, it offers us room for contemplation or, we might even say, thinking. Can painting offer us such a retreat? Henri Matisse famously compared a good painting with a comfortable armchair in which we find rest. Isn't De Witte's interior a perfect example of a similar kind of calm retreat in which the viewer can be at ease, in harmony with the environment?

The idea that painting enables the beholder to somehow enter its space and dwell within it has been explored since antiquity, and examples run from the vivid *ekphrases* of Philostratus to an episode in Akira Kurosawa's *Dreams* (1990), in which an aspiring painter literally walks around in Vincent van Gogh's paintings. Denis Diderot wrote a now famous description of his long promenade through the landscape paintings of Claude-Joseph Vernet in his *Salon* of 1767 (fig. 12).[2] The philosopher gives an enthusiastic account, in six distinctive "sites," of his excursions through fields and over hills and his experience of breathtaking vistas. He even records his small talk with the locals and enters into a Socratic dialogue with a tutor named Abbé on the extent to which the machinery of language falls short of describing the rich variety of human feelings—only to reveal, at the end of his forty-three-page ramble, that all this time he has been standing in front of Vernet's pictures in the Louvre. After this confession in the last part of his essay—a seventh description, not of a "site" but of a "picture"—Diderot forgets for a moment his philosophical struggle with language's shortcomings and shows himself to be the literary artist he so often is: in lively and colorful terms, he passionately describes one of Vernet's moonlit harbors. Even as he has declared himself to be standing in front of this night scene, Diderot, as before, is still roaming around in a pictorial landscape—following an esplanade up a hill, pausing to look at sailors rolling dice, continuing past fishermen who are casting their

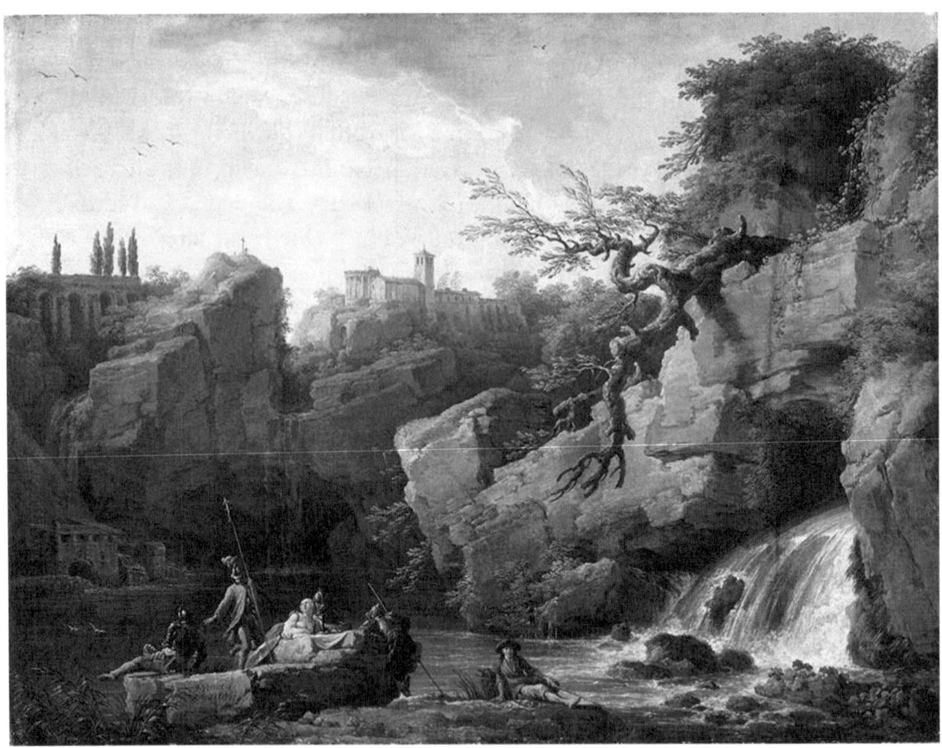

FIGURE 12 Claude-Joseph Vernet, *Romantic Landscape*, c. 1746. Oil on canvas. Moscow, Pushkin State Museum of Fine Arts.

lines.[3] Ultimately he asserts that this is a painting that he would truly like to own, not so much because of its beauty or its potential to be a shrewd investment but rather because it is so much more than the sum of its parts. It is not merely a painted scene but a vehicle that allows Diderot to transport himself imaginatively to a different place. Not only can he "enter" Vernet's scene, but its vivid images, in their turn, can take possession of his thoughts, penetrating his mind as they come alive in the fever dream that came over him in the wake of his Louvre visit. In fact, he wants to possess this painting as much as it has possessed him, drawing him in so that he does not want to leave. The painting has become for him a dwelling place, a place to "be," where he can go—inwardly—for philosophical reflection. Diderot may have wanted to hold onto this painting as a way of keeping this peaceful retreat so that he could return to it as he pleases.

Though far from being a vast landscape in which one might wander expansively, De Witte's painting similarly opens up a space for retreat, a place of peace and quiet. This is a homey interior where one will find, especially in the room at the very back, a place to be free from troubles and to gather one's thoughts. In his essay "Of Solitude" (c. 1580), Montaigne outlines his ideas on modern stoicism and recommends that "we must reserve a backshop [*arrière-boutique*], wholly our own and entirely free, wherein to settle our true liberty, our principal solitude and retreat."[4] In order not to let our happiness depend on possessions and a family, Montaigne uses an architectural metaphor to describe the sense of an inner space, so private that no one else can ever reach it. This innermost sanctum can be likened to a kind of study where we find, besides our own true solitude, a philosophical home, or differently formulated, a home for the philosophical subject.

In this chapter, I argue that paintings such as De Witte's domestic interior can serve as such a philosophical home; they act as objects that are evocative, serving as a contemplative aid that lets thinking get through. Such paintings not only offer us a space to dwell, as Vernet's offered Diderot, but also provide a metaphor for mental processes—an *image* of the spatiality of thought—by which thinking can be visualized as much as activated. Following Gaston Bachelard, I suggest that without such images, we would lack a model for mental retreat. Absorption in thought is accompanied by a mental movement of retreat, as Montaigne would have it, or as a "drawing in or drawing toward" as Heidegger would say. I am interested in the "housing" of philosophy, so to speak, or rather, its housing problems.[5] In particular, I raise the issue as to what extent an understanding of a new articulation of interiority, in the seventeenth century and beyond, has been allowed by the models we possess for mental retreat: actual spaces (such as Heidegger's hut) and the metaphors they helped generate, as much as representations of houses and rooms. I am interested to what extent paintings such as De Witte's—as well as early modern dollhouses, which will soon join the discussion—have similarly provided us with images, in Bachelard's sense of the term, through which we have come to understand the dialectics of outside and inside, the drawing of a borderline between public and private, and the determination of what is intimately ours and what is the world's. In the same vein, I explore the significance, in philosophical writing, of architectural metaphors, such as the house, as representing a space where one finds oneself at home to think. My question is less about what thinking actually *is* and more about how artworks have enabled us to find an interior space to house our thoughts—and our subjectivity. I demonstrate that painting can serve as a pathway to find a space where thinking can take place. My discussion of the metaphors of architecture and building in Descartes, Heidegger, and Bachelard will lead us from houses to cabinets to the dollhouse as a house cabinet providing a space for reflection. Lastly, I will compare the warm depictions of home such as by De Witte with the early twentieth century's bare interiors of Vilhelm Hammershøi, where no rest or solitude is found.

At Home with the Subject

Das Denken baut am Haus des Seins.

MARTIN HEIDEGGER

In the fall of 1619, a young soldier traveling through Germany after attending the coronation of Ferdinand II in Frankfurt found lodgings in what probably was Neuburg-on-Danube. His name was René Descartes, and he famously spent an entire day "shut up alone in a stove-heated room, where I was completely free to converse with myself about my own thoughts."[6] The night following, a dream changed the course of his life. Apparently, his conversation with his thoughts inspired such excitement that "a fire gripped his brain" and Descartes fell prey to a feverish three-part dream, which contained, as it happens, most of the dominant metaphors of his later metaphysics.[7] The source for information about this transformational moment, however, are some lost autobiographical writings in Latin that were transcribed (probably not at all accurately) into French by his early biographer, Adrien Baillet (1649–1706). After having two nightmares, the first of which caused him to awaken with a sharp pain on his left side, Descartes dreamed of the mysterious appearance in his room of two books: a dictionary and an anthology of classical verse, which fell open to a poem beginning "Quod vitae sectabor iter?" ("What road shall I follow in this life?").[8] A stranger entered and presented Descartes with a poem beginning "Est et non" ("Is and is not"), which Descartes claimed was written by the fourth-century Christian poet Ausonius, though he searched in vain for the poem in the anthology. He then offered to find an even better poem—namely, "Quod vitae sectabor iter?"—but was distracted by a series of engravings in the book, which now seemed to be a different edition (the dictionary, too, was no longer complete and had moved to the other side of the table). The man and the books soon vanished, leaving Descartes, not yet awake, to interpret the dream's meanings. Whatever the dream's peculiarities, it clearly emphasizes (at least in the account we have of it) that Descartes had arrived at a defining moment in his life. It was there, in that room, that he found his vocation, his way in life, or, more precisely formulated, his *method* (from *meta*, after, and *hodos*, road or journey).

Referring to this crucial moment in *Discourse on the Method* (1637), written almost twenty years later, the philosopher refrains from mentioning his nightmarish dream, but he does make a point of describing, perhaps with too much detail, the characteristics of the quarters where "the onset of winter" had detained him. The place was lonely, and there were no distractions and no one to converse with; but the probably rather small spare room must have provided a warm welcome. Likely to have been inspired by Montaigne and the seclusion of his *arrière-boutique*, Descartes found a home away from home, a comfortable room to rest from his travels through a cold Germany, a place where he could think. It is therefore not a coincidence that the first thoughts he discusses concerned the design of buildings, apparently evoked by his hyperawareness of being alone in this room.[9] Building projects governed by a single architect, Descartes reasons, are better planned than those involving many different craftsmen, and usually those starting from scratch are better proportioned than those made from a patchwork of existing parts. Continuing this line of argument, he applies to himself the metaphor of building construction. If he wishes to reform himself, he should follow the pattern of erecting a building from the ground up, so to speak, so as to construct his thoughts "upon a foundation which is all my own," and not one patched together from the received opinions of others.[10] Drawing his famous analogy likening his body to a container in which thinking takes place, Descartes compares the development of a thought to the erection of an edifice: the old foundation must be demolished to allow the realization of a brand-new building plan. The scrutiny of knowledge about himself is what Descartes declares to be a method of thinking, akin to what happens in the process of building when existing foundations are obliterated. And it is this process of "building" a new method that he wishes to record in the *Discourse*. Rather than teach his reader this new method for obtaining self-knowledge, he wants to picture himself finding it. Describing the paths he has followed so far, he uses another metaphor taken from the visual arts to illuminate this process: that of painting. He writes that he wants to "reveal in this discourse what paths I have followed, and to represent my life in it as if in a picture, so that everyone may judge it for himself."[11] Very much like Montaigne claiming that he himself is the subject of his *Essays*, Descartes intends the *Discourse* to be a kind of self-portrait, which, while still in the making, is being held out for its reader's judgment, in the expectation that the commentary made on its "picture" will provide yet another means of self-instruction.

Having literally chosen paths while traveling that turned out to be a period of intensive self-scrutiny, Descartes decided to settle down and create a written self-portrait in the *Discourse*. Just as you need to move somewhere else when your house is being rebuilt, Descartes writes at the beginning of part 3, you need to relocate in order to write about yourself. Moving to Holland in 1629 enabled him to live the life of a recluse amid the bustle of city life. In Descartes's eyes, the Dutch were too much concerned with their own affairs to express curiosity about the life of others, which suited him, as he was able there "to live a life as solitary and withdrawn as if I were in the most remote desert, while lacking none of the comforts found in the most populous cities."[12] Descartes had found—in life—the conditions that had comforted him so much in his little stove-heated room in Neuburg-on-Danube: his day cloistered in his room had become a miniaturization—indeed an image—of the lifelong retreat he made to rebuild his house from scratch.

I am less interested in presenting the building of this "house" (first as the writing of a text and second as the painting of a self-portrait), and more in the apparently seamless metamorphosis of one process of building into another: from an architectural metaphor to a pictorial and literary one and back. The metaphor of writing as if composing a painting—indeed an image—has facilitated this transition. The little room in Germany may once have been a reality; but Descartes transformed the secluded space into an image that joins the apparently contradictory states of being on the open road and being at home.

Both Descartes's actual travels and his written account of them are presented as philosophical trajectories toward formulating a method, which, in turn, would be the starting point for a philosophical undertaking. The method is both the result at the end of the road—the clear representation of one's thought to oneself that Descartes is looking for—and itself a pathway toward further inquiry into the nature of this thought for oneself. We could say that the method is both the home of the philosophical subject and the way toward it, an ambiguous home at once architectural drawing and finished building, design and realization, traveling and dwelling—and, ultimately, building and its *un*doing.

The construction of a house as a metaphor for philosophical method thus stands at the beginning of modern philosophy as a kind of rudimentary comparison. The house metaphor has become a recurrent trope in philosophy, yet whereas all metaphors in philosophical writing can be said to be slightly problematic, the house metaphor is especially complicated, in particular because a metaphor is, by definition, transformative in the sense that it effects a displacement. To stand in for something else is to somehow be in contradiction with the stable home that the philosophical house is meant to provide. This tension between the placement of a house and the displacement inherent in the rhetorical figure we have already seen in Descartes—finding a home while traveling, building a house while residing in another—as a clash between the familiar and the foreign. This tension is further confirmed by the very definition of metaphor. In his *Poetics*, Aristotle defined metaphor as a form of analogy whereby an unfamiliar term is applied to another one.[13] Whereas other rhetorical figures merely adorn speech, Aristotle reasons, a metaphor brings about learning because the listener, in comparing the two terms, finds out something about each of them. In his book on tropes, published in 1730, the French grammarian and philosopher César Chesneau Dumarsais pushed the conjunction of foreign and familiar even further in his definition of metaphor, which he understands to be a term that takes on something other than its proper sense. Remarkably for our discussion here, he relates metaphor to a house: "it is, so to speak, in a borrowed residence," he writes.[14]

A metaphor's proper sense is always elsewhere, it seems, never under the same roof of the borrowed residence, which makes the house, as a metaphor, into what in fact *precedes* metaphor. The borders of the house metaphor must therefore always be transgressed in order to get closer to the figure's proper meaning.[15] In other words, the house, as a philosophical metaphor, can never quite be occupied in a "proper" way—its meaning can never be fully appropriated as it lies by definition *outside* its rhetorical boundaries. The way toward its proper meaning is always a way *out* of its housing, *toward* another one; in a nutshell, this dynamic neatly sums up the to-and-fro movement of Descartes's journeys, traveling *toward* home and finding it en route all the while. This is the clearest instance where we see how the method—being on and after this road—*is* the home for the philosophical subject, a place that provides a foundation from which a thought process can be set in motion.

As we will see, although Heidegger departs from Descartes in his philosophical project as a whole, he picks up on Descartes's metaphor of method as a kind of philosophical housing and holds firmly to it even as he attempts to dismantle the very tradition it has established. Ultimately, he claims that language is the dwelling of being, urging a return to a linguistic residence. Yet, if we assume that language is, after all, essentially metaphorical, as all words are borrowed residences that never fully appropriate meaning, we are sure never to find a proper home and the subject will remain effectively homeless. While this is precisely Heidegger's point, as we will see in the next section, it is also the very reason why the only way to build a philosophical house is by deconstructing it, in Jacques Derrida's sense of the term. For Derrida, deconstruction is precisely the process of tracing the house metaphor in philosophical discourse. What he revealed was what Heidegger had already discovered: that a departure from a tradition is not really possible, that in using language, one cannot simply abandon one metaphor by creating another, and that therefore, one never can quite leave a borrowed residence in order to find the proper meaning of the term. What Derrida points out, over and again, throughout his monumental oeuvre, is that a philosophical trajectory, always, takes place in and around the metaphorical house as a process of appropriation.

The question I raise is whether this extends to painting, specifically to Dutch seventeenth-century interior scenes—a new category at the time—during a period when the house had become a charged space within the freshly established republic, metaphorically as well as literally. As Annik Pardailhé-Galabrun, Philippe Ariès, and others have demonstrated, the history of private life can partly be traced to changes in house design. I will demonstrate that likewise, seventeenth-century paintings of interiors will play a revelatory role in such a tracing. The typically Protestant longing for intimate spaces to reflect upon the self is not all that visible in actual house design. However, we clearly see this desire for reclusion portrayed in painted interiors, and, as I will argue, in dollhouses of the time as well. For that reason, De Witte's interior and seventeenth-century dollhouses can shed fresh light on philosophy's housing problem because, I suggest, they both visualize this double-bound trajectory of placement and displacement, of thinking as being underway, all the while providing an image (rather than a metaphor) where we can reside in order to think. Before I return to De Witte's interior, I will first elaborate on the house metaphor and its central position in the work of Martin Heidegger.

Heidegger's Hut

Philosophy can never be free from architecture.

ANDREW BENJAMIN

In *Being and Time* (1927), Heidegger makes a fresh attempt to tackle the question: What is the meaning of being? In phenomenology he finds a place—or rather a possibility of thinking—where this question can be addressed. Criticizing the spatial metaphors introduced by Descartes so as to release the question of being from subjectivist determination, Heidegger develops an "architectural rhetoric" (to use Mark Wigley's term) in which being, dwelling, building, and thinking are deeply intertwined.[16] Composing his magnum opus in a cabin high up Todtnauberg in the Black Forest that he fondly called his hut, he argues that philosophy to a certain extent entails the construction of a house as a way of "housing" being.[17] Being, for Heidegger, is anchored in location, and he speaks of being *there*, *in* the world, which he calls *Da-sein*. However, and here he departs from Descartes, the awareness of I-am-in-the-world, the *cogito*, comes at the price of a full realization of its nothingness, or rather, its nowhereness. In the course of living our daily life, we are unconscious of the futility of the things around us, or indeed of our own "thinghood." To a certain extent the houses in which we live our quotidian lives conceal ontological underpinnings and detach us from Being, as we are usually not conscious of why exactly we are where we are and exist the way we do. Only when we fully see ourselves as "in" the world does everything that usually seems to be part of our normal life suddenly take on an uncanny aspect. Apparently, the everyday reality we live in does not fully "house" our being; that which we experience as reliable and ordinary becomes unfamiliar, such that we no longer feel at home in our own lives: we are homeless in our world at the moment we realize that we are "in" it. This results in feelings of angst or dread. We are not afraid *of* something, but rather, dread is born precisely from *Da-sein* as the awareness of being such.[18]

In a double-bind gesture typical of Heidegger, he declares that what is disclosed to us in *Da-sein* is precisely that which we find dreadful, and from which we want to turn away: we dread being in the world, and one of the reasons we do is because it comes with this fundamental experience of not being at home. Through *Da-sein* we become highly individualized: we are being there, in the world, yet isolated and alone. The consequence of fully experiencing Being shakes our foundations—*Da-sein* exposes us to utter freedom in its most profound sense without anchor or restraint, which results in our feeling homeless, which Heidegger calls *unheimlich*, uncanny. However, there is an antidote to the homelessness we experience while living our ordinary, domestic lives. We can attune ourselves to the idea that being anxious is the condition of being thrown into the world, namely by its building an ontological rather than ontic house for ourselves—that is, by thinking.

In his essay "Building Dwelling Thinking," originally delivered as a lecture in Darmstadt in 1951, Heidegger explains the interrelatedness of thinking with building and dwelling. He is not interested in the simplistic opposition of interior and exterior that an architectural metaphor entails (and that we see in Descartes's description of his rented room). As a consequence, he rejects the division between means and end to turn building, dwelling, and thinking into practices in their own right, or crafts as Heidegger would have it, rather than being processes toward the construction around which interior and exterior get organized. Obviously, in order to dwell we need a building to dwell in; however, Heidegger demonstrates that through the words' etymologies, building as such already means dwelling. Referring to the cultivation as well as the erection of edifices, building is a way of being on earth, it is habitual—we inhabit it, or as Heidegger says, it is the habit, the *Gewohnte* (referring to the German word *wohnen*, which means to live). He notes that the German *ich bin* (I am) is derived from the root *bauen*, which means "to dwell."

Heidegger uses the term "building" both in a traditional way, denoting a shelter, and as a thing that connects and gathers, for example, a bridge, which creates a location by gathering the banks of a river, which eventually leads to a gathering of stream and banks and land, of earth and sky, *in* the landscape. For the philosopher, one does not "map" space in a cartographic way. A plan for a building always already comes with its proposed elevation, and it is this intersection of horizontal and vertical structures that produces for Heidegger a location. A location is never already there before an edifice is built; instead, it comes into existence by virtue of clearing away space for a building to be erected, allowing the opening up of "spaces" where we as human beings can dwell. These spaces provide us with a sense of safety and offer a certain feeling of being at home. "To dwell," Heidegger says, "is to be set at peace."[19] The fundamental character of dwelling is found in the double gestures of opening and keeping, clearing and preserving, not so different from Descartes, who, in reforming himself, wanted to build something new or open up new spaces.

The question now arises whether painting can provide such a sense of opening up space in order to preserve something. In the introduction, we saw how Van Gogh's painting of a pair of shoes is a thing and yet more than a thing, as it makes Heidegger feel "immediately alone with it." I want to leave aside for the moment the hot debate spurred by Heidegger's discussion of another pair of shoes painted by Van Gogh in his essay "The Origin of the Work of Art" (1935)—strongly criticized by Meyer Schapiro in 1968, prompting Derrida to deconstruct both arguments at length in "Restitutions of the Truth in Pointing" (1978)—so as not to lose sight of the significance of what is actually said here. Being alone with this painting means *entering* it. What *is* in this painting, is us—all but literally stepping into these peasant shoes, slipping them on to walk away in them, indeed, "homeward." Like Diderot, Heidegger sees the painting as an invitation to enter it, and just as Diderot had been sauntering around in Vernet's landscapes, his chatter with passersby ultimately revealed as a conversation with his own thoughts, Heidegger is alone with the shoes, walking from the *unheimlich* toward the *heimlich*. This being alone is not found in the thingness of the object. Rather, the painting offers us a kind of space in which we can walk, in which we can be alone. What *is* in this painting is *us in it*, and us being alone with it. In a way, walking home in these peasant shoes means already having found a home. And this kind of dwelling, of being alone while en route, of walking homeward as a way of conversing with one's own thoughts, is what is possible in painting. We may even say that this blending of walking, thinking, and dwelling as a peaceful preservation and keeping of the self is possible *only* in painting. Is this what Heidegger means when he states that art is a way of overcoming metaphysics and a protection from the anxieties of *Da-sein*? Is this what caring for the dread caused by *Da-sein* entails?

If we return to De Witte's painting (plate 4), we can perhaps better understand the extent to which it is possible to dwell in painting. Spaces open up, Heidegger says, by their being allowed into the dwelling of man.[20] It is not that we *face space*: we are not on one side, with space on the other—a notion, by the way, clearly suggested by De Hooch's theatrical interior paintings but contested by De Witte's work. For Heidegger, to dwell is not to be *in* spaces but to go *through* them, thereby *anticipating* the upcoming spaces that we draw near to us while they are still distant from us. In his Darmstadt lecture, Heidegger declares: "When I go toward the door of the lecture hall, I am already there, and I could not go to it at all if I were not such that I am there. I am never here only, as this encapsulated body; rather, I am there, that is, I already pervade the room, and only thus can I go through it."[21] In fact, in contrast to De Hooch's *tableau vivant*, De Witte's painting shows us this "going through" visually, in the sense that we virtually *foresee* our presence in the rooms toward the back of the house. While "here" in the room with the bed and the spinet, we are also "there," nearing the water pump and the servant. Whereas our body may be, strictly speaking, outside the painting, we have already pervaded the room and are going through it.

Heidegger uses the down-to-earth example of the lecture hall door to make a similar point. His definition of dwelling as a process of going through spaces is deeply intertwined with his understanding of building and thinking. And when he invites his audience to think of the old bridge in Heidelberg, he argues that this thinking toward that location is not just an experience occurring *inside* an individual; rather, the lecture hall audience is transported to the bridge: "it belongs to the nature of our thinking *of* that bridge," Heidegger says, "that *in itself* thinking gets through, persists through, the distance to that location."[22] Going through space is in fact being drawn toward a location, without ever properly arriving.

In *What Is Called Thinking* (1952), Heidegger utilizes the same dynamic that occurs with *Da-sein*: turning away from *Da-sein* for fear of dread, we are nonetheless drawn toward it. The confrontation with *Da-sein* is precisely the care we have to take of ourselves, the way we have to keep ourselves: however, as with space, we cannot *face Da-sein*, as it always draws away from us. In that respect, *Da-sein* is always already *ahead* of itself, "beyond itself," Heidegger writes, and our thinking about it is running behind. More precisely formulated, the structure of our awareness of *Da-sein* as the "being ahead of itself" is similar to the way our thinking (of the bridge, for instance) is always ahead of our location, persisting through the door even before we could make a first leap forward.[23] Heidegger's cryptic assertion that "what gives us to think is thought-provoking, yet what is most thought-provoking is that we are still not thinking" should be read in a similar way.[24] The thought-provoking thought always lies ahead of us, and turning toward it so as to start thinking about our being there makes our dread about the confrontation with *Da-sein*—which we want to shelter ourselves from—the cause of our concern. And this cause constantly slips away from our grasp: even when we want to think about *Da-sein* and address our existential homelessness, it withdraws from us, yet by doing so it sets out a course for us to follow. That which must be thought about somehow turns away from us; it withdraws from us, all the while drawing us along by its very withdrawal.[25] And this journey toward thinking that turns away from us is what Heidegger calls dwelling; that is, it is the process of building a philosophical home for ourselves to gather our thoughts about being there.

If we translate this into visual terms, we could say that entering De Witte's painting means being lured into the farthest room, which seems to move away from us, recessing further into the pictorial space as we approach it, pulling away all the while drawing us along. We are drawn to what is furthest from us, summoned toward the open window that we will never be able to reach. Evidently, this kind of drawing-in is the essence of perspectival painting, which directs our eye into the depths of the pictorial space toward the vanishing point. Paradoxically, the point to which our eye always turns can never be reached, or for that matter seen, to the extent that it is vanishing. What we see in painting is how the entire pictorial composition is drawing toward that withdrawing point and is revolving around it. Reading Heidegger's text and looking at De Witte's painting side by side, we see how De Witte's interior offers us an apt picturing of this sense of withdrawal, which happens not in space but at a location, a "dwelling," as Heidegger would have it. "When man is drawing into what withdraws," Heidegger writes in his typically convoluted style, "he points into what withdraws. As we are drawing that way we are a sign, a pointer. But we are pointing then at something that has not—yet—been transposed into the language that we speak."[26] This gesture of pointing toward something that cannot quite be translated into language (that what provokes thought but has not yet been shaped as thought) becomes visualized to a certain extent in De Witte's painting, by way of its offering us the house's little back room as an opening and a keeping. Assisted by this painting, we can better understand how for Heidegger the house stands as a joint between the ontic and the ontological, how the house of Being is hooked onto the picture of a home.[27] Having entered it, we are not only protected and sheltered by its warm atmosphere, but we are also en route, which is for Heidegger the condition for the revelation of real thoughts.[28] We are moving through the series of rooms toward the window in the back room, the location we are drawn to even as it eludes us, to the extent that it is vanishing. It is from there, the unreachable point that we are drawn toward, that we may see through the window a glimpse of Being.

De Witte's welcoming home evidently fits within the ideology of the home in seventeenth-century Dutch culture, yet it is perfectly capable of illustrating Heidegger's concerns. He insists that the feeling of being at home in our lives is a fiction, and that we hide behind our daily business as a way of not having to think about the nature of our being. Our preoccupation with the everyday shields us from the alienation and homelessness on which our life is based. We need to start learning to think, by moving through space. But even though we have moved through the painted interior, we have not yet started thinking. Learning for Heidegger means, in fact, unlearning. Perhaps in response to Descartes, who wanted to rebuild himself but only on new foundations he would lay himself, Heidegger contends that learning how to think means putting aside what thinking has traditionally been. And it is precisely by doing so that we come to know it. Thinking is in that sense comparable to craftsmanship, when you learn what to do in response to the very stuff that you work with. In *What Is Called Thinking* Heidegger gives the example of a cabinetmaker's apprentice, who learns to build a cabinet not just through practice and acquired knowledge but also via his own answering to the wood and the other materials he works with. It is in this answering to what is given by the wood that the cabinetmaker's apprentice is crafting. "Perhaps thinking, too," Heidegger muses, "is just something like building a cabinet. At any rate, it is a craft, a 'handicraft.'"[29]

The aspiring cabinetmaker referred to here, and the cabinet as the future fruit of his craft, are far from innocent examples. For centuries, cabinets have served as metaphors for the storage of knowledge or the gathering of memory and the process of thinking and have left a deep resonance in philosophical and literary writing. We know all too well from Frances Yates's *The Art of Memory* or Mary Carruthers's *The Craft of Thought* that in medieval times the trope of building was used as a mnemonic device, and that the metaphor of the strongbox was utilized as a place for the safekeeping and storage of memory. Admittedly, such metaphors stood in for memory rather than the kind of provocative thinking Heidegger has in mind, but his word choice reveals his affinity with this tradition. In the seventeenth century, cabinets of curiosities became emblems for the gathering of encyclopedic knowledge from the Old and New Worlds. Closer to Heidegger's own time, in 1894, Edmund Husserl had rejected Locke's interpretation of the mind as an empty cabinet, and with it the notion of the mind's solitary self-enclosed awareness only of itself and its thoughts and sensations, when he posited his concept of intentionality.[30] And a decade later, Henri Bergson had a cabinet of drawers serve as a metaphor for the mind, a comparison that was sharply criticized by Bachelard, who in 1958 revealed himself as a most radical thinker in *The Poetics of Space: The Classic Look at How We Experience Intimate Places* when claiming that spaces like wardrobes and cupboards are models of intimacy, whereby our mental processes of retrieval such as remembrance, contemplation, and reflection are understood. Investigating our experience of intimate spaces and the effect of this kind of spatiality on our thought, Bachelard draws parallels between architecture, furniture, and objects and closely studies the nature and meaning of various intimate spaces that he considers to be linked, such as houses, cabinets, dollhouses, even shells. Arguing against Bergson's example of a chest of drawers as an all-too-dominant metaphor for classifying thought, he posits that a house offers us shelter, allowing us to daydream in its attics or its corners, with the consequence that in our memory, our thoughts begin to inhabit these dwelling places. Similarly, a wardrobe or drawer where we store intimate things provides our intimate life with a *model* of intimacy. Like Heidegger, but with completely different results, Bachelard ultimately examines how our existence in spaces is a kind of dwelling that structures our thoughts. We should notice here that for Bachelard, a cabinet is neither an example nor a metaphor for thinking but rather its *image*. He is not interested in the wardrobe as a vehicle for *storing* or classifying thoughts or concepts, but he sees these as spaces of solitude that we live *by*. They are fundamentally creative, as they open up a particular dimension in our thought.

No matter how much Heidegger was influenced by the history of the metaphor of the house, his notion of thinking goes far beyond the opposition between the world on the one hand and the interiority and privacy of the conscious mind on the other. He wanted to show that learning how to think was a craft comparable to that of a cabinetmaker: in thinking as in cabinetmaking, we answer to the material. In addition, Heidegger stresses how learning always involved an element of unlearning. To that extent, we can see how he evokes the slightly dilapidated metaphors of building a cabinet or a house, so that such figures can be used as fresh new building blocks for the house of Being. I am interested in the aspect of concreteness Heidegger is so fond of using in his comparisons, and I will further explore his metaphor of thinking as cabinetmaking on the basis of a little-studied, concrete object that fuses cabinet and house and clearly resonates with interior painting: the seventeenth-century Dutch dollhouse. As I will demonstrate, in this extraordinary type of building we see the fusion not only of cabinet and house but also of craft and thinking, of building and dwelling, and of caring and preserving. Dollhouses were quite popular throughout the seventeenth and eighteenth centuries in Europe, but the Dutch version is exceptional in that the miniature house is concealed within a cabinet. Instead of having a detachable façade, the Dutch dollhouse ingeniously hides behind wood-inlaid doors and sometimes even fake drawers and can be opened and closed like any cupboard. Usually considered to be the feminine equivalent of a cabinet of curiosities, or a peepshow displaying the interior of a house (like the one by Samuel van Hoogstraten in the National Gallery in London), both of which are generally seen as elements of typically male pastimes, the dollhouse is far more complicated than what it is usually taken to be: an object of a wealthy woman's leisure. When approached as an image of the dialectics between inside and outside (the dynamic that Bachelard discusses in his consideration of intimate spaces), and seen in the light of the rich tradition of metaphorical cabinets in philosophical thought, the cabinet dollhouse, as I will argue, becomes a very strong image indeed for the craft of thinking.

The Dollhouse

In the 1680s, Petronella Oortman started an ambitious twenty-five-year-long building project: a rather monumental three-story dollhouse (plate 5), probably a fairly accurate copy (or at least a version) of Oortman's residence on the Warmoesstraat in Amsterdam, at that time one of the city's most prominent streets, graced with shops selling the most sumptuous silks and *laken* (wool).[31] Oortman, who as a young woman had lost her first husband, remarried the successful textile merchant Jan Brandt and started her building project in the year of their marriage in 1686. This was clearly not a mere hobby undertaken by a dynamic and imaginative housewife, but the couple's serious means to assemble an art collection. The carefully crafted pieces of miniature furniture, tiny silverware, and minuscule paintings often made by known artists and craftsmen that we find in Oortman's dollhouse were not just amusing, small-sized duplicates or "toys" (in the eighteenth-century sense of the term). They were meant to be regarded as rare treasures and genuine curiosities in their own right. The dollhouse and its contents were on display not just to entertain but also to stimulate the intellect and provoke curiosity about the virtuosity of the artists (the delicacy of the tiny paintings, the minuscule needlework, and the woven baskets are breathtaking), the technology of building (some dollhouses had operational fountains or pumps), and the skills of the carpenters who carved the furniture. Friends and visitors of Oortman and Brandt must have marveled at the accuracy of the contents of the house, all made of the finest silver, shining walnut, and heavy textiles. Close observation of the small wonders in this exquisite model household surely satisfied a desire for visual complexity and the keen interest in the various materials that had their origins in various places all over the world. For unlike most European dollhouses, which largely contained items produced locally, Oortman selected, in addition to typically Dutch household assets such as tin pitchers and finely braided baskets, numerous items made from imported materials. She even commissioned objects to be made overseas: for instance, the blue-and-white plates were especially ordered in the East Indies to decorate the kitchen, where we also find Chinese-style painted silk window-covers (*voorzetramen*).

The earnestness of this collection is also signaled by its being referred to in seventeenth- and eighteenth-century documents as a *poppecas* or *Poppe Kas*, a doll *cabinet* rather than a house. Among the handful of extant Dutch examples, Oortman's dollhouse stands out for its glass doors, which invites viewers to approach the house as a display case. The theatrical aspect of presenting this doll cabinet as a special showcase was further emphasized by the yellow curtains, now removed, that hung over the glass doors to protect it from the light. These strategies for showing (and showing off) proved to be highly effective, as by the early eighteenth century the dollhouse was mentioned in several documents as an "excellent art work" or "art cabinet," indicating its artistic value.[32] The owners must have been well aware of the exceptionality of their creation, as they commissioned the Amsterdam painter Jacob Appel to portray it (plate 6). Appel's depiction reveals not only the curtains, which reached to the floor, but also shows us that initially, the house was inhabited: a series of wax dolls, dressed to perfection for their particular roles as lord, lady, or maid of the house, were apparently positioned in the house's various rooms. Whereas early inventories show that up to the present day, not a single item has vanished from the house's contents, it is somewhat uncanny to realize that the only thing that has gone missing over the centuries are these wax figures, leaving the house essentially vacant.

This "excellent art work" started to attract tourists from within the Netherlands and beyond. Apparently, not everyone was allowed to see it, as records show that some highborn visitors who had come a long way to see the cabinet house were refused at the door. Visiting the Warmoesstraat in 1718, the

German Uffenbach family had better luck. While enjoying tea with the widower Brandt and his daughter (Oortman died in 1716), they studied the nine rooms closely and were deeply impressed by them, as we read from Zacharias von Uffenbach's record of the visit. He describes the layout and the various items in great detail, noting that Oortman's wonder was likely the most valuable dollhouse in Europe, having cost between 20,000 and 30,000 guilders, an amount equal to or exceeding the price of a house along one of the city's major canals.[33] The Uffenbachs were further awed by the paintings they found hanging all over the various rooms, all produced by well-known masters (Zacharias insists), some of them rendered in trompe l'oeil or grisaille. As his description emphasized, virtually every surface in the dollhouse had been worked over, from the upholstering of chairs and the leather or silk patterned wallpaper and marble floors, to the wood inlay cover of a tiny sewing box (4 × 1 cm) with a working bottom drawer, to the engraved silver pitcher with a small tap in the laying-in room, to the illustrated pages of the minuscule, leather-bound books in the library. Every surface, thus, offered something exciting to a visitor to gaze at and to marvel at how it was made on such a small scale. Even the outer construction of the cabinet was highly wrought: manufactured from expensive tortoise with tin inlay, it was likely built by a cabinetmaker who, as *maître ébéniste* had worked for the French court in Versailles.[34]

The argument that dollhouses were miniaturized female equivalents of cabinets of curiosities overlooks the essential position of the house in Dutch society at large, its value as a retreat, and its importance as a source of pride for men and women alike. Only when we take this into account can we get a real insight in the significance of the Russian nesting doll effect at work here: an actual residence housing a doll cabinet, housing, as we will see, a miniature cabinet of curiosities within it.

The House as Retreat

> [I]n the peace and quiet of his home . . . he can enjoy himself among the castles, towns, and estates, and see cattle, cows, villages, and towns; oaks, fields, hedges and fences; springs and waterfalls—all in his own room.
>
> JOOST VAN DEN VONDEL

The founding of the United Provinces of the Netherlands marked the establishment of the first modern republic. While a great role continued to be played by the princes of Orange as the stadholders of Holland, the republic's dominant leaders, their powers were relatively limited and they were, as a consequence, in constant conflict with a newly formed class of rich merchants (like Brandt) who resided in the cities. The Dutch elite was composed not of aristocrats but of burghers who prided themselves on having *earned* their riches rather than having been born into wealth, and who slowly learned to recognize themselves as the new ruling elite fully responsible for the prosperity of their country-in-the-making, which they were helping to build. A firm handle on one's own life and business could therefore directly influence the republic's interests and politics, and vice versa. A new set of (Calvinist) virtues developed whereby good housekeeping became a metaphor for good government, and the family house was seen as the place where children—as the country's future governors—were to be raised in preparation for their lives as hardworking citizens. The home, therefore, was effectively understood as the nursery for the young republic as it looked toward its maturity and future prosperity.

The home became a kind of showcase, a source of great delight and an indication of economic success that many a citizen, male and female, liked to show off. Architectural design revealed the desire to exhibit the link between the prosperity of house and the flourishing of the nation through the so-called front room (*voorhuis*), which bordered the street and was fitted with huge windows that allowed passersby to peep in. Foreign visitors famously remarked on paintings and other treasures amassed in front rooms for semi-public display.[35] This room, as much as the façade as a whole, and the stoops in front of it, were kept spotlessly clean. If we are to believe these accounts, the cleanliness of the Dutch housewife bordered on obsession, and baffled foreigners commented frequently as well on her strong position as ruler of the house, ordering her husband around. Indeed, Dutch housewives often oversaw the administration of their husband's businesses and handled money and trade in the same self-confident manner as their spouses did, often in the *voorhuis*, which doubled as office space. Because decorating the interior was largely the task of the wife, she and not her husband was often responsible for buying paintings and other decorative objects. The explosive production of interior scenes (coined *kamergezicht*, or "roomview," by Arnold Houbraken in 1718), genre paintings, and other indoor compositions such as kitchen pieces and food still lifes can partly be explained as satisfying a particular demand for domestic scenes that appealed to an exclusively female group of art buyers. What probably especially appealed to this group of buyers was the way in which Pieter de Hooch, Pieter Janssens Elinga, Johannes Vermeer, Quirijn van Brekelenkam, and others raised the everydayness to the level of the monumental, making, in fact, a philosophical argument about the sublimity of seemingly uneventful daily life.[36]

As the front room developed into an exhibition space, the need grew for a back room where one could retreat from public view. Privacy gained unprecedented authority: the rise of Protestantism had encouraged silent reading as well as inward moral scrutiny to great effect on the industrious merchants and their diligent wives and offspring. Many a head must have been daily bent over, if not the Bible, than one of Jacob Cats's emblem books, which presented moral lessons as amusing picture-puzzles, often on the basis of objects that could be found directly in the domestic sphere, or indeed those employed for housekeeping. For instance, the broom features prominently, both in emblem books and interior scenes, cleaning the corners of the house and the mind alike from dust and dirt. The broom as symbol of domestic health gained further resonance when Admiral de Ruyter, who here clearly saw the personal as the political, incorporated the broom into his personal device, making it no secret that he intended to sweep the seas of the republic's enemies.

This preoccupation with attaching moral dimensions to household utensils, making the everyday significant in every way, seems to reach its apotheosis in *Het leerzaam huisraad* (*Instructive Household Effects*), an emblem book exclusively devoted to household objects that was published in 1711. Poet and emblemist Jan Luyken (1649–1712) published this book as a series of fifty moral poems on buckets, brushes, bookcases, stoves, and the like, each accompanied by a print of the given item in its position in a domestic setting, and captioned by a biblical quotation and other mottos outlining the object's metaphorical significance. Expressive in a typically baroque fashion, Luyken's trivial objects are transformed into metaphors that, in his poems, start living a life of their own. Naturally, his collection includes entries on the broom, as well as on the cabinet, which is central to every successful household. In "The Cabinet" (fig. 13), he wags his finger at the decadence of showcasing a collection of curiosities at home. The engraving displays figures studying the content of a large cabinet of curiosities, while Luyken's poem opens with the statement that the heart is a real cabinet of *rariteiten* (the Dutch word for "curiosities" is *rariteiten*, which means rare and extraordinary things) because, after all, only real virtues are truly exceptional. The poem continues to instruct its readers that showing off one's collection, as we see being done in the image, should be compared to children playing with "empty shells" (*leege schellen*). Real riches can only be found when they are safely stored in the cabinet of the heart.[37]

It is interesting to see how Luyken challenges the limits of metaphor, turning it inside out, so to speak: it is not just that the cabinet stands for decadence, but that the heart itself *is* a cabinet. In contrast to his celebration of the broom, in which he likens the cleaning of the house to the cleansing of

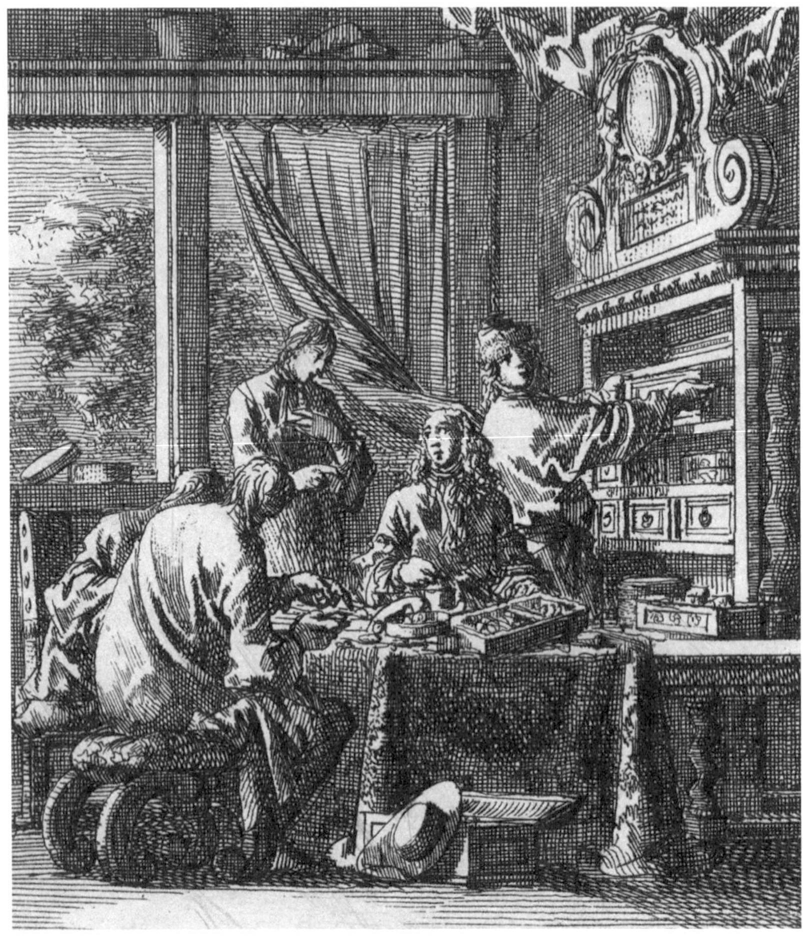

FIGURE 13 Jan Luyken, "The Cabinet," figure 67, from *Het leerzaam huisraad*, ed. P. Arentz and K. vander Sys (Amsterdam, 1711). Photo: Rijksmuseum, Amsterdam.

the soul, Luyken does not compare the cabinet to a heart, but the heart to a cabinet, moving from the metaphorical to the concrete rather than the other way round. This oscillation in Luyken's book between concrete and abstract, thing and what it stands for, referent and reference, occurs too in the house metaphor of Descartes and Heidegger. The distinction between the cabinet and its metaphoricity seems to dissolve, laying bare an intertwined structure, typical of the seventeenth-century allegorical way of thinking and perceiving the world, in which concept and thing, container and contained are continually changing places to such an extent that it is no longer possible to differentiate between the terms. The metaphor of the cabinet as a chamber of empty materialism seems to have been waiting to undergo a metamorphosis into the multichambered heart suddenly filled with virtue, or into the reality it was always supposed to be.

These dynamics of reversal raise the question of the status of Oortman's dollhouse in this web of figurative language so characteristic of seventeenth- and early eighteenth-century thought. In fact, Oortman's dollhouse is an even more complicated case, further blurring the distinctions between metaphor and what it stands for, all the while maintaining its status as a material object—and a historical document—as well as a container for the storage and display of concrete things. It is this clash between a concretization of metaphor and a metaphorization of the concrete that makes it such an excellent site for exploring the metaphoric potential of "housing" as such. On the one hand, Oortman's dollhouse should be placed firmly in the cultural-historical and economical context that produced it, allowing a privileged view of a household anatomy loaded with symbolism. Yet on the other hand, it raises pressing questions as to whether the dollhouse endorses the centrality of housekeeping in seventeenth-century Dutch culture, or rather articulates an escape route from which one's position within this culture could be rethought. Does the deep care for this miniature house, and the apparent scrutiny of its contents, intensified by its shrunken size, demonstrate an anxiety about the strangeness, if not of the objects as such, usually overlooked in daily use, but of the ontological issues that a study of this mini-house raises? Is this house meant as a finished product, or was it a life's project? Is it intended as an exemplar, a model, or a study of what this model actually comprises? Could this, from a twenty-first-century perspective, be seen, perhaps, as a very elegant deconstruction *avant la lettre* of the house as philosophy would have liked to build it: as a route toward its realization as much as its actual erection, yet surrounded with anxiety regarding the presence of ideas, so profoundly preconceived that one hardly recognizes them as such? It is this dialectic between withdrawal and exposure, and between the dollhouse's seemingly contradictory state as both showcase and retreat, that I further explore here.

As we have seen, the new sense of privacy resulting from the Protestant advocacy for self-teaching and self-instruction generated a growing sense that a subject's interiority was seated "in" the body as container. Portraits of the period testify to this new, private identity, as sitters made great efforts to present an outer façade that would offer glimpses of a deeper sense of self, using the surfaces of their bodies as sites for projecting such a self-identity. As Ann Jensen Adams and Joanna Woodall have argued, Dutch citizens found in portraiture a mode of expression of their new reputation as members of a powerful rising bourgeoisie.[38] In addition, egodocuments, such as family albums and diaries, started to reveal a widening of the gap between professional and private identities. One of its most prominent examples, inspired by Montaigne, is Constantijn Huygens's autobiographical poem *Dagh-werck* (*Day's Work*; 1639) in which he fondly describes how after a day's work he leaves his troubles at the doorstep to enter the realm of domestic bliss. His later poem *Hof-wyck* (1651) is even more explicit in its tribute to domesticity, imbuing his need for a retreat from public office. In this poem, he celebrates his country estate outside The Hague as the retreat (*wyck*) from the court (*hof*), where he, as the secretary of the princes of Orange, was heavily burdened by the problems of the republic.

With this desire for retreat comes the demand for a closet or small study at the back of the house, away from the noise and activity of street life; a counterpart, in fact, to the semipublic space of the *voorhuis*. Just as portraits start to show an inner life breaking through the façade of one's appearance, *kamergezichten* (*gezicht* means both "view" and "face") reveal glimpses of intimate closets embedded within them. It is essential to point out here that it is in painting, rather than in actual architectural design, that this space gets articulated as a deeply seated "back room" at the far end of a house. Indeed, as De Witte's *Interior* shows us, the house extends to an incredible length in order to create a deep space into which our gaze can plunge, all the way to the end of the series of rooms. As Martha Hollander and Willemijn Fock have convincingly demonstrated, the enfilade in De Witte's painting (and others like it) is largely fictitious.[39] Though they may be based on actual models, *kamergezichten* are not accurate recordings of real-life living spaces, yet through their fictionalization, they do show, as Hollander asserts, that the border between the public and the private was not sharply drawn, and the definition of solitude and retreat was still very much in flux. I suggest that the inaccuracy of De Witte's painting only emphasizes more strongly that what was meant to be represented was a fictional haven, a pictorial refuge making up for the lack of a real sanctum for retreat. It is somehow fitting within the philosophical discourse of the house, being simultaneously a concrete entity as a condition for thinking and the essential metaphor for both the structure and the process of thought, that painting (or, for that matter, Huygens's poems) articulates this idea of retreat better than actual architecture ever could. The notion of the house, heavily charged already as we have seen with specific meanings about nationalism and family pride, embodies a typically Dutch ideal of citizenship, yet it is in its pictorial or literary representation that we see a desire and ambition to address its ontology and a keen awareness of the dialectics of inside and outside, familiar and foreign. It is this aspect of the *kamergezichten* that gains new resonance in the context of my discussion of Heidegger's linking of dwelling, building, and thinking. Paintings like De Witte's visualize a kind of retreat that was hard to achieve in reality. Indeed, this painting itself has probably served *as a retreat.* Just as Heidegger was able to step "into" Van Gogh's painting as a way of being there, viewers of De Witte's painting can "enter" it and use it as an incitement to contemplation about what is *in* the world and what falls outside it, and where the thinking subject is within it, or outside it, and whether it ever finds a true home.

In this light, Oortman's dollhouse may serve a similar purpose as De Witte's painting or Huygens's *Hof-wyck*, yet it offers a specific, concrete case in point here. The twenty-five-year period of building this house—which, if not a duplicate, very much resembled the residence in which she lived—represents a single, continuous reflection on what it means to dwell—literally as well as figuratively. The apparent correspondence between the interior of the house and the mind that the dollhouse evoked was obvious enough at the time. In a 1631 broadsheet advertising the instructive qualities of a dollhouse she had built, the German widow Anna Köferlin wrote that "a house that is in disorder reflects the disorder of its housekeeper's mind," confirming the current ideology about housekeeping and morality.[40] Oortman's dollhouse, I suggest, elicits a much more sophisticated form of contemplation than Köferlin's more narrowly defined, pedagogical undertaking. Oortman's building project may have been initiated by an obsession with possession common to many owners of cabinets of curiosities, but it has also turned into a kind of egodocument in the manner of Huygens and Montaigne. It reveals a deliberate crafting of a (miniature) domestic space in which one can dwell only imaginatively—all the while showing a very concrete household in perfect order: the linen (bearing her initials and Brandt's, intertwined) is all neatly hemmed and ironed, the silver is sparkling in the miniature drawers, the polished wood surfaces are shining.[41] Evidently, this is an example of an orderly mind as Köferlin would have it, yet it has a deep, ontological undercurrent as an image—not of an orderly mind, but of thought. Oortman cared deeply for this house that doubled as a place to store and display its treasured content; it was not intended primarily as a conspicuous example of perfect housekeeping. In a Heideggerian way, we could say that she cared and preserved this house as a way of living with it without living *in* it, as a way of reflecting on her daily life without keeping a diary, as the creation of an image of herself, without a likeness. The objects are all very familiar—after all, their life-size originals are right there in the house—but are also made strange and exotic because of their small scale. Peering into the various rooms, one gets completely absorbed in this miniature space without ever having the chance to get in. Susan Stewart and Bachelard have each brilliantly observed in their discussions of the miniature that when one bends over to look at something tiny, the world is canceled out. Once you tend to the miniature house, the world seems to shrink, and you are sheltered from it, so to speak, by your attention to the minuscule.[42] Bachelard goes even further when he remarks that, in fact, attention works like a magnifying glass. Under our absorbed eye, the small rooms of the dollhouse gradually start to inflate, slowly begin to fit themselves to the contours in our imagination, filling us while we fill them with our gaze. We are in the dollhouse, mentally and optically, while our body remains outside; in other words, we leave our outer shell behind us when we roam through the various rooms, going through them. The dollhouse serves, in that sense, as a concrete metaphor—a metaphor we live by and live *with*. As Bachelard would argue, the dollhouse is not merely a metaphor that stands for something else but an insightful *image* that provides us with a model for thought.

It is this specific connection that makes the doll cabinet an excellent site to further explore the process of thinking as a craft and its connection to building and dwelling that Heidegger has in mind. Indeed, in light of his theory of the housing problems of being, what would it mean to erect a house within a house, to "collect" everyday objects, and moreover, to spend a fortune on it? What must it have meant for Oortman and Brandt to lead their visitors to a cabinet that, when opened up, revealed itself to be a small-scale version of the very location they were in, housing an assemblage of very expensive miniature reproductions of the domestic utensils that they were already surrounded by? What is the meaning of dwelling (in Heidegger's sense of at-home-ness, or *heimlichkeit*) when one erects a house within a house as a lifetime project? If we for the moment assume that thinking is a kind of craft and a means of being underway, in the sense of going through one space to arrive in another, then looking into this dollhouse is utterly thought-provoking in precisely Heidegger's down-to-earth sense. Can we say in Heideggerian terms that the dollhouse, as an artwork, opens up as well as sets up a world?[43] Oortman appears to have attempted to articulate a superlative of the private: an interior in an interior, in which one could dwell by way of crafting things and thoughts alike as a way of finding a retreat. There are two elements in this dollhouse that further support my argument that this dollhouse in particular offers a contemplation on the dialectics of inside and outside, or, more precisely formulated, a *philosophy* of housing, in concrete and visual terms: the decoration of the drawing room and the little cabinet of curiosities in the tapestry room. Let us use our attention like a magnifying

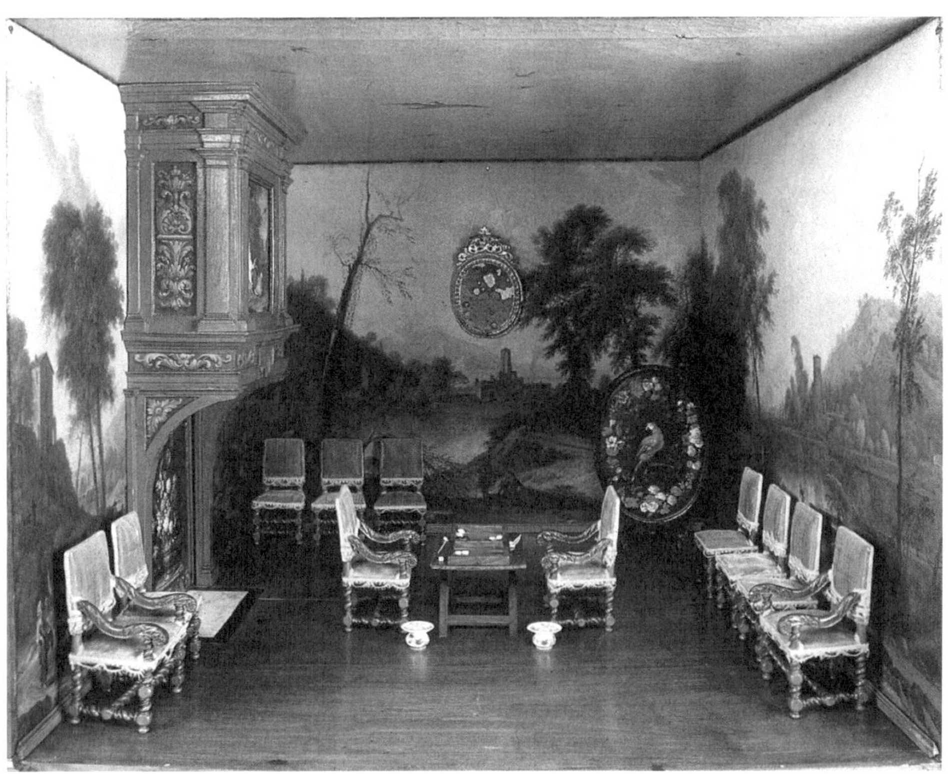

FIGURE 14 Dollhouse of Petronella Oortman, 1686–1710. Detail: the drawing room. Amsterdam, Rijksmuseum.

glass and bend forward toward these rooms to cancel out the world. Let us enter the drawing room (fig. 14).

A Concrete *Mise-en-Abîme*

Arriving in the drawing room on the second floor to the left, we find it fully decorated in accordance with the rules of interior decoration formulated by Gerard de Lairesse in his *Great Book of Painting* (1707): from floor to ceiling, its walls have been covered by a monumental Italianate landscape painting, exquisitely rendered by Amsterdam-born artist Nicolas Piemont, who signed his four-part miniature painting not once but twice. In this room meant for "withdrawing" (in the sense of a drawing room), the notions of exterior and interior have become so entangled that for anyone bending forward to look inside this dollhouse, the experience of visually entering the room cancels out the rest of the world. This windowless room appears to be a kind of a slightly claustrophobic instrument, much like a perspective box, through which notions of embodiment and the dialectics of inside and outside have been played out and investigated. It is as if the world has turned inside out: as a kind of panorama *avant la lettre*, the monumental nature scene continues over three walls with barely any interruptions from borders, frames, or windowsills. Unlike De Witte's painting that—being a commodity—is typically small-sized and thus portable, Piemont's landscape cannot be removed from its location and is a permanent feature of the room it inhabits. The notion of dwelling "in" painting should been taken quite literally here: the wall painting has come to designate a whole space as such. We could say that, indeed, dwelling has turned into painting from which there is no escape: even the ceiling has become part of its totality, as it has been covered with a cloudscape punctuated by flying birds.

The Italianate landscape shows monastery-like buildings on the shore of a large lake in the background, while in the foreground, a road runs along the shore on which various figures walk—a few seem to have stopped to chat with each other. Though obviously we cannot actually stand in this miniature reception room, we can easily imagine how it must be to sit on one of its chairs, all the while being transported into this landscape, taking the same path as the calmly walking figures. When sixty years later Diderot described how he "entered" the paintings of Vernet, he must have had something like this in mind. There are enough elements in the room to prevent complete absorption in the illusion: a large mantelpiece adorned with paintings of a chicken and flowers is clearly out of tune here. Yet this is less about illusionary effect and more about being transported into another world even as one remains in the same location, just as Heidegger explained how thinking works when he gave the example of the bridge at Heidelberg. The room turned inside out only reinforces the strange awareness of what it means to be inside and outside at the same time. In addition to Piemont's wall painting, another item evokes reflection on the nature and essence of "housing," and more specifically on the movement of withdrawing and retreat. This can be found when we move to the tapestry room.

Located on the first floor, the tapestry room is named for its rather modernist-looking zigzag wall decoration, and it hides an ingenious surprise: a small Japanese-style cabinet, in black and gold lacquer, is placed against its back wall, standing on legs, very much like the dollhouse itself (fig. 15). The Russian nesting doll effect reaches its pinnacle in this tiny piece of furniture, labeled in a late eighteenth-century description of the dollhouse as an "East-Indian art cabinet" (*Oost-Indisch Konst-Cabinettje*): the cabinet house within

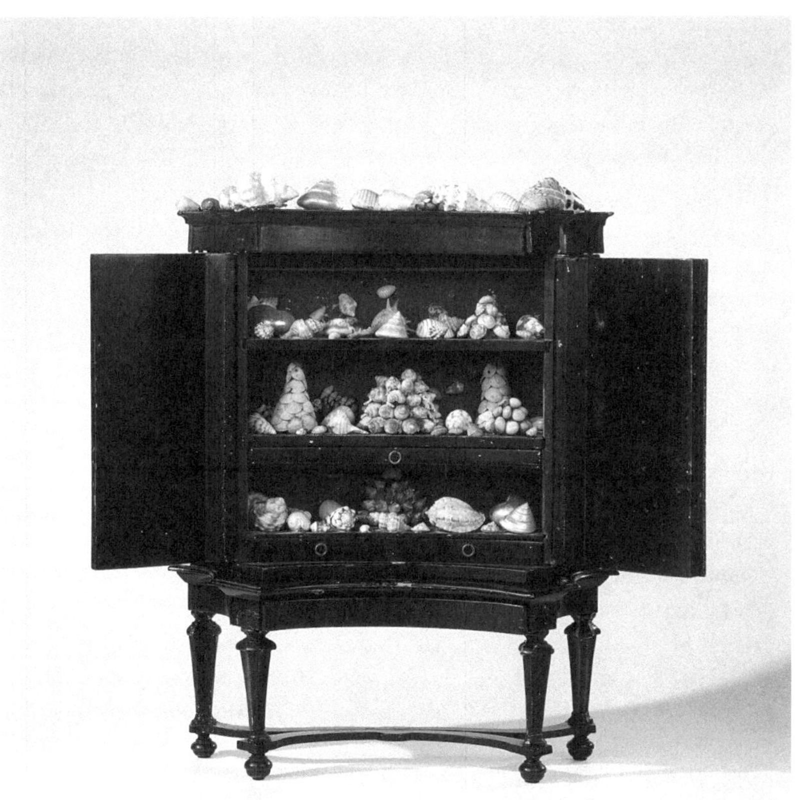

FIGURE 15 Dollhouse of Petronella Oortman, 1686–1710. Detail: East-Indian art cabinet with miniature shell collection. Amsterdam, Rijksmuseum.

a house houses a cabinet. But this spiraling downward toward a further interiority exceeds all expectations when the doors of this mini cabinet open to show an impressive collection of shells, nicely laid out on three shelves. In the drawers underneath we used to find yet more shells, along with eastern horns and glass pearls, "all very small and real," the eighteenth-century inventor assures us.[44] The presence of a collection of shells at the heart of this dollhouse reveals dramatically the extent of a visual argument being made, which can be unpacked on at least three different levels.

First, the shells' placement in a cabinet fits with contemporary collecting practices. Shells were considered collector's items, and amateur scientists and other enthusiasts eagerly gathered them to marvel at the wonderfully natural artistry of their intricate shapes. In literature, emblem books, and art theory, the shells' luster has sometimes been celebrated as a natural shine that no painter could duplicate, though apparently, many still life painters took up the challenge: numerous still lifes with shells, having a particular concentration on the rendering of their sheen, were produced during the course of the seventeenth century. Their presence here in the tapestry room is fitting, so to speak, as an incidental musing about these issues.

However, this musing is interrupted by the play with scale immediately apparent in the shells' presentation. Von Uffenbach remarks that these miniature shells had been collected by someone who had spent forty years in the East Indies, an observation that must be correct, as almost all of the items are from the archipelago.[45] Their display on these miniature shelves underscores the owners' imperialist reach, which is centered in their privileged bourgeois residence and extends outward to the far corners of the world. Compressed within the cabinet space is the distance from Amsterdam to the beach the shells came from, as well as the potential scientific knowledge about that part of the world contained within them. As we know from Norman Bryson's brilliant reading of two shells flanking a bouquet of flowers set against a view of a landscape painted by Ambrosius Bosschaert around 1618, the shells' profiles set against the distant vista underscore how the vast landscape can be dwarfed by the small scale of the shells; this game of scale results in a complete dislocation of the objects involved.[46] The miniature shells in Oortman's minuscule cabinet are mostly juvenile versions of mature specimens, which make them even more interesting in terms of scale.[47] Therefore, like Bosschaert's painting, Oortman's miniature collection incites its viewers to think about the fitting placement of the exotic shells in the cabinet—a placement that is simultaneously a displacement.

Moving beyond these reflections on proper and improper placement, we should note that a shell, within the discussion of the house that we have developed here, is a particular case in point worth elaborating on. As the house of a sea creature that accompanies it wherever it goes, offering a retreat and protection at any moment, a shell raises issues about the potential mobility of a house, and about how one might find a home while being en route (as we have seen in Heidegger's notion of dwelling, for instance). The shell also prompts thoughts about exotic natural wonders washed ashore on East Indian beaches and their incongruous placement as precious *objets d'art* in an upper-middle-class Amsterdam townhouse as their new, or borrowed, home. Indeed, Bachelard, in his chapter "Shells," describes how a shell creature is dialectical *par excellence* as an image of continuous withdrawing. If we consider for a moment that this dollhouse, along with being a building project, is also both a metaphor and an instrument of retreat, the baby shells become

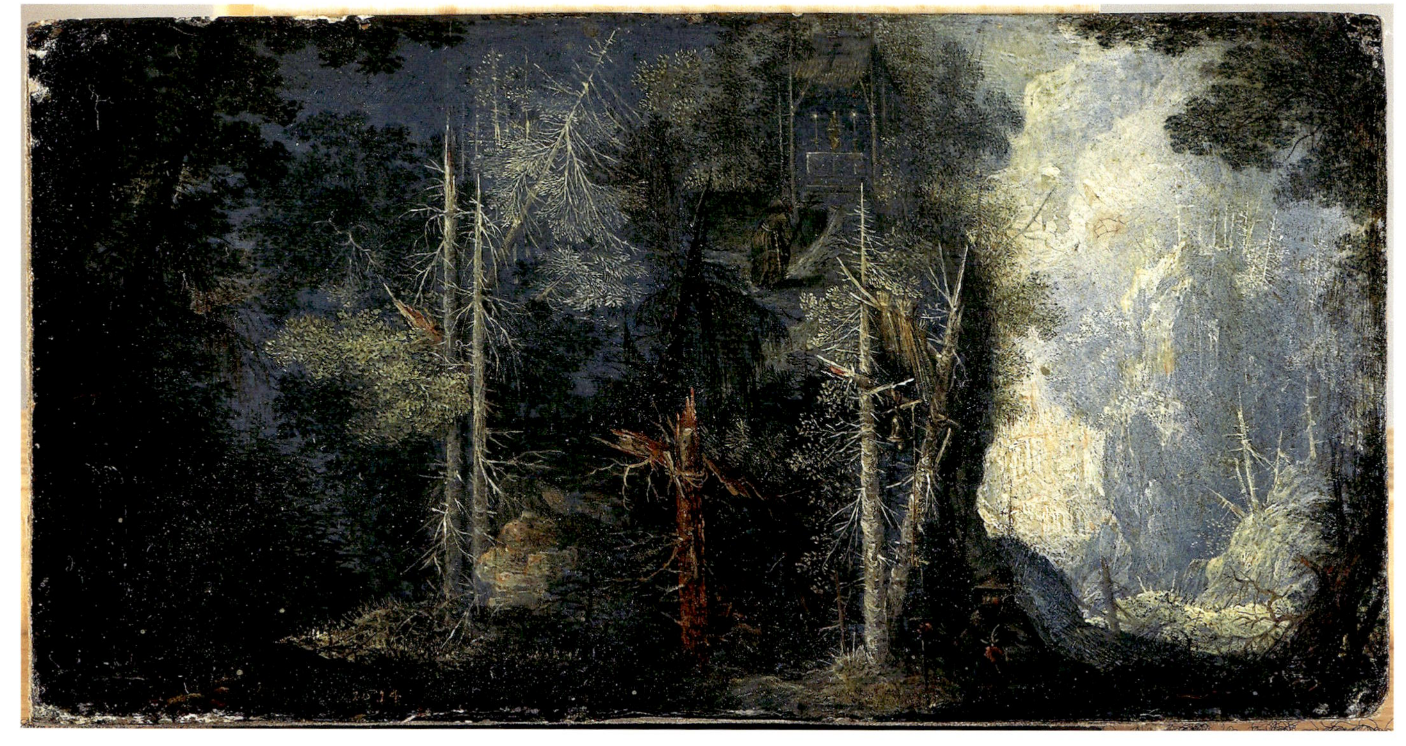

PLATE 1 Pieter Stevens, *Wooded Landscape*, 1614. Oil on cardboard; 6.9 × 12.8 cm. Frankfurt, Städel Museum. Photo © Städel Museum / ARTOTHEK.

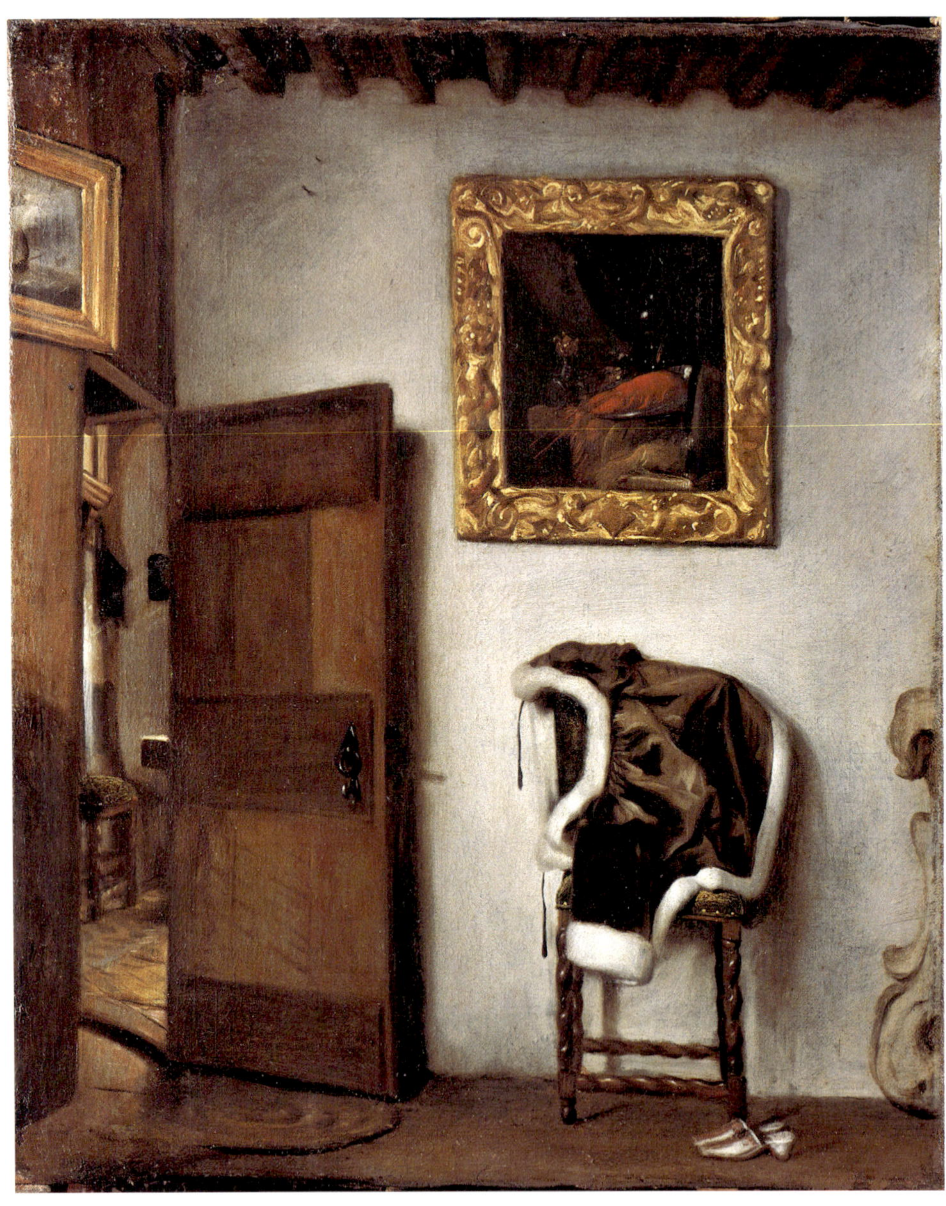

PLATE 2 Cornelis Bisschop, *Interior with a Jacket on a Chair*, c. 1660. Oil on canvas; 47 × 37 cm. Berlin, Gemäldegalerie, SMB. Photo © bpk / Gemäldegalerie, SMB / Jörg P. Anders.

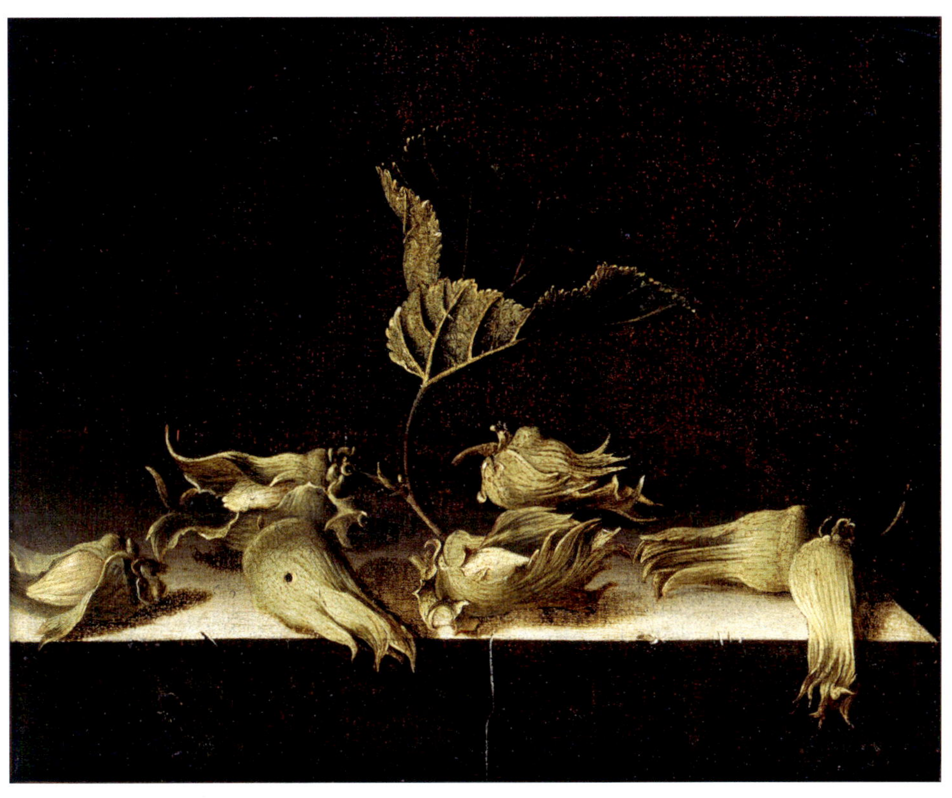

PLATE 3 Adriaen Coorte, *Still Life with Hazelnuts*, 1696. Oil on paper; 16.5 × 20 cm. Oxford, Ashmolean Museum. Photo © Ashmolean Museum, University of Oxford.

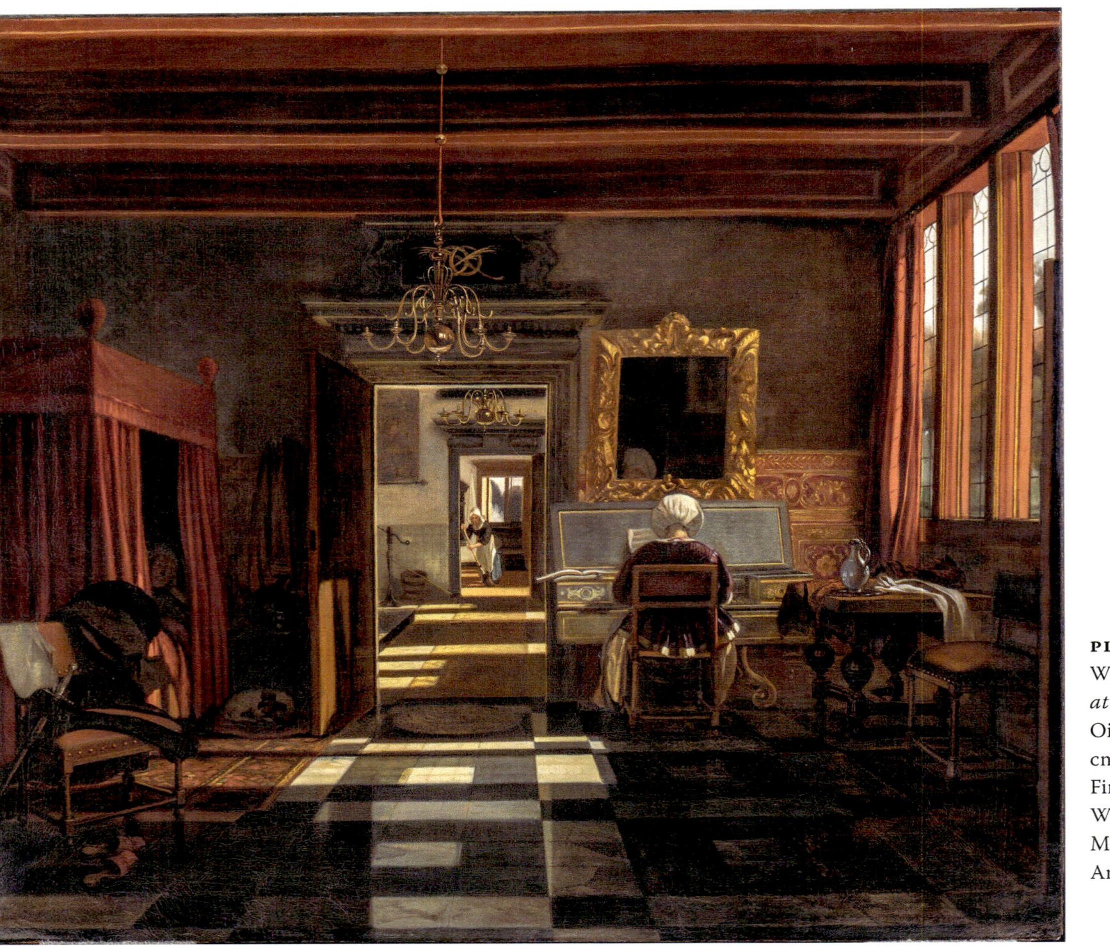

PLATE 4 Emanuel de Witte, *Interior with Woman at a Virginal*, c. 1660–1667. Oil on canvas; 97.5 × 190.7 cm. Montréal Museum of Fine Arts, purchase, John W. Tempest Fund. Photo: Montréal Museum of Fine Arts / Christine Guest.

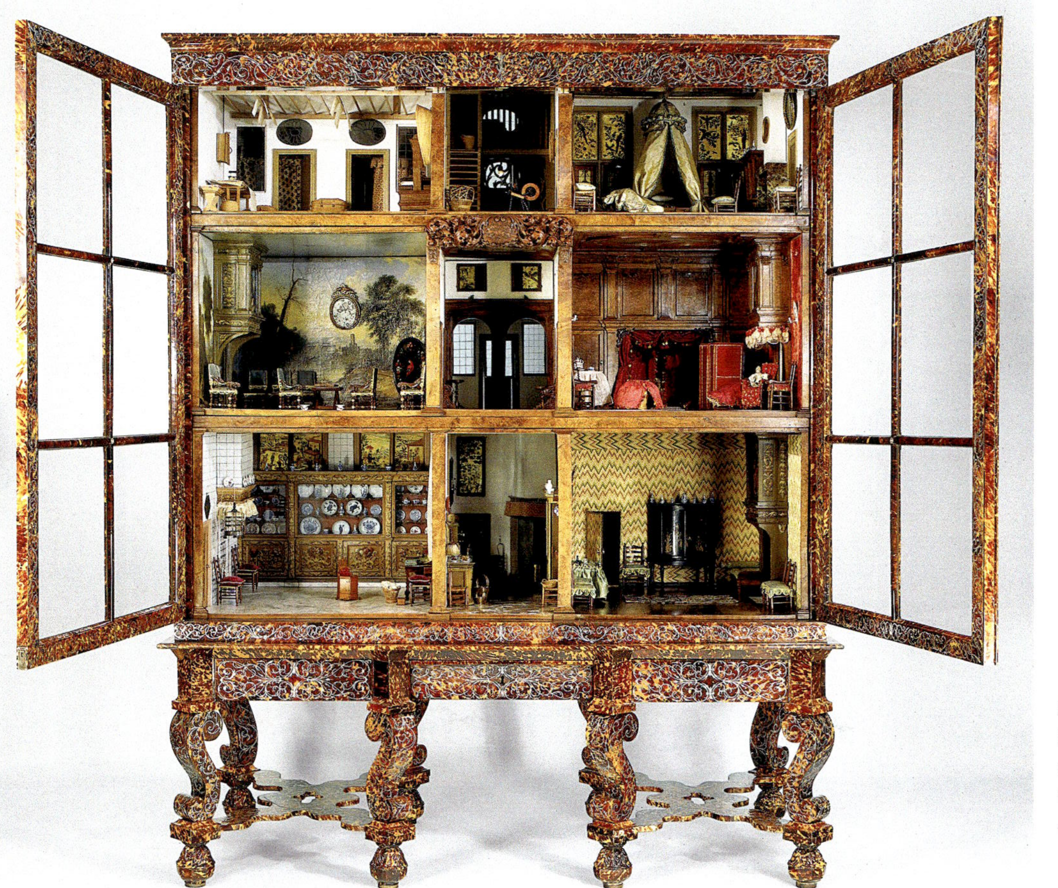

PLATE 5 Dollhouse of Petronella Oortman, 1686–1710. Wooden case, various materials, 255 × 190 × 78 cm. Amsterdam, Rijksmuseum.

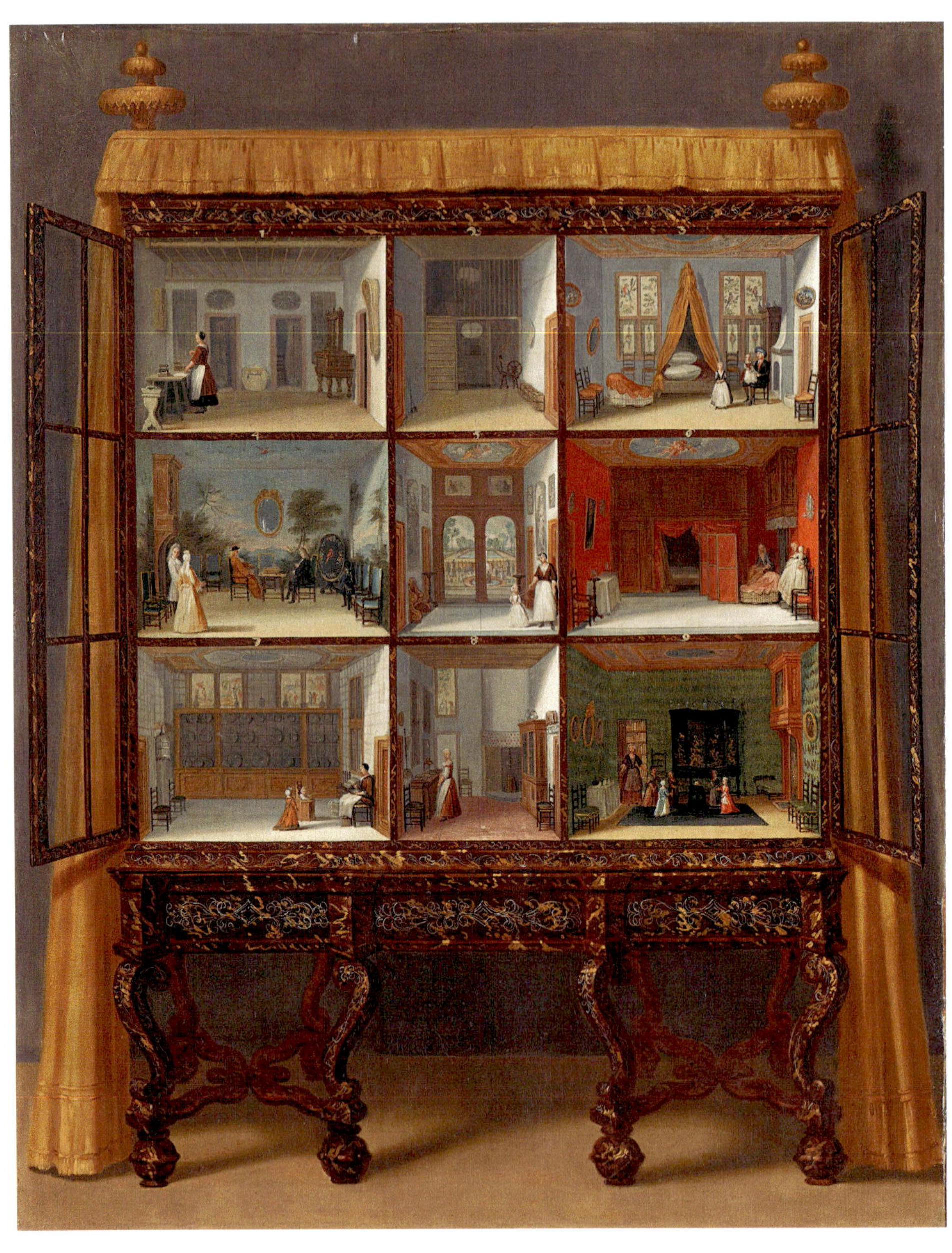

PLATE 6 Jacob Appel, *Painting of the Dollhouse of Petronella Oortman*, 1710. Oil on parchment and canvas; 87 × 69 cm. Amsterdam, Rijksmuseum.

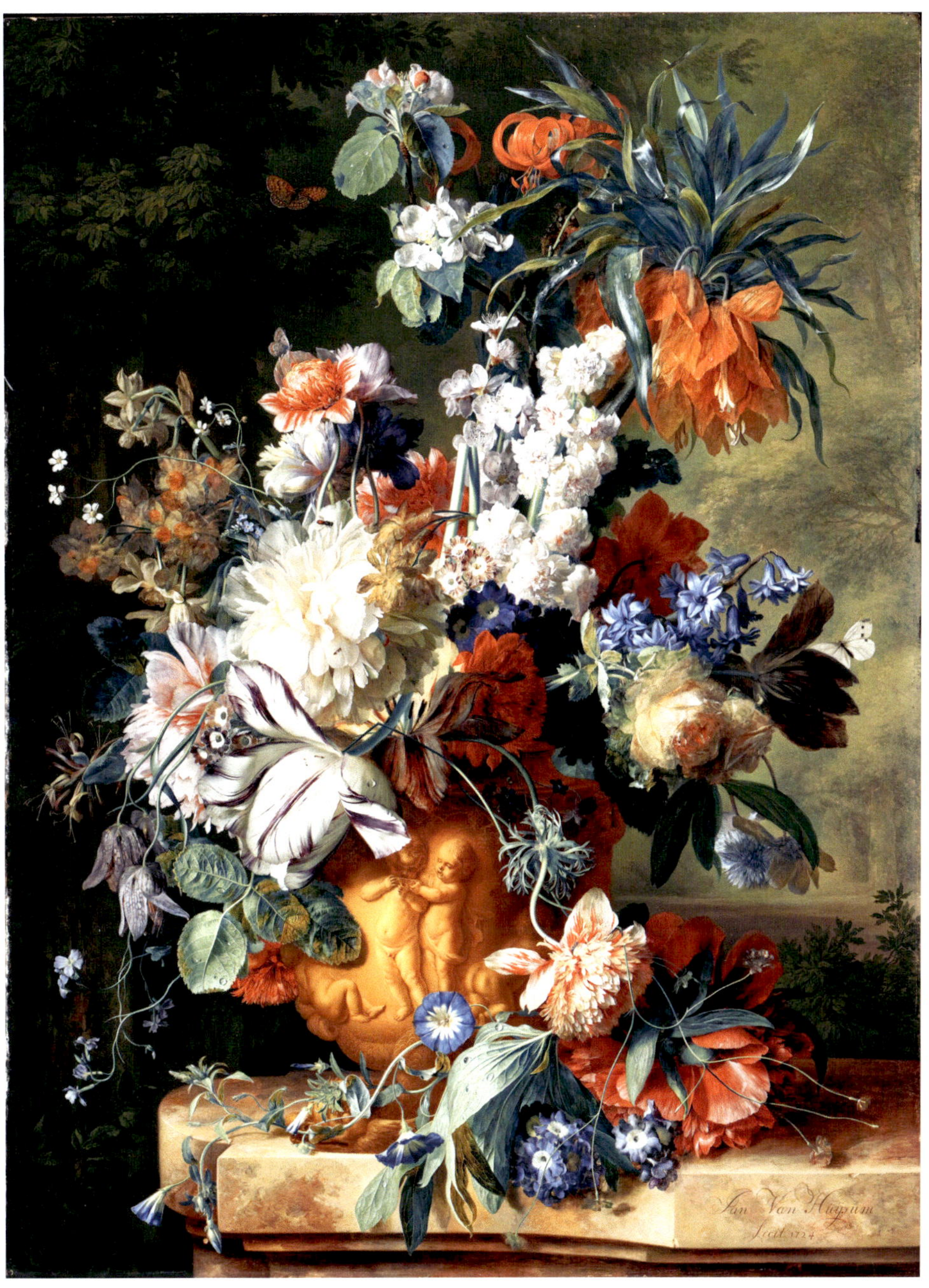

PLATE 7 Jan van Huysum, *Bouquet of Flowers in an Urn*, 1724. Oil on panel; 80 × 59 cm. Los Angeles County Museum of Art, gift of Mr. and Mrs. Edward William Carter, M.91.164.2. Photo © 2021 Digital Image, Museum Associates / LACMA / Art Resource NY / Scala, Florence.

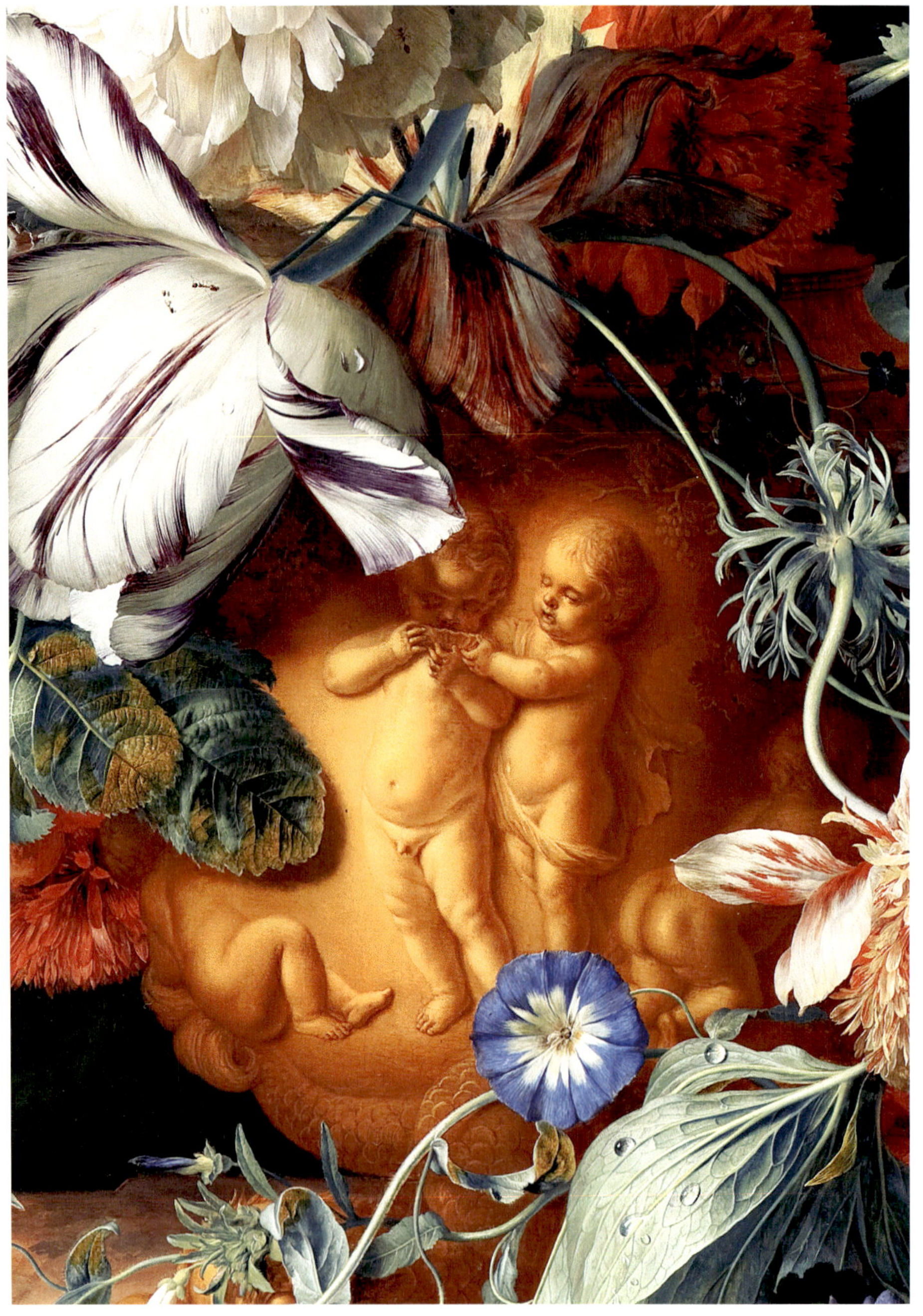

PLATE 8 Jan van Huysum, *Bouquet of Flowers in an Urn*, 1724. Detail: tulip petal. (See plate 7.)

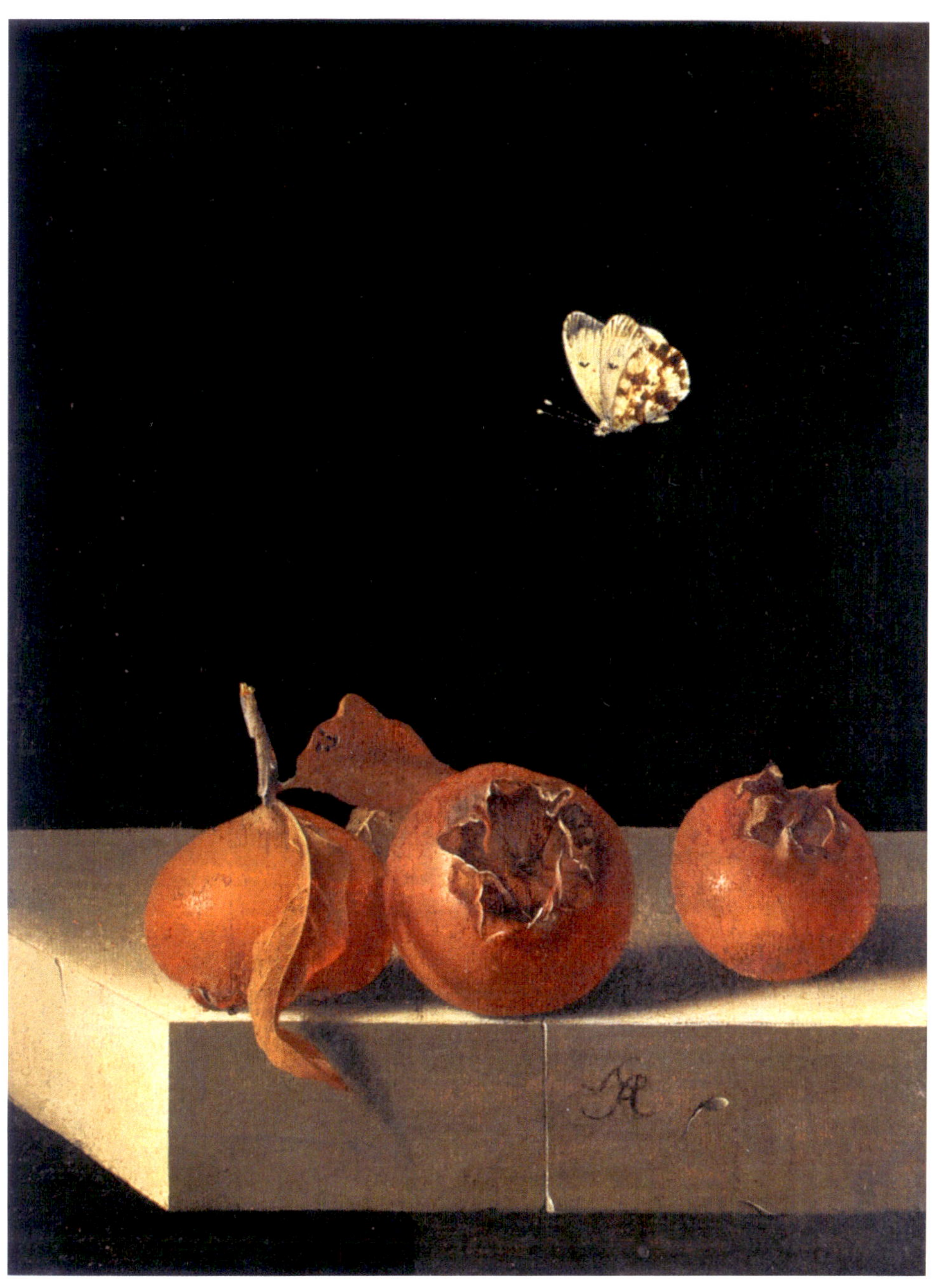

PLATE 9 Adriaen Coorte, *Three Medlars with a Butterfly*, c. 1693–1695. Oil on paper mounted on panel; 27 × 20 cm. Private collection.

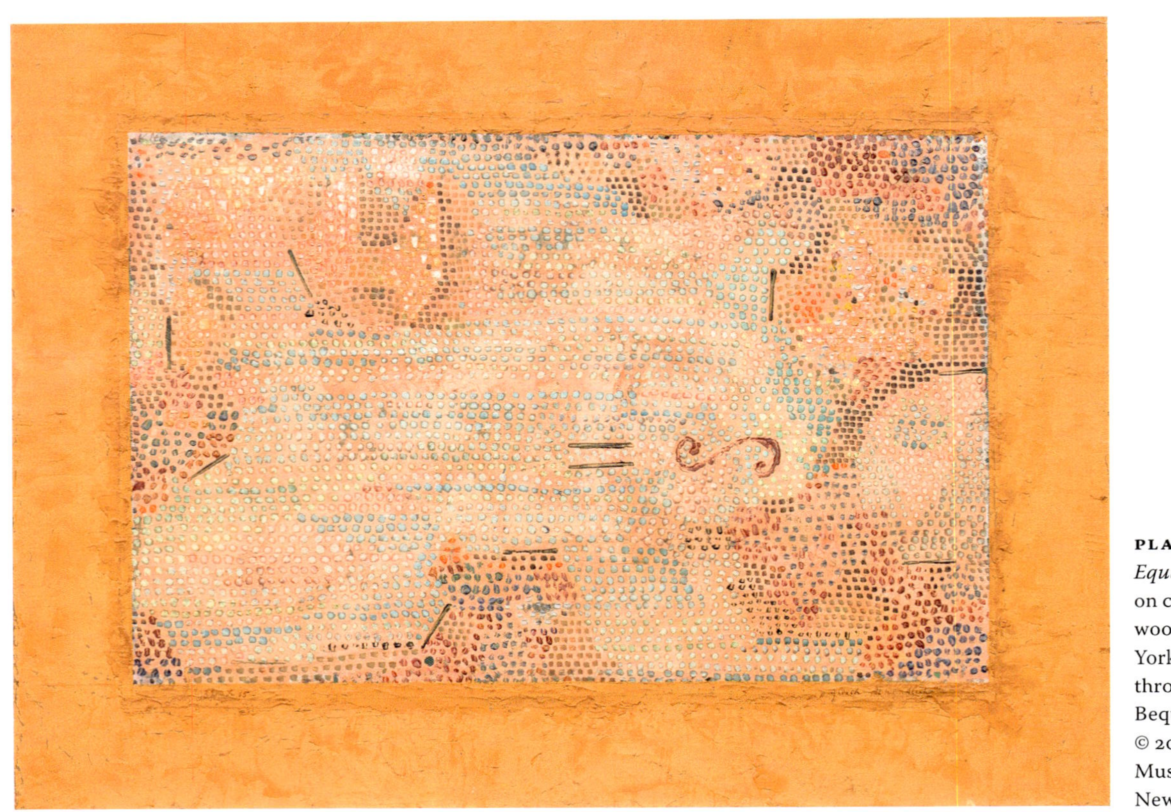

PLATE 10 Paul Klee, *Equals Infinity*, 1932. Oil on canvas mounted on wood; 51.4 × 68.3 cm. New York, MOMA, acquired through the Lillie P. Bliss Bequest, 90.1950. Photo © 2021 Digital image, The Museum of Modern Art, New York / Scala, Florence.

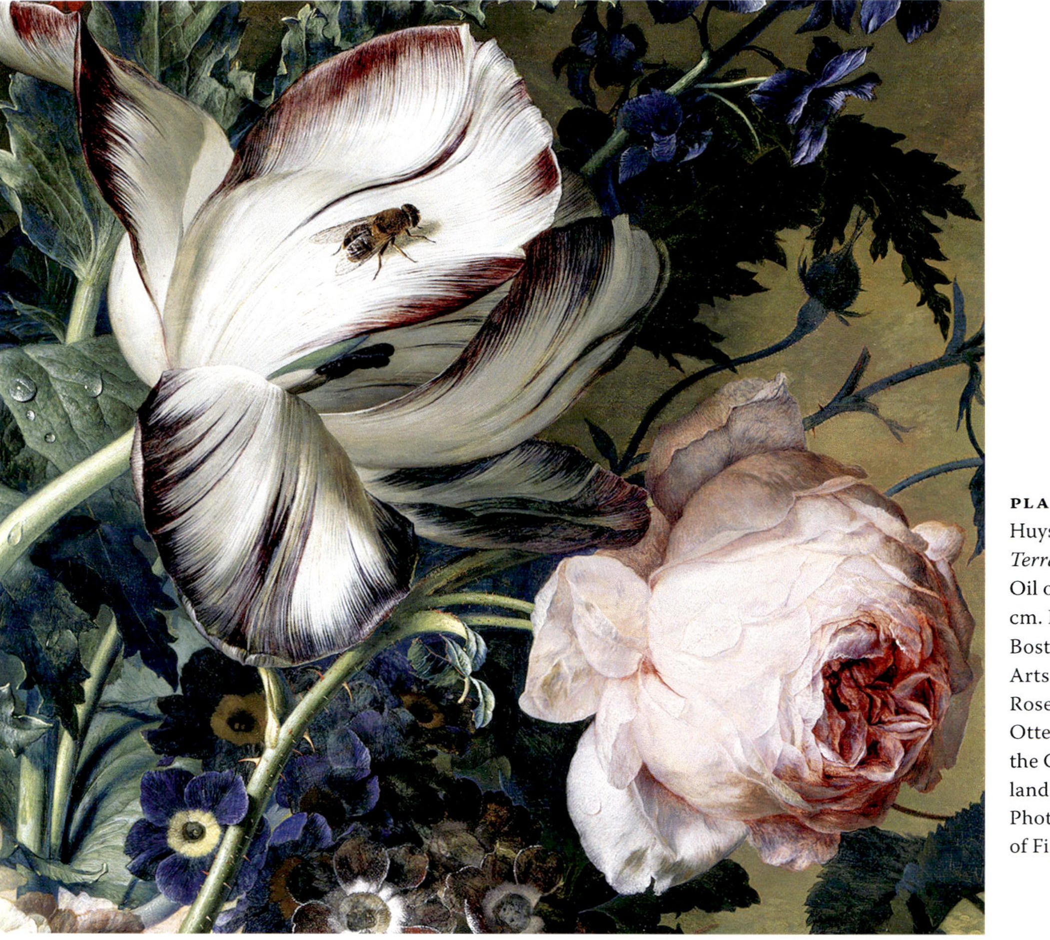

PLATE 11 Jan van Huysum, *Flowers in a Terracotta Vase*, c. 1730. Oil on panel; 80 × 61 cm. Detail: tulip petal. Boston, Museum of Fine Arts, promised gift of Rose-Marie and Eijk van Otterloo, in support of the Center for Netherlandish Art, L-R 13.2019. Photo © 2021 Museum of Fine Arts, Boston.

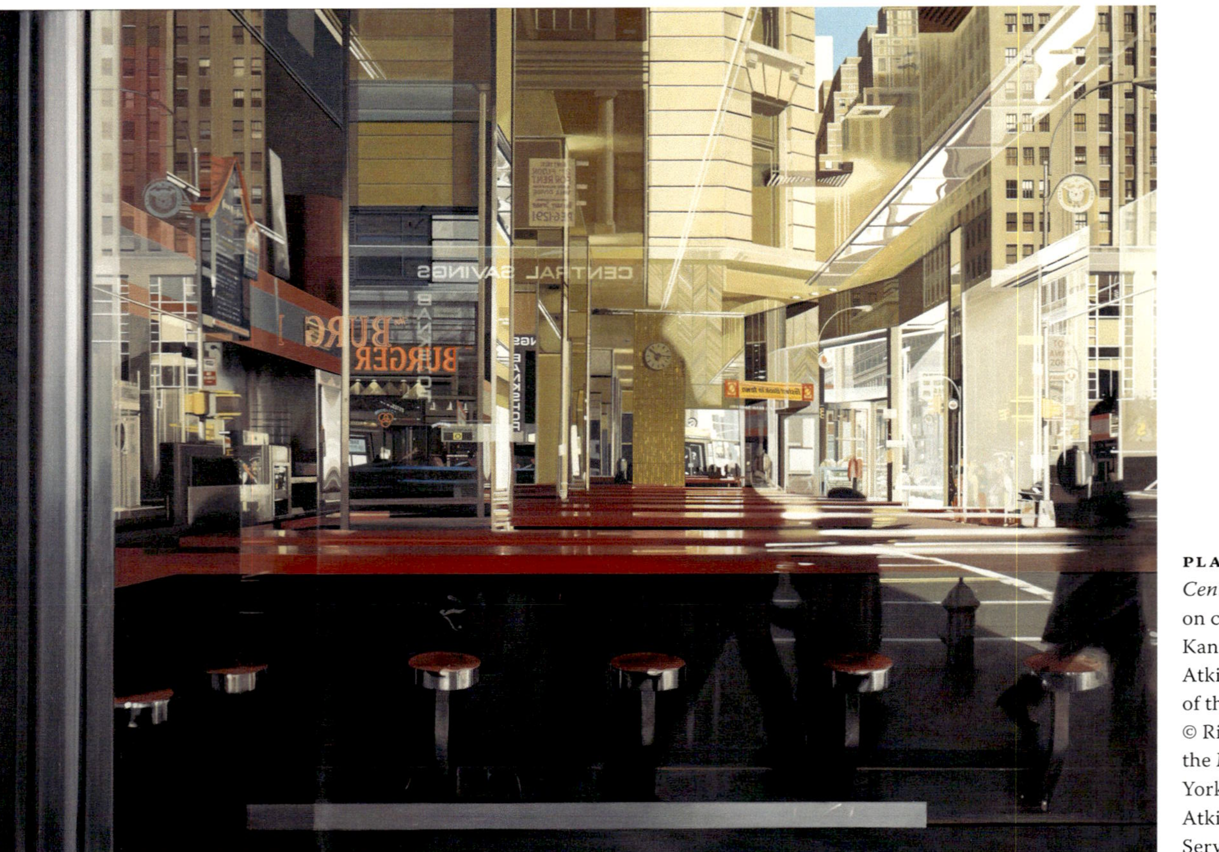

PLATE 12 Richard Estes, *Central Savings*, 1975. Oil on canvas; 91.4 × 121.9 cm. Kansas City, MO, Nelson-Atkins Museum of Art, gift of the Friends of Art, F75-13. © Richard Estes, courtesy of the Marlborough Gallery, New York. Photo courtesy Nelson-Atkins Museum of Art, Media Services / Jamison Miller.

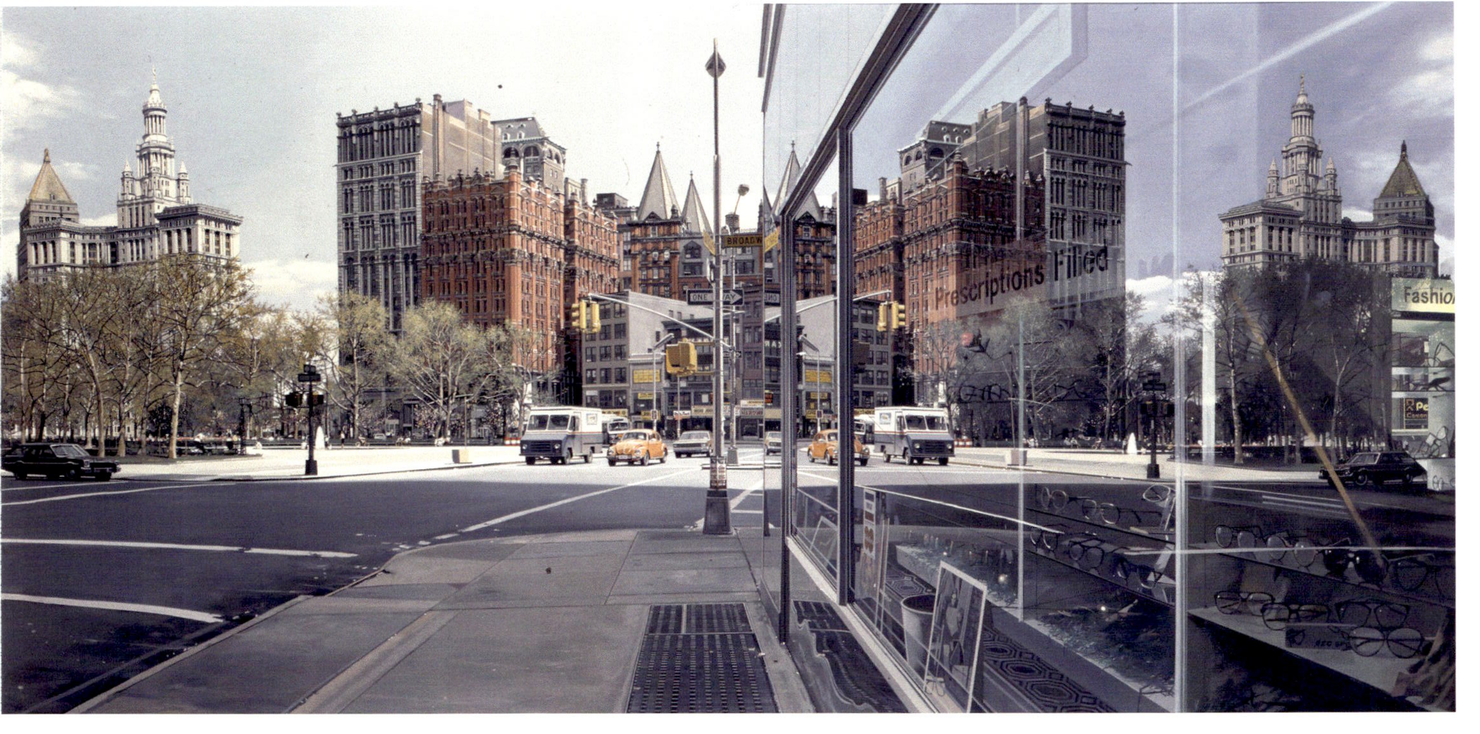

PLATE 13 Richard Estes, *Prescriptions Filled*, 1983. Oil on board; 36 × 72 in. © Richard Estes, courtesy of the Marlborough Gallery, New York.

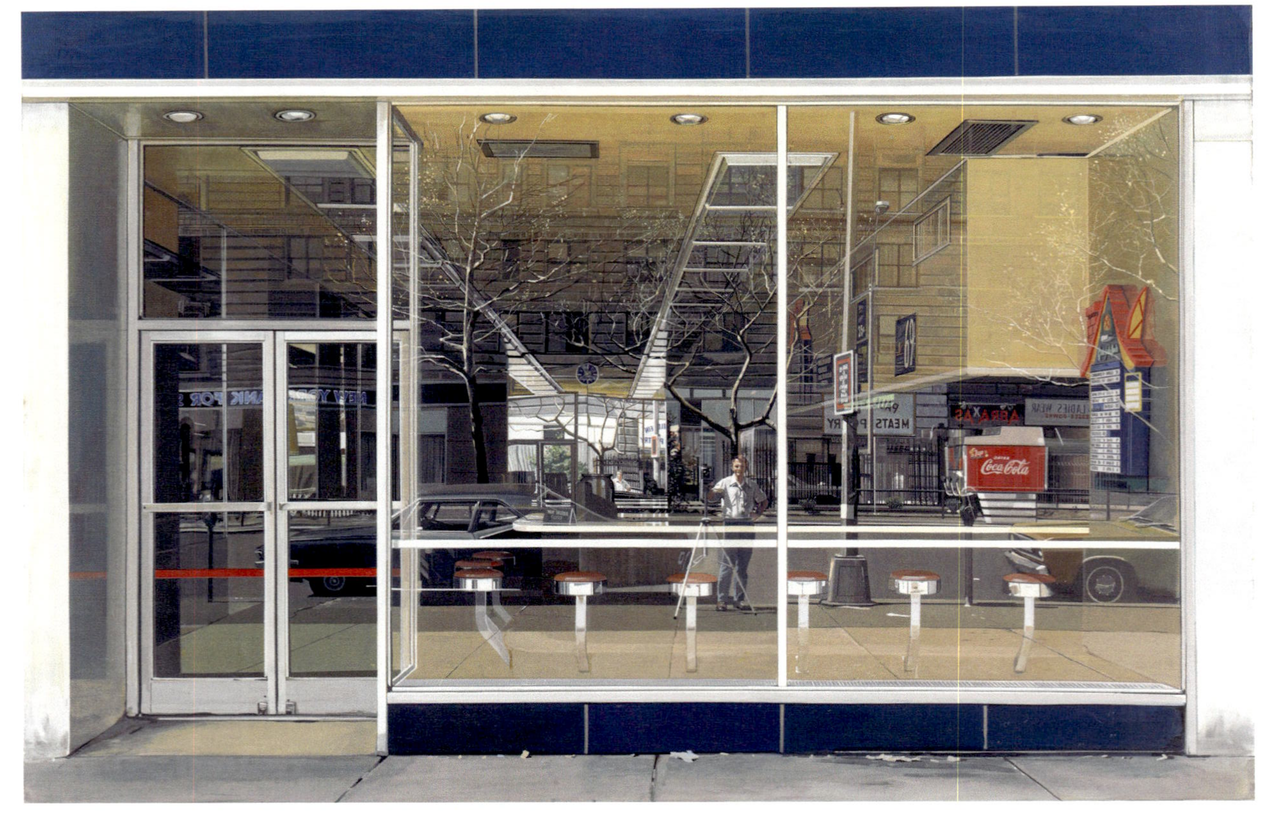

PLATE 14 Richard Estes, *Double Self-Portrait*, 1976. Oil on canvas; 60.8 × 91.5 cm. New York, MOMA, Mr. and Mrs. Stuart M. Speiser Fund. © Richard Estes, courtesy of the Marlborough Gallery, New York.

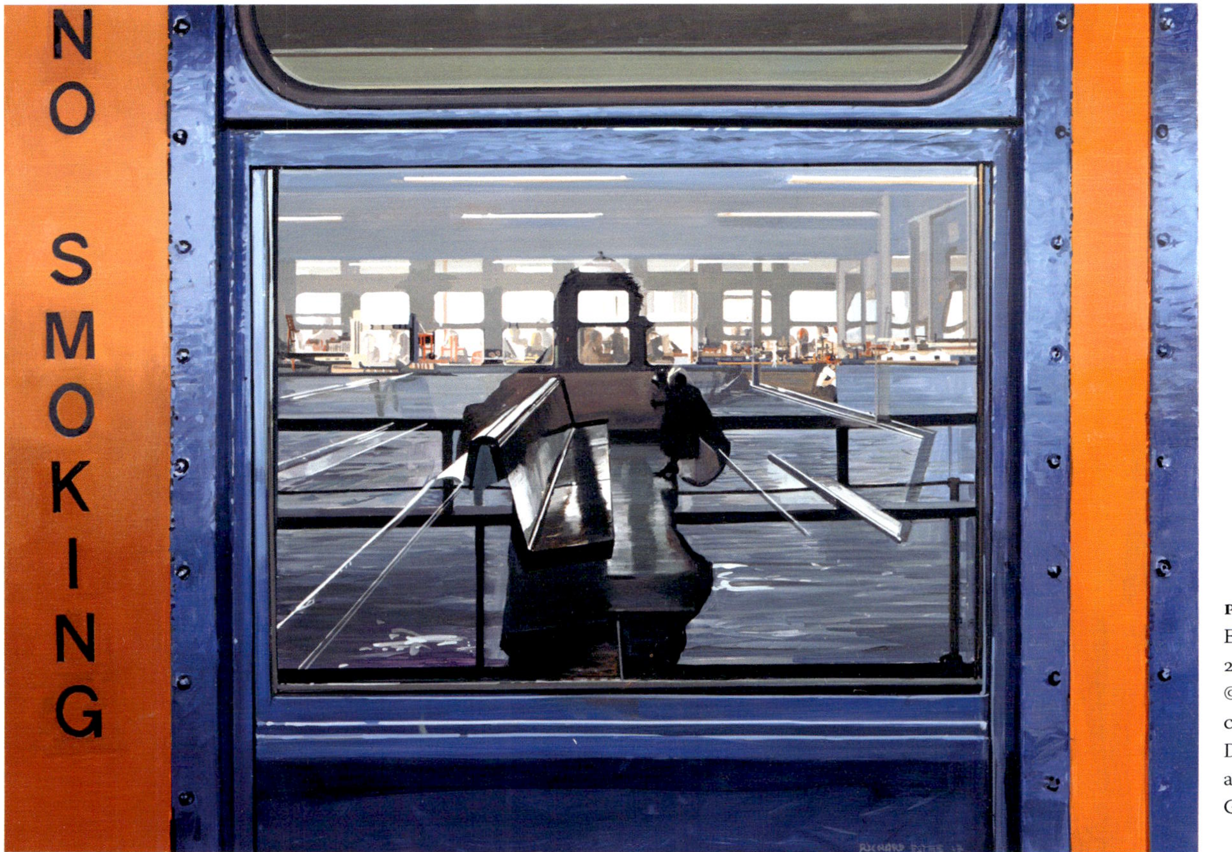

PLATE 15 Richard Estes, *Self-Portrait*, 2013. Oil on board. © Richard Estes, courtesy of Ann and Donovan Moore and Marlborough Gallery, New York.

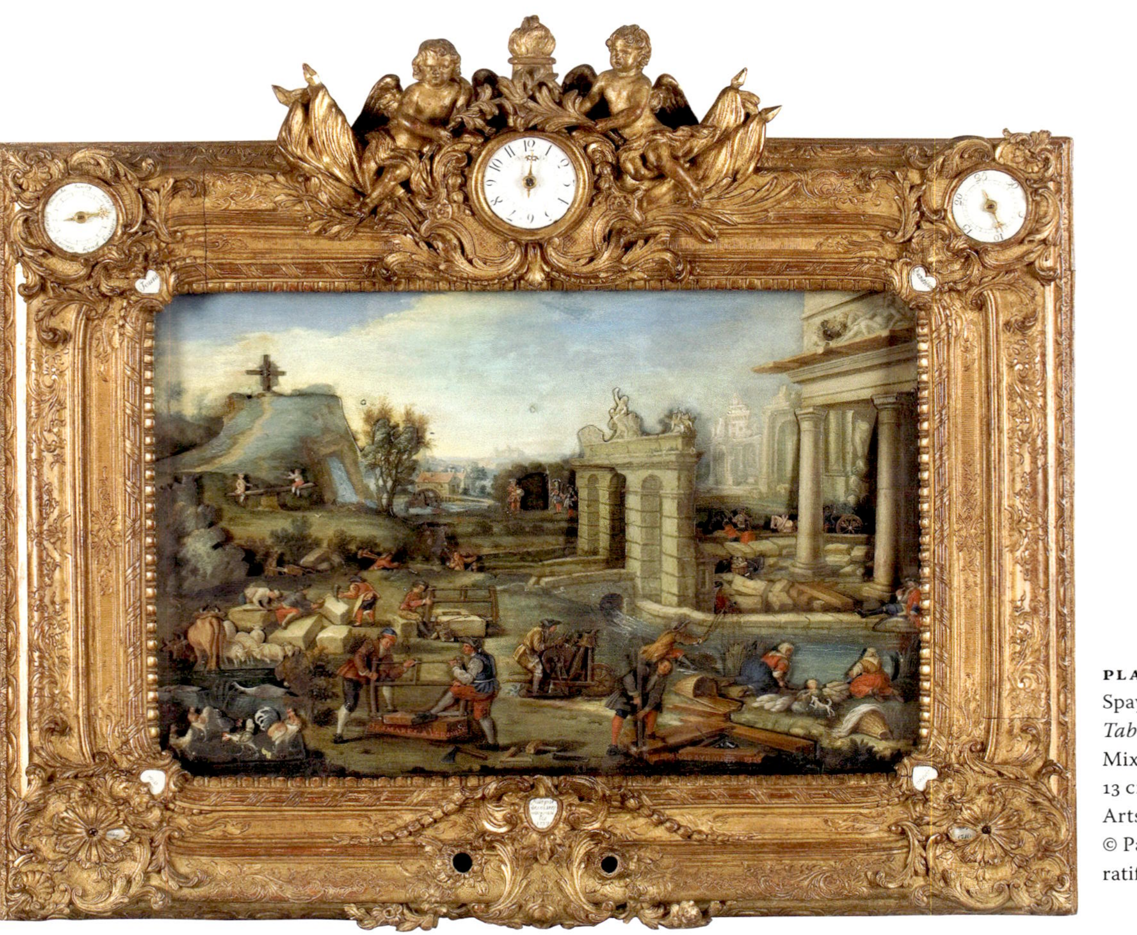

PLATE 16 Nicolas Spayement and Desmares, *Tableau Mécanique*, 1739. Mixed media; 79 × 91.5 × 13 cm. Paris, Musée des Arts décoratifs. Photo © Paris, Les Arts Décoratifs / Jean Tholance.

provocative objects, stirring thoughts about what it means to be housed as a curiosity in a cabinet within a cabinet. Like Descartes, whose first thoughts in his rented room concerned the structure of architecture in relation to the method of thinking, and also like Heidegger, whose thoughts in his secluded hut go out to the house of being, we can imagine Oortman arranging her shells on the miniature shelves—according to a decorative pattern still visible on the bottom of the drawers—as a way of articulating her thoughts. Wittingly or not, by the act of putting the baby shells on shelves, she has, in fact, created a concrete *mise-en-abîme*: the shell as an abandoned house is placed in a cabinet which in its turn is placed in a cabinet house, which stands in her own residence. However, unlike her own house, or the dollhouse at the time still inhabited by wax dolls, the shells are vacant; they are the empty houses of deceased sea creatures, now laid to rest as mere exteriorities of what used to be living spaces, closely fit to the creature that inhabited it. This ideal house with a perfect running household might not quite provide the home that we need. Filled with things, it has at its heart an emptiness, exemplified by the shells, that, no matter how deeply it is stored away, cannot but fill us with dread. Ultimately, this house has only been a borrowed home, a metaphor. It is this awareness of *Da-sein*, the utter strangeness of our ordinary life and our place in it, that fills us with anxiety and dread for which there is only one antidote. It is only when we really start thinking that we will feel underway to our philosophical home.

Painting as Dwelling and Thinking

In 1905, the Danish painter Vilhelm Hammershøi (1864–1916) created *Open Doors* (fig. 16), a view of an apartment at Strandgade 30 in Christianshavn, Copenhagen, that he and his wife Ida had inhabited since 1898. From the moment they moved in, Hammershøi found a fresh topic for his work, which gradually garnered an admiring audience in Denmark and beyond. He had specialized in intimate and small-scale scenes of interiors, where lone figures appear absorbed in needlework or reading, but his apartment at Strandgade 30 inspired him to remove even the solitary figure and the sparse array of furniture from his paintings. In what would become one of his most empty (and most famous) paintings, we see three rooms *en enfilade* toward a bright window in the rear. The floor is composed of wide, dark brown boards, the walls are painted a dark gray, and the doors and their frames are cream colored. The rooms are completely empty. Besides a glimpse of what seems to be a decorative panel over the door in the center, we see mostly space. Space, and three wide-open doors, which suggest more emptiness behind them,

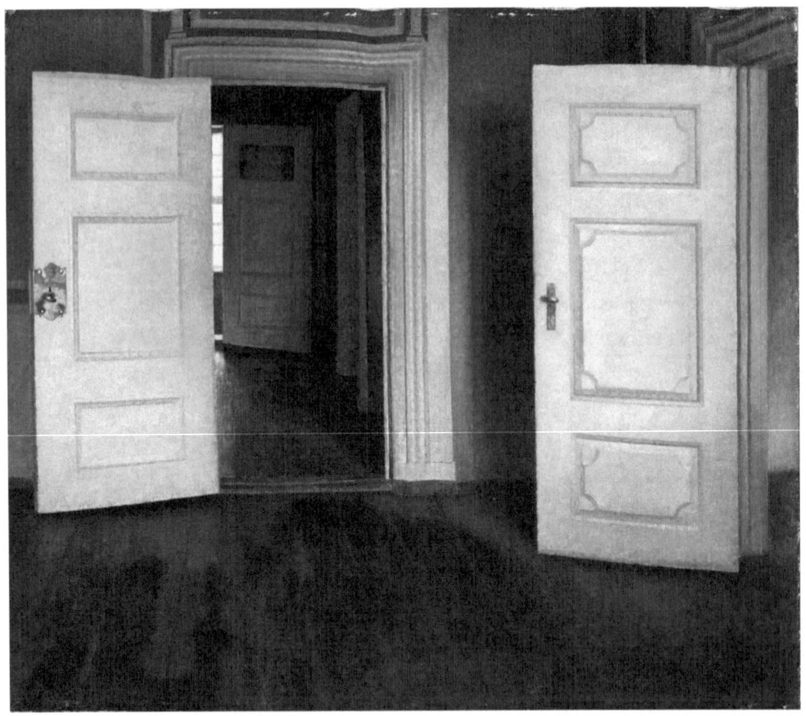

FIGURE 16 Vilhelm Hammershøi, *Open Doors*, 1905. Oil on canvas; 60 × 52 cm. Copenhagen, The David Collection, B309. Photo: Pernille Klemp.

and which are less inviting than their openness seems to convey. In addition to the three open doors, a fourth opening is visible in the middle room, the door of which is either closed or is swinging open to the other side. Clearly, no one lives here, and we, as viewers, are only visiting, passing through, while noticing only the few moments that break through the monotony: a handle different than the others, a slight variation in the surface pattern of a door.

Although all paintings featuring the interior of the Strandgade apartment are accurate in terms of the floor plan, Hammershøi's versions have been heavily edited. Compared to photographs of the painter and his wife in their apartment, the paintings have been cleared of people, clutter, wall decoration, and, most notably, chairs. There are few places to sit in these emptied interiors, and so we are given few opportunities to rest or carry out a task. We, as viewers, are meant to roam around, not to stay; we are asked to go through, walk around, not to sit down. The emptiness evokes a great sense of silence. As has been pointed out by past and present commentators, Hammershøi

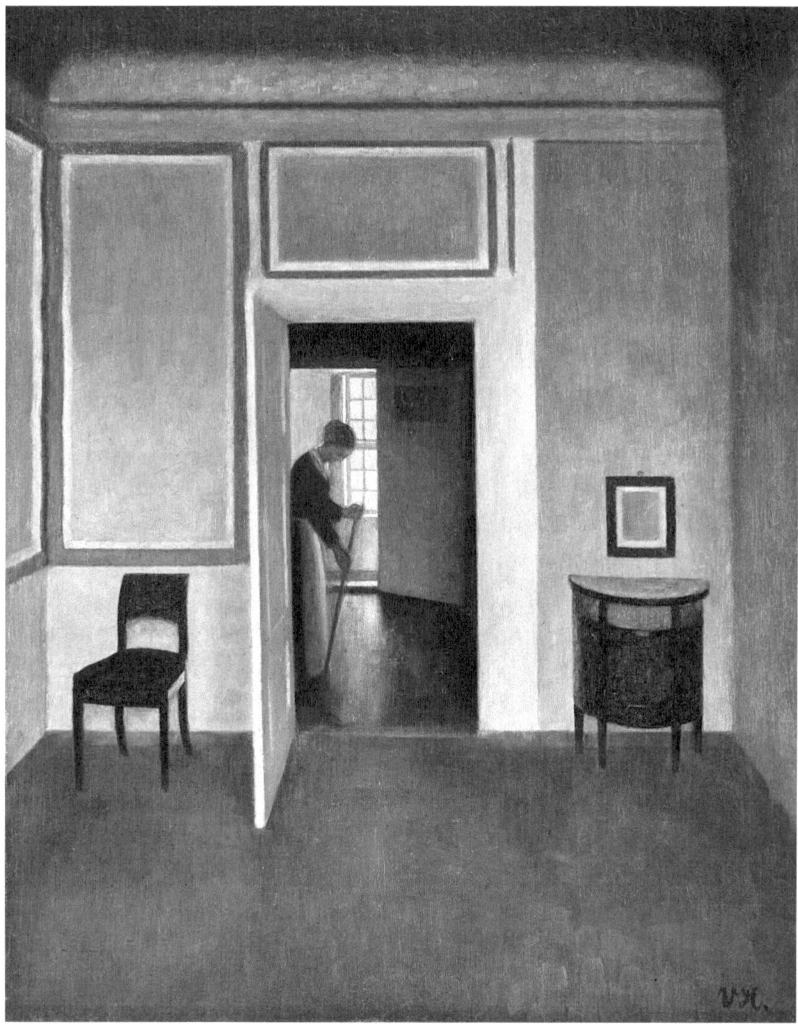

FIGURE 17 Vilhelm Hammershøi, *Interior, Strandgade 30*, 1902. Oil on canvas; 41 × 33 cm. Private collection. Sold at Sotheby's, December 12, 2018.

may have been influenced by the Romantics, and his empty rooms may well be a reflection of his private feelings. But it is also clear that he was heavily inspired by seventeenth-century Dutch interior painting, and very much like De Witte, he created a fictionalized version of his home. Even though the atmosphere, and the kind of subjectivity we find in his work, are very different.

If we look at *Interior, Strandgade 30* (1902; fig. 17) we see that its composition is clearly influenced by De Witte, but without the warm sunlight and the orange-red palette of the Dutch painter. Grays and off-whites dominate the scene, revealing strong architectural contours of the walls and door openings. It is as if he has set off to finish something that his Dutch predecessors have left untouched. Indeed, we could say that Hammershøi's work rephrases, in clear and plain language, what Dutch interior painters like De Witte were so passionately trying to articulate: that the need for solitude can probably never been found in actual architectural space, that the pursuit of a back room in one's head most likely ends in a fictional space rather than anywhere else—be it a poem, a painting, or a dollhouse—and that only there do we find room to start thinking while underway. However—and this is fundamentally different from seventeenth-century conceptions of the home—Hammershøi's rooms are filled with anxiety instead of bliss about the transformation of the familiar into the unfamiliar. There is no anchorage here, no comfortable place to sit down. This is a solitude that is distressing and uncanny. Not even the picture on the wall provides us with familiar faces, as they appear as ghost paintings, merely showing a gray field on white. Though De Witte was an excellent example to visualize Heidegger's notion of thinking, Hammershøi's work depicts an image of the dread of *Da-sein*, recognizing the extraordinary of ordinariness: we cannot call this place home. Even though we inhabit it, we do not quite belong here. Modernist subjectivity has been given another image of thought.

Hammershøi's work brings out, more than any Dutch painter could have, the grid of space, the skeletal linework of a building as such, rather than what it contains. Whereas the apartment has obviously been completed, its habitation is unfinished. Most of his works show how living has not yet begun in the bright chambers but may be about to start: there is a single piece of furniture, or a solitary figure has turned up but remains detached from his or her environment. These elements seem as if they do not yet belong. The outline is definitive, not its content.

In one of his rare interviews, Hammershøi confirmed his interest in the architectural skeleton of his rooms: "what makes me choose a motif is as much the lines in it, what I would call the architectural stance in the picture. And then the light, of course. It is naturally also very important, but the lines are almost what I am most taken by. But when I choose a motif I think I mainly look at lines."[48] This emphasis on grid lines makes the apartment seem not haunting or uncomfortable, but rather clean and dust free. The place is ready for us to move in and to put our stuff here.

In a little-known text, "Art and Space" (1969), Heidegger raises the question as to how we can find the special character of space, as there is nothing "behind" it, nothing more is there to which it can be traced back. "Before space, there is no retreat to something," Heidegger writes.[49] Evidently, space *is* this retreat, which can only be made visible when we are clearing-away all that is in it. "Clearing-away is release of places" and, for Heidegger, a condition for dwelling.[50] Hammershøi's paintings show his home as cleared away of all his possessions. Only when this is done, he seems to insist, can this space turn into the kind of dwelling Heidegger has in mind. But perhaps the best image that brings out space's *articulation*, is Lucy McKenzie's installation *May of Teck* (2010) comprising canvases of trompe l'oeil walls mimicking Georgian interior walls covered with scenes of cloudy skies. Different from Oortman's dollhouse drawing room that brought the outside indoors, here we have both. Or neither: the point is less whether we are inside or outside, and more that we are—as philosophical subjects—continuously lost.

CHAPTER FOUR

The Profundity of Still Life

So this is why we philosophize: because there is desire, because there is absence in presence, deadness in life, and also because there is our power that is not yet power; and also because there is alienation, the loss of what we thought we had acquired and the gap between the deed and the doing, between the said and the saying; and finally because we cannot evade this: testifying to the presence of the lack with our speech. In truth, how can we not philosophize?

JEAN-FRANÇOIS LYOTARD, *WHY PHILOSOPHIZE*

The Depth of a Dewdrop

Flower still lifes such as Jan van Huysum's abundant bouquet of 1724 confront us with a methodological quandary: how might we make sense of the sheer splendor of the blossoming flowers, the almost blinding freshness of the colors, or the breathtaking transparency of the canvas effected by the artist's technique of fine painting, the secrets of which he jealously guarded (plate 7)? How do we look at this overwhelming tableau, which, apparently, despite its abundance of species, richness of color, and meticulously rendered detail, does not immediately answer to the conditions of pictorial legibility demanded by figurative painting? Any concrete starting point for a reading of this painting is denied, yet our gaze may creep in, welcomed by the dwarf morning glory in the lower left corner that is suspended from the marble stone ledge holding up the terracotta pot containing the bouquet. Climbing over the peony leaves and the white-and-red anemone, our eye is suddenly arrested by the peculiar position of the tulip, which has taken a nosedive. The tulip's inverted direction is further emphasized by the slight diagonal starting in the stem that is continued in the red streak on the tulip, the sprig, and the delicate twig of the honesty. Following the tulip's stem, we arrive at the center of the arrangement that, remarkably, shows a cut: the tulip has snapped, its stem's bare ends exposed.

The displacement of the tulip has left an indentation in the floral arrangement, which opens up in the upper left corner to the wooded background. If the tulip had not been snapped, it would have completed the symmetry of the floral arrangement as a counterpart to the fritillary on the right. The snapped flower could be a biblical reference to Job 14 that has often been associated with flower still lifes: "He comes forth like a flower and fades away," yet in Dutch translation reads "He comes forth like a flower and is *cut off*" (*Hij komt voort als eene bloem, en wordt afgesneden*). In that sense the tulip may relate not only to the brevity of man's life but also to his status as fallen. However, this interpretation is not entirely convincing given how opportunistic Van Huysum deals with a snapped flower, embracing the artistic and formalistic possibilities it offers him.

Our reading of this image may have been arrested by the tulip's upside-down position, but our wanderings have not quite come to a full stop. Something is pending in this image. Are we called upon to settle it? It is as if despite our arrested reading something else has been set in motion, an ultimate meaning that apparently this painting kept in reserve. What exactly does this still life wish to show by means of the snapped tulip at its composition's heart? The painting as a whole reveals a kind openness that does not necessarily call to be "filled" with meaning in an iconographic interpretation. Rather, the indeterminacy of the picture's lack gestures toward an understanding of this painting as governed by a more abstract or theoretical paradigm that offers us room for contemplation, or we may even say, for a *thought*.

Van Huysum seems to have been intrigued by the effect upside-down flowers have on traditional compositions. In other paintings, we also see how plunging stems allow him to create lovely jumbles of flower heads and leaves. These playful instances indicate Van Huysum's fascination with the very limitations of painting. The setting on the edge of a marble table frames the bouquet as much as it seems to tame its wildness, yet some twigs naughtily transgress these boundaries. By the time Van Huysum started his practice around 1710, the century-old history of still life as a genre had shown a continuing challenge to the restrains of pictorial space. In the so-called breakfast still lifes by Willem Claesz. Heda and Pieter Claesz and their followers, knife handles stick out and napkins crumble forward, ready to be picked up by the approaching viewer, while in *pronkstillevens* by Abraham van Beyeren and others, rims of plates filled with oysters lean dangerously over the table's edge, protruding out into the viewer's space as if offering the shellfish for immediate consumption.

Van Huysum goes further. If we look closely at his intricate composition with the diving tulip at its heart, we become aware of a game played out on the surface of the leaves, or rather, on the plane of the painting. The tulip may seem as if it has been displaced by sheer chance; however, it has triggered a series of consequences, including that its upside-down position has caused a dewdrop on one of its petals slowly to slide off (plate 8). Gravity's effect, often at work in still lifes, as we will see, is well depicted by Van Huysum: the tiny dewdrop is about to roll off the petal, apparently straight into the scallop that the female putto, on the relief adorning the terracotta pot, offers her male companion. The presumed accident of the snapped flower has been carefully planned. By letting the drop roll off from its petal into the scallop, Van Huysum is playfully shifting mimetic registers, creating a realm of fanciful fiction within his hyperrealistic mastery of pictorial resemblance, delving deeply into the notion of a faithful image as such by means of a virtually moving dewdrop. This may look like a rather frivolous diversion, a hidden bit of narrative told purely in visual terms, a kind of wink of the artist virtuoso to only those sharp-sighted art lovers who would care to see. In this chapter I will take up this dewdrop's theoretical challenge as capable of reflecting on the very act of painting, as such. I am interested in the way in which, through these dewdrops, Van Huysum's flower pieces philosophize about the nature of their representation.

Dewdrops have been considered the hallmark of Van Huysum's celebrated technique. In an ode written at the time of the artist's death in February 1749, the artist's biographer, Johan van Gool, describes Van Huysum's paintings in terms of fruit plants that were richly laden with silver dew, like "night drops sweated by blond Apollo during the summer."[1] The dewdrop was at the time a recurrent motif in art-theoretical writing, and already in the second century, the Greek Sophist Philostratus (c. 170–245) characterized the dewdrop as the sign *par excellence* of pictorial realism, advising artists purporting to create absolute verisimilitude to paint dewdrops on their flowers.[2] Whether wittingly or not, Van Huysum followed Philostratus's recommendation by scattering many pearly drops on the waxlike foliage—too many, in fact. While his work can be termed excessive in color palette and composition (combining his flower arrangements with deep garden views—a novelty at the time, and according to Van Gool the artist's invention), his abundant use of dewdrops is overdetermined. If we start to pay attention to them we suddenly see that like the snapped flowers, they have become tiny instruments by allowing Van Huysum to create another level of articulation beyond the realistic one. The dewdrop on the tulip's petal seems to literally shift registers, "sliding" off the dominant mimetic level and onto a minor, fictional level of the relief; or rather, it is tending toward such a shift of register, that in literary terms can be typed as an anacoluthon, which for Paul de Man "designates any grammatical or syntactical discontinuity in which a construction interrupts another before it is completed."[3] Is Van Huysum's painting contemplating the possibility of certain details to escape their status as mimetic elements, to become something more concrete, more independent or more substantial? Is this drop at least "thinking" about it?

Van Huysum's dewdrops and highlights show how blobs of paint seem to "lift" themselves from their support, creating an in-between space. This kind of thickness allows for a meditation on surface and ground, on transparency and realism, and on the status of a pictorial sign that has transcended its representative function to make a philosophical statement *in paint.*

The analysis of Van Huysum's painting will be framed by Hubert Damisch's notion of the "underneath of painting," explored in a discussion of Paul Klee's painting *Equals Infinity* (1932). I will argue on the basis of a juxtaposition of Klee's *Equals Infinity* to Van Huysum's flower still lifes that the work of both artists touch on similar issues, or more precisely formulated, that their work, in a comparable operation, attempts to think though issues of finitude and infinity through the application of dots of paint on a surface, however different the results. But before starting with a comparison between Van Huysum and Klee, I will make the case for still life as the most philosophical of genres—or rather, that for centuries, still life has been making this case itself.

The Most Philosophical of Genres

At the beginning of the 1690s, Adriaen Coorte painted a small still life scene of three medlars on a stone ledge, placed against a black background (plate 9). A small brown butterfly flutters over the fruits, its astute feelers conspicuously poised against the black backdrop. In contrast to the nocturnal darkness stretching out behind it, the stone ledge bathes in a shaft of early morning light, which enters as if it were falling through a narrow opening that splits the otherwise closed curtains. The little butterfly seems to have sought out the bright light, having just come into its narrow beam. Chipped here and there at its edges, the ledge is adorned only by Coorte's signatory intertwining initials and a single, surprisingly straight crack.

And yet its simplicity does not make it any easier for us as viewers to take it in. Unlike the experience of theatrical and hyped excitement offered by the likes of De Heem and Van Huysum—so bombastically performing for us—we have to make an effort to actually *see* Coorte's painting: we have to move closer and bend toward it in order to study the neatness of the fruit, the liveliness of the ordinary butterfly. Is it only then that we start to feel ourselves lost in this little painting? Is it only then that we are startled by the sudden thought that there might, in fact, be more in this image than is actually being offered to us? Is it only then that we see that the perpendicular crack in the ledge does not stand alone but is part of a fundamental fissure that cuts invisibly through the image's darkness, sharply defining the butterfly's precise position to its right by a hair's distance from its feelers? Where is the little butterfly going anyway? Is it attempting to escape from the yawning darkness surrounding it, a void filled with total nothingness, by dragging itself to the light?

If we bend toward it and peer closely, what is otherwise quite a sweet picture turns into a rather disconcerting image. The medlars on the ledge's edge slowly begin to lose their familiarity as fruits we might pick up and eat. They do not lie there quietly but threaten to plunge into the depths of the image, as if hanging from invisible threads. Though a vague indication of the stand underneath the table offers some sense of stability, we are not sure how much more darkness surrounds this little place that appears as if it were a corner not of a table but of the world itself, with the universe expanding around it. This is no ordinary kitchen table. Where exactly are we?

Coorte seems to have been genuinely interested in issues of suspension, balance, and approximation. Some early pieces from the late 1680s depict fruits or nuts beneath hovering sprigs of fruit trees dangling from a thread. The suspended branches were eventually displaced by a butterfly, but later even that transformative insect disappeared, and only darkness stretched out behind his delicately painted fruits and shells.[4] Whereas Coorte's life is largely shrouded in mystery, his work enjoyed considerable attention from a steady stream of clients, as we know from the many detailed mentions of his work in inventories; these buyers were almost exclusively from the vicinity of the city of Middelburg in the province of Zeeland. It is likely that he served as an apprentice in the studio of Amsterdam painter of birds Melchior d'Hondecoeter, as Coorte almost exactly copied one of the older painter's landscapes with a pelican and other birds, now in the Ashmolean Museum in Oxford.[5]

Most of the sixty-odd paintings known to have been made by Coorte follow a pattern of composition that must have been commercially lucrative, as he repeated it over and over again: a stone ledge, very similar to what is featured in our image, that shows fruits or other objects laid out on its edge as if they were about to tumble off of it. Grapes, spears of asparagus, peaches, nuts, and even shells are presented to us from the same stone ledge as if they were there for our taking. However, most of these offerings reach far over the edge, as if about to tumble down. For instance, in the still life with gooseberries, a spray of the beautifully translucent fruits hangs over the edge in precarious balance (fig. 18). Whereas the little earthenware test with wild

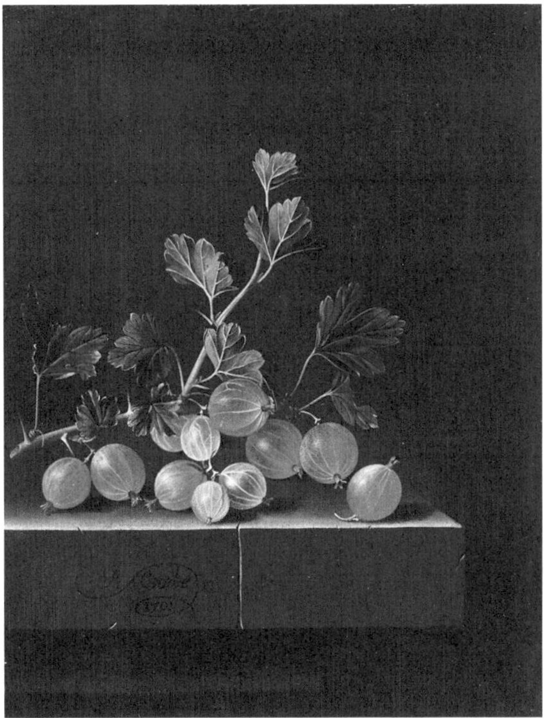

FIGURE 18 Adriaen Coorte, *Gooseberries on a Table*, 1701. Oil on paper mounted on wood; 30 × 23 cm. Cleveland Museum of Art, Leonard C. Hanna, Jr. Fund.

strawberries, a common feature in Coorte's oeuvre, stands firmly on its little legs, there is always something that undermines a sense of overall stability: a sprig dangerously hauling over the edge, or a loose strawberry that has rolled to a full stop just beyond it.

In addition, whereas most modest still lifes such as the breakfast pieces by Pieter Claesz and Willem Heda (said to have been Coorte's model or inspiration) show tabletops running across canvases that are wider than they are tall, the portrait-style format of most of Coorte's pictures allows just a corner of the table to show and thus emphasizes the nothingness surrounding it on two sides. Simon Schama later interpreted the precarious balance in still life compositions as a symptom of the "embarrassment of riches"[6] felt by Dutch Calvinist merchants when contemplating the wealth of their possessions as citizens of a young republic constantly at war. Schama's brilliant reading is very apt for larger still lifes such as breakfast pieces or for the messy compositions in which very expensive *objets d'art* are thrown together with costly exotic fruits, but they do not yield much insight into the tiny pictures by Coorte, which offer us something very specific that remains to be articulated. A comparison with still life's traditional role as allegory might assist us in defining Coorte's work as what it is not.

In his *Groot Schilderboek* (1707), Gerard de Lairesse identifies the genre of still life as particularly useful for the expression of abstract concepts, such as theology or jurisprudence, through an arrangement of carefully selected objects. The art theorist has little patience of still life painters who do not stick with the genre's allegorical function and blatantly dismisses "messy" compositions in which objects are thrown together without a clear motivation or meaning. He accuses Willem Kalf of such carelessness, even though he admits that the "famous Kalf excelled in still lifes as no other."[7] To set a better example, and in a normative tone typical of his writing, he instructs artists how to arrange a variety of objects so as to express concepts such as "war" or "fame," explaining the meaning of each of the objects exhaustively as if it is a course in iconography.

De Lairesse could not have approved more of Maria van Oosterwijck's *Still Life* (1668; fig. 19) that he probably had called a religious scene due to its careful selection of *vanitas* and theological symbols so as to exemplify a pious lifestyle by following Christ. Just as De Lairesse later would recommend artists to use, we see a marble tabletop placed in a dark niche, laden with attributes that each has a singular symbolic meaning. The center of the composition is taken up by an account book that serves to record and make up the balance of all deeds in one's life. The quill nearby used for adding entries is freshly inked, indicating that one's account is written up throughout the course of one's life, and not just at the very end. Lightly touching some cut flowers and an hourglass, the quill is leaning on a book entitled *Overcoming the Self* (*Self-Stryt*), suggesting that the records should be inspired by the exercise of restraint and the awareness of brevity of life. The typical skull is resting with its teeth on the cover of the account book as if intending to leave an imprint of its deadly bite signifying that a life led by the remembrance of death will lead to heaven, the withering flowers and a celestial globe literally back up this message to indicate life's course. Van Oosterwijck permits herself some artistic freedom by assigning the butterfly, a symbol of resurrection, a central role, by placing it right in the middle, but it is not clear what exactly it is doing there. In this scene where nothing is left up for speculation, the butterfly's position is ambiguous: has it landed on the upturned corner of the account book, or rather ascended from it? Its shadow seems to merge with the heavy shade the book's cover casts on the still blank page underneath, as if to suggest that Christian resurrection hovers over all man's deeds, even those still to come.

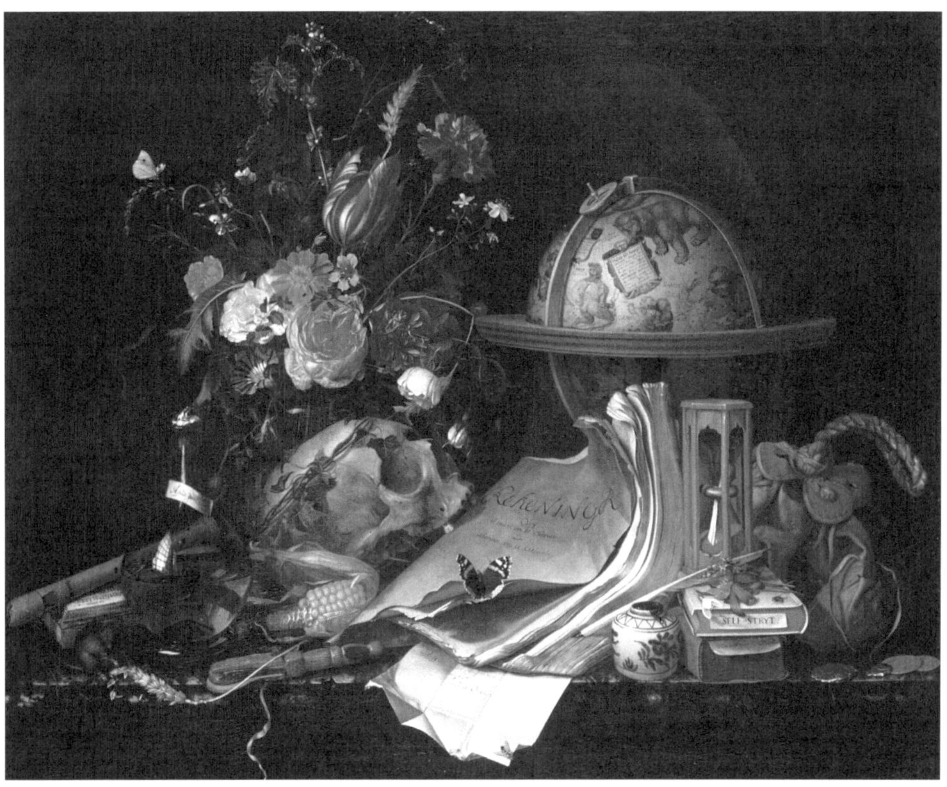

FIGURE 19 Maria van Oosterwijck, *Still Life*, 1668. Oil on canvas; 73 × 88 cm. Vienna, Kunsthistorisches Museum. Photo: KHM-Museumsverband.

Adapting a popular trend employed by still life painters since Clara Peeters started it around 1610, Van Oosterwijck captured her likeness in the flask with *aqua vite* on the left—a reference to the fountain of life from Revelations 21:6, whose water is lifegiving. This expression of the concept of "theology" is also the image of her life. Following Thomas a Kempis's *De Imitatione Christi* on the left, which—significantly—"supports" the book on self-struggle by having been placed underneath it, Van Oosterwijck presents her life as closely mirrored to that of Christ as she gets reflected in the flask. If we look closely, we see how the vague contours of the artist's figure sitting behind her easel with palette in hand are not only projected on the glass but on the filled part so that her image is mirrored in the life-generating water. The act of painting this painting is giving her life, she seems to say. Indeed, this painting *is* her life's work, in the double sense of painting it and living in Christ's image.

As apparent of Van Oosterwijck's intricate compositions, still lifes in general, and *vanitas* images in particular have often been described as capable of visualizing complex ideas (as De Lairesse would have it) by raising ontological questions on life after death, or pondering the differences between (God's) creation versus (the artist's) imitation of the world, as we have seen Van Oosterwijck do. Philosopher Wayne Martin has argued that seventeenth-century Dutch still lifes are phenomenological studies of the experience of things around us. The common motif of a reflection of an artist's self-portrait in the so-called breakfasts by Pieter Claesz and Willem Heda he interprets as instances of Cartesian self-awareness. A panel by Claesz entitled *Vanitas Still Life with Self Portrait* (c. 1628), featuring books and writing implements flanked by a skull on the right and a silver sphere mirroring the artist on the left, is considered by Martin as illustrative of Descartes's mind/body dualism. The locus of the self, contained in the sphere, is separated from the outside world of the senses, Martin explains. The fact that Claesz's painting precedes Descartes's *Discourse on the Method* by a few years is of no importance to Martin. After all, the relation between image and philosophical idea can never be one to one. Even though his argumentation is somewhat muddled, Martin rightly states that "philosophers do not invent their philosophies out of whole cloth . . . rather [they] distill and articulate their philosophical views from the cultural practices in which they are embedded."

Going beyond Martin in this respect, I suggest that still life is capable not just of illustrating philosophical ideas but of *articulating* them. If we look, for instance, at Coorte's butterfly we see that its presence is no longer as clear cut as in Van Oosterwijck's still life. It seems to have successfully uncoupled itself from the burden of Christian symbolism. Even though it is very *like* the other butterfly, and the Christian symbolism of resurrection may still resonate, there is nothing in the picture that support it as such. This does not mean that it is without importance. On the contrary, we could say that its intriguing position marking an invisible line cutting this picture in half creates a "fracture" through which a wholly different significance "underneath" the black paint breaks through.

It is through this invisible line that *Three Medlars with a Butterfly* reveals an astonishing vastness at the heart of its diminutive composition. If anything, perhaps through this invisible cut, the blackness projected behind the little innocent butterfly opens up to an immeasurability. Something is larger than life here, or is at least too large for the tiny picture to contain: a kind of monumentality—for lack of a better term—that is at odds with the composition's smallness and sophistication. The combination of the suspension, the subtle threat of the medlars rolling off the edge, and the utter loneliness of the butterfly pictured against this void, making its course toward the unknown turns this composition in a speculation on infinity, or perhaps rather an approximation of it. We know little about Coorte, who was a bit of an outsider artist. Active in Zeeland near Middelburg but apparently without an established practice, he was once fined one Flemish pound by the Guild of St. Luke for selling paintings without having registered as a master.[8] Though his work must have sold well around Middelburg, as inventories demonstrate, his technique of using oil on paper and the limited size of his paintings make him an unorthodox figure. His outside position actually may have assisted in his attempt to find a new language of forms that is, as I argue, deeply philosophical.

However unpretentious these pictures of medlars might be, their inexplicable vastness evokes Blaise Pascal's meditations on where we, as human beings, find ourselves in the universe. Inspired by perspectival painting among other things, Pascal places us between the dazzling firmament sparkling with distant stars and the ultimate minuteness of a miniature atom, between, in mathematical terms, the infinitely large and the infinitely small. If we imagine, Pascal writes, the imperceptibility of our body as a speck within the universe's infinity, we can equally imagine our body's colossal proportions when compared to the nothingness beyond our reach in, for instance, microscopic elements. "I want to show [man] a new abyss," Pascal writes, and not only does he show us this abyss, he shows us our position in it. Man is at "a middle point between all and nothing . . . equally incapable of seeing the nothingness from which he emerges and the infinity in which he is engulfed."[9] Reformulating this middle point between all and nothing in the fragmentary notes grouped under the title "Vanity" in his *Pensées*, Pascal claims that perspectival painting can somehow designate such a middle point between two infinities, two extremes, or two versions of immeasurability. Linear perspective is a geometrical method that creates a sense of recession and depth on a two-dimensional picture plane by placing the painting's surface at the intersection of converging lines running from the point of view outside the painting and from the vanishing point within the painting. If drawn out, a perspectival configuration looks like two cones meeting at their bases, and this invisible network of perfect proportion underlies all pictorial representation. As it places man on a defined, plotted locus between the point of view and the vanishing point, painting therefore gives us a handle to hold on to, a sort of blueprint that situates us between the infinitely large and the infinitely small, as it directs our gaze from the point of view toward the vanishing point—sometimes termed the infinity point—that continues to recede into a depth that is beyond comprehension.

Obviously, Coorte's paintings are not to be regarded as illustrations of

Pascal's theory, but they possess a kind of abyssal quality as if his paintings want to capture the notion of the infinite, the bottomless, yet in minimalistic and finite ways. If we tune in to this painting by bending over and losing ourselves for a moment into the infinite depth stretching out behind the little butterfly, we may encounter a similar kind of limitless in our own mind that pushes us toward the realm of the unknown. This painting is as much about the beauty of a butterfly or a bunch of medlars as it is about the void that stretches out behind them.

Different from the religious still life of Van Oosterwijck, in which all elements serve as symbols, each neatly linked to a specific, unquestionable meaning, here we find no meaning behind the butterfly or medlars, only darkness. Coorte has managed, through the combination of composition and minute dimensions of the picture plane, to articulate not vastness as such but our idea of it. Neither a symbol nor a concept, Coorte's vastness might be best described in Deleuze and Guattari's terms as an affect, an image of the sense of bottomlessness by which we as viewers can comprehend it. Indeed, by looking at this image, it somehow changes size and shape and becomes so much more than a butterfly and a few pieces of fruit. This little painting is growing on us—there is something we start to understand, even though it lies beyond meaning, beyond any (iconographic) code—indeed, full well beyond our comprehension. Perhaps it is that the infinite, no matter how boundless, can somehow be shaped against the delicate outline of medlars and a butterfly to let it slowly come into visibility. Two hundred and fifty years later, Paul Klee would make a similar attempt at shaping the infinite with finite means, however with a radically different result. Comparing Klee's painting to early modern still lifes in general, and Coorte and Van Huysum's in particular, will further demonstrate how images can be pensive, and how "thinking" in painting may takes place.

The "Underneath" of Painting

Chaos can be structured as non chaos.

EVA HESSE

In 1932, Paul Klee created *Equals Infinity* (plate 10). We see an "S" on its side that is preceded by the mathematical equalizer, surrounded by a confusing assemblage of dots running from pale blue to light orange to purple that have been placed in orderly yet imprecise rows. The pattern applied to a salmon pink background is reminiscent of a geographical map, the blueish parts standing out as continents against a slightly darker sea of dots. Short sticks of the exact same length as those making up the equal sign here and there emphasize the borders between "continent" and "ocean." The composition is painted in oil on canvas that is attached on a rough wooden mount that more resembles a narrow box than a proper frame. On one of the edges of this boxlike construction, along with Klee's signature, and a serial number as if it is a print, is its title, that invites us to read the signs "= ∞" in the center in mathematical terms as "equals infinity."

In a dense essay originally published in 1973 in *Fenêtre jaune cadmium, ou, les dessous de la peinture*, Hubert Damisch wonders to what extent all Klee's marks should be considered figurative, or in contrast be read as signs.[10] If the latter is the case, Damisch raises the question as to what precisely constitutes a reading here. Clearly, Klee is making a statement, a proposition even, when claiming with this painting that something equals infinity. But what elements in the picture are here equal to infinity as such? In addition, we are not sure that the "S" on its side is a proper mathematical sign, as strictly speaking, as it only resembles the mathematical sign ∞, but does not equal it.

Moreover, Damisch explains, the "S" shape could be read figuratively as the sound holes of a violin, and as such refer to the work of Braque and Picasso. Alternatively, it roughly compares to Klee's example, in his volume of pedagogical writings, entitled *The Thinking Eye*, of a dynamic movement that he calls an "active line," which, in its turn, resembles Hogarth's famous line of beauty. Damisch continues (writing in 1973, before the linguistic turn in art history) that the S-shaped sign is not a fixed entity but operates in different registers, or rather, it lets these various registers clash. Considering its placement in between this sea of dots, Damisch assumes that the "S" is Klee's version of the vanishing point.

Damisch's radical reading is, interestingly enough, essentially *figurative* when he finally explains that Klee has turned traditional, perspectival painting inside out by showing its very structure. Whereas in realistic painting such as Van Huysum's flower piece, linear perspective is used to annihilate the flat surface of the canvas or panel so as to make it into a window onto the world, in Klee's work, we see how its configuration—its armature, Damisch writes—has been laid bare and made visible on the picture plane. If we want to fully understand the theoretical claim of *Equals Infinity* (and the breath of Damisch's reading), I suggest we first look at Klee's theoretical writings and at his investment in Alberti's perspective. As we will see, in his oeuvre, and particularly this work, Klee deliberately wants to find a pictorial mode of thinking.

From the beginning of his career as a painter, Klee had been interested in developing a system of pictorial thinking based on what he called "concrete research." In his art as well as his pedagogical writings (the two practices are deeply linked), he intended to establish as series of "visual concepts." Influenced by Hegelian philosophy, he claims that such visual concepts only make sense in relation to their opposition, by nonconcepts. His most prominent example is the concept of "chaos" that, no matter how unweighable and unmeasurable, can be put into perspective, in art, through its nonconcept. The pictorial symbol for this nonconcept is a point. Klee explains that like a zero, this point is neither positive nor negative, and though falling outside any dimensions, it creates a certain order within chaos by generating a sense of direction around itself, such as above or underneath, left or right. Therefore, Klee concludes, drawing a point on a piece of paper is an attempt to put chaos *in perspective.* It brings into being space, dimensions, and ultimately art as such. A point is pure genesis, Klee claims, it is not a product of any kind but it brings into being. He calls it the gray point.

Neither white or black, but somewhere in between, the gray point does not have its own location but is always somewhere in between up or down, left or right. More precisely formulated it is always on the move. It does not quite have its own entity or substance either. Evidently inspired by Hegel's notion of *aufheben*, Klee describes the gray point as "between coming-into-being and passing-away."[11]

For Klee, there is an underlying mobility in visual art through this order brought about by the gray point that "produces" lines and shapes. A tension between a point and another point materializes as a line; a baseline and a point above realizes a triangle, and so on. We could say that his work is partly driven by the question of what underlying tensions let a shape come into being.[12] For instance, his 1922 water color *Separation in the Evening* explores contradictory forces visualized by the arrows who aim toward each other while the color gradations pull them apart. *Le Rouge et le Noir* (1938) demonstrates how the pulling and pushing of the dots is given an additional direction through their color with the result that they seem to be moving or circulating around each other, articulating the space around them.

Even though the still life painting is figurative, it likewise demonstrates tensions between objects that result in the articulation of space. We have found that in Van Huysum, gravity is pulling the water drop off the petal—its clear direction further emphasized by the poignant narrative detail of the putti holding up the cup, and in Coorte we saw how opposite forces built up between the medlars and the table's edge, or between the sucking power of darkness and the fluttering little butterfly apparently defying it. If we juxtapose Coorte's and Van Huysum's pictorial tensions with Klee's, we see more clearly what he is trying to do.

In *The Thinking Eye*, Klee writes that mathematics assists us in learning to see "what flows beneath" the visual. "[W]e learn the prehistory of the visible. We learn to dig deep and to lay bare. To explain, to analyse."[13] His visual work presents this analysis by laying bare these—essentially mathematical—internal structures. That is why, in his work, he is not interested in delivering finished products but in ongoing processes. He wishes to explain the function of the shapes, lines, and colors, their tensions "underneath."[14] If anything, we see this underneath surfacing in *Equals Infinity*. Whereas in both Coorte and Van Huysum's work linear perspective's armature produces a sense of real space, either filled with a niche and a garden, or intensified by blackness, Klee turns perspectival painting inside out and takes the vanishing point, and any other coordination point of the perspectival grid, forward to lay it out on the surface of the canvas. The result is a reversal of perspectival depth that lays bare the underlying perspectival "skeleton" in painting that is still firmly in place in Coorte and Van Huysum.

It seems that with his gray point, Klee is essentially looking for a new kind of vanishing point in painting, one that creates a realm of order on the picture plane that is alternative to what perspective does for figurative painting. Like the gray point, the perspectival vanishing point, while never really "there" (to the extent that it is "vanishing") enables geometry to come into existence so that the illusion of the third dimension can be generated. And like the gray point, the vanishing point creates a realm of mathematical order and clarity on the picture plane. It is the degree zero of realistic representation.

In that light, grasping the infinite in the finite as Klee tried is nothing new to painting, as linear perspective has been utilized as a system of representation which does precisely that. As a finite mode of representation, linear perspective embraces infinity in its configuration laid out by the point of view on the one side of the picture plane, and the vanishing point within. In this system, infinity is inscribed under the guise of a point, a trace in paint on the picture's surface that marks the limit of representation within its system. Despite the fact that it is called the vanishing point, this mark is—as Klee argues—not a proper *point* at all, if we follow Alberti's theory on perspective. Alberti writes at the very beginning of his treatise that "I hear call sign anything that belongs to the surface such that the eye can see it."[15] In the same breath, he insists that "a point is a figure which cannot be divided into parts."[16]

We may now wonder, with Damisch, whether the vanishing point is a sign, or a point, as it cannot be both according to Alberti's definitions. If it is a sign, it should be marked on the painting's surface, and as such be visible and legible. However, if it is a point, it should be "indivisible" and as such indistinguishable from its support, to the extent that it is not visibly present. A point that is vanishing is therefore truly a point. However, if we understand the vanishing point as a *sign* of infinity or its symbol, it should be visible in painting as a tiny dot that differentiates itself from the surface to which it adheres, as well as from the support that it now "marks and grooves," Damisch says.[17] To become visible in painting, the infinity point should therefore "depart" from its support, so to speak, and it is this differentiation that gives a sign its metaphorical character. However, the "departure" from its support makes it divisible rather than indivisible and, as such, it will not qualify as point according to Alberti's definition. Damisch argues that the vanishing point is thus theoretically split, and the practice of perspectival painting precisely conceals this split. In theory, the convergence of the orthogonals we see only in painting, however, the point of convergence cannot possibly be visible *as point* to the extent that it is vanishing, till infinity. We may imagine this split between the vanishing point and its support as a division continuously leveled by the picture's ground, as if the painting's support, in the process of depth's recession, is constantly moving a tiny bit away from us so as to not coincide with the dot of paint that signals it.[18] Perspective is essentially a system to represent the infinite in the finite. This is what the history of figurative painting, ever since the discovery of perspective, has struggled with, Damisch argues. And this is precisely what Klee's painting is about by showing linear perspective as it actually *is*, as a naked truth so to speak, no longer clothes by realistic representation. Klee's dots are signs, marks in paint applied by the tip of a brush, making up a geometrical system, one that does *not* disappear under a realistic representation but instead remains a figure "standing out" from its ground. Operating within the bounds of the figurative, Klee's dots try to remain theoretically split, or rather, they attempt to "think" this split by expressing infinity within a finite mode of representation, just as linear perspective has done. However, whereas in perspectival painting this structure remains hidden underneath the realistic representation, Klee brings it to the fore, laying it out on the very surface of the painting, by giving the points all substance instead of letting them vanish.

In his essay on Klee, Damisch raises the question of what it means for a painter to think. This question is in fact the starting point for what eventually would become his magnum opus, *The Origin of Perspective*, in which he claims that painting is a mode of thinking and that linear perspective is a kind of pictorial grammar through which statements in painting can be made. Evidently, Klee's *Equals Infinity* has been used by Damisch as a modernist filter through which he was able to look at Renaissance painting afresh. He consciously approaches perspective's origin from a vantage point that is "turned inside-out." By looking back at history through the lens of Klee's painting, he is searching for perspective's point of origin—as if it were a kind of vanishing point deeply buried in the past—only to discover that there are multiple points of origin. We could say, therefore, that *Equals Infinity* depicts a more accurate picture of perspective than Piero or Massaccio could ever have done. He concludes that there is no one historical account of perspective, but that there are many, each trying to create its own graspable picture of the chaotic world by determining the interminable.

Before I claim, following Damisch, that Van Huysum's still life is doing precisely that with his dewdrops, I first want to point out how essential Damisch's essay on Klee has become for Deleuze and Guattari's famous dictum that art is a mode of thinking.

The Thought of the Dewdrop

Two drops are not the same, two eggs, two pears,
Nor two countenances either

CONSTANTIJN HUYGENS, 1647

In *What Is Philosophy?*, Gilles Deleuze and Félix Guattari take Damisch's essay on Klee as their major source of inspiration for their radical claim that art is a mode of thought. No matter how blunt and insufficiently worked out some of their assertions are, and how confusing their associative (one might say unedited) writing sometimes is, their redefinition of art remains an important consideration for the discipline of art history and is very helpful for further formulating the nature of the thoughtfulness of still lifes. In addition to art, Deleuze and Guattari present science and philosophy as the two other modes of thought that are complementary to one another, however without any form of hierarchy between them. Though philosophy has been presented sometimes as the only discipline where proper thinking takes place, the writers insist that "no one needs philosophy to reflect on anything," implying that artworks are capable of philosophizing in their own right. As a consequence, they are opposed to the idea that art needs to be interpreted or that it needs a method of analysis to reveal its meaning. They disregard any mode of signification that transcends art's form: the meaning of an artwork need not be found "behind" its representation but is contained *in* its material. It is the notion of thought as substantiated in the artwork's material that I am interested in as an alternative to interpretation. Coorte's expanding vastness, and Van Huysum's pulling gravity are two instances, I suggest, where we see that painting "thinks" the impact of opposing force or the boundlessness of space.

Damisch's lengthy exegesis of Klee's painting is their main source of inspiration, and one sometimes wonders whether this essay has been their single point of reference altogether for their last chapter, "Percept, Affect, and Concept," in which they explain the main strand of their theory on art. They follow Damisch, or for that matter, Klee, to the letter, when they consider art as attempting to "create the finite that restores the infinite."[19] We don't look at painting in order to "recognize" an image and interpret it, the authors explain, but see the lines and points comprising that force themselves upon us, confronting us. We can better understand this by sensing, for instance, how Klee's two dots in *Le Rouge et le Noir* "look" at us, or how his arrows force our eyes to follow their track. Alternatively, we can think of how Cézanne's apples seem to tremble, about to slide off the table, how Coorte's medlars threaten to roll over, or how Van Huysum's dewdrop start to slide. It is this force startling us somehow, arresting us in our paths, that Deleuze and Guattari call sensation.

Their theory on art is based on the premise that painting is a "bloc of sensations," a modality through which sensations can be persevered. These preserved sensations are not expressions of experienced sensations by someone, but rather a kind of monument to such feelings, a magnified and visualized version of it. A spark of joy as captured in the eyes of a sitter in a seventeenth-century portrait continues to shine up till today, independent from its sitter or the intention of the artist. The fact that it *still shines* is what makes it art. Therefore, an artwork should not be seen as a recording of someone's perception or affection; it but encompasses a bloc of desubjectified sensations that they term "percepts" and "affects." A percept is a perception made into a monumental image. An example they give is a landscape by Cézanne that is painted as if no one is there to look at it, or Virginia Woolf's Mrs. Dalloway, who passes through London like "a knife through everything" and while perceiving the city as such, becomes herself imperceptible.[20] It is what a city or landscape looks like without anyone looking at it. Likewise, an affect is a growing, inflating feeling of becoming, as we see Emily Brontë creating in the image of rudimentary kinship between Cathy and Heathcliff, that is way more than the sum of their experiences, continuing to grows to monumental proportions to encompass rocks and moors as well. Peter de Bolla would see such affect in the paintings by Pierre Bonnard whereby the blush starting out on the cheeks of some of his sitters would grow to take over the entire picture.[21] What we see, De Bolla argues, is not a figure blushing, but the "blush of the world."

For Deleuze and Guattari, art is thinking through sensations, and the making of art is an attempt to preserve blocs of sensations for eternity, that is, for the duration provided by the medium in which it is preserved, and which we always take (or hope) to be eternal given the way we care for works of art. Art therefore is an attempt to restore the infinite (or eternity) in the finite, the authors claim. Closely following Damisch's theory on perspective, they distinguish between two poles in art, first, realistic painting like Van Huysum, whereby sensation is realized *in* the material and second, modernist (or abstract) work like Klee, whereby the material as such passes *into* sensation. Following Damisch, they see Klee's "thickness" as a collapse of the imaginary space between foreground and background, ground and surface, or point and support still in place in the work of Coorte or Van Huysum. In abstract art, the material has thus "ascended," they argue, thickening the painting's background into an opaque entity, a process that has resulted from the breakdown of the perspectival system which is the invisible skeleton of composition *par excellence*.[22] Evidently, Klee's work reveals a trace of linear perspective, or rather, of its removal. In modern painting one no longer paints *on* but *under*, Deleuze and Guattari write.[23]

At the other end of the scale, Van Huysum's exquisitely rendered flower painting is clearly an instance of painting on rather than under. Called the "phoenix of flower painting," Van Huysum was the master of what has been called *fini*, or finish, the extremely polished surface on which brushstrokes become truly invisible. Indeed, Van Huysum as an embodiment of an artist who paints *on* rather than *under* is evident in the culmination of his breathtaking "fini" technique in his dewdrops. If we look closely at his dewdrops we see how he manages to create the ultimate blob of transparency through a very precise placement of highlights in lead white. Literally left as a last finishing touch by Van Huysum's brush, his highlights are not themselves transparent but generate in the dewdrop a high level of pictorial transparency. His breathtaking technique is even more apparent at moments when the thickness of the rim of white paint (indicating reflecting light) casts an *actual shadow*, as we see here on the rose petal of the flower piece (fig. 20).[24]

As a motif, dewdrops have followed their own micro course in the grand narrative of the history art while remaining at all times at the very surface of painting. Among the most prominent instances are *The Water Seller of Seville* (c. 1617–1623; fig. 21) by Diego Velázquez. On the belly of the huge jug in the very center of the painting, already bulging out of the frame so it seems, we see big beads of moisture so fresh and cool that viewers might feel inclined to lick them off the surface. In *Still Life with Fruit and Oysters* (1660–1679), Abraham Mignon renders drops of liquid as falling from a plate of oysters as if caught in their descent (fig. 22). The blobs are so glittery that we almost smell their saltiness. Samuel Pepys was similarly taken in when in 1669 he was

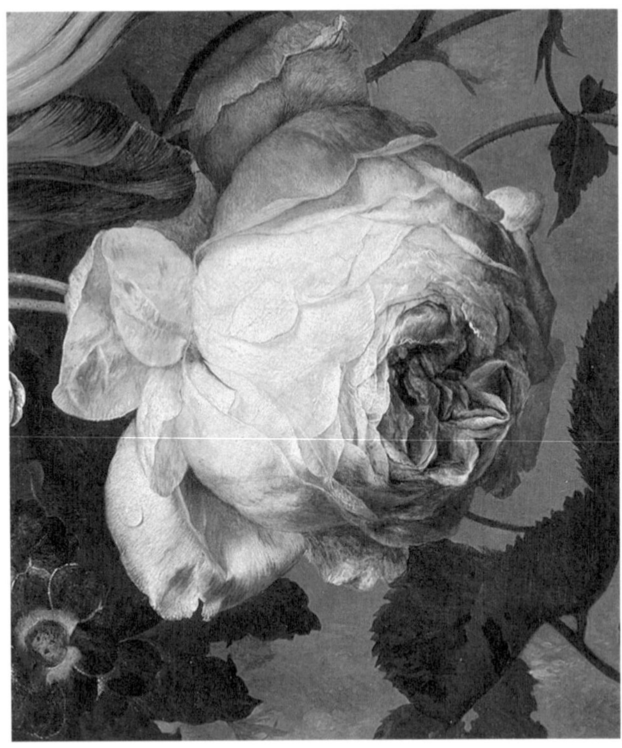

FIGURE 20 Jan van Huysum, *Flowers in a Terracotta Vase*, c. 1730. Oil on panel; 80 × 61 cm. Detail: rose petal. Boston, Museum of Fine Arts, promised gift of Rose-Marie and Eijk van Otterloo, in support of the Center for Netherlandish Art, L-R 13.2019. Photo © 2021 Museum of Fine Arts, Boston.

standing in front of a flower piece by Simon Verelst (1644–1721), barely able to suppress the inclination to wipe a drop of dew of one of the flower's petals.[25] In art-theoretical writing dewdrops continue to be the focus of attention, as we saw with the poem quoted by Johan van Gool in his biography of Van Huysum, or mentioned as a hallmark of realism in Goeree's *Inleyding* (1668). Leonardo was intrigued by its perfect curvature and how it was able to hold its own, even after one would insert a grain of millet in it.[26] Already in antiquity were dewdrops in painting observed, as we have seen in Philostratus's *Imagines*. In particular in his famous description of a painting of Narcissus bending over a pool that "painted" his face, the Greek Sophist writes in awe that "it even shows drops of dew dripping from the flowers." He continues to praise the picture's realism by describing how in addition to dewdrops "a bee settl[ed] on the flowers,"[27] leaving it undecided whether it is a painted bee, or a real one

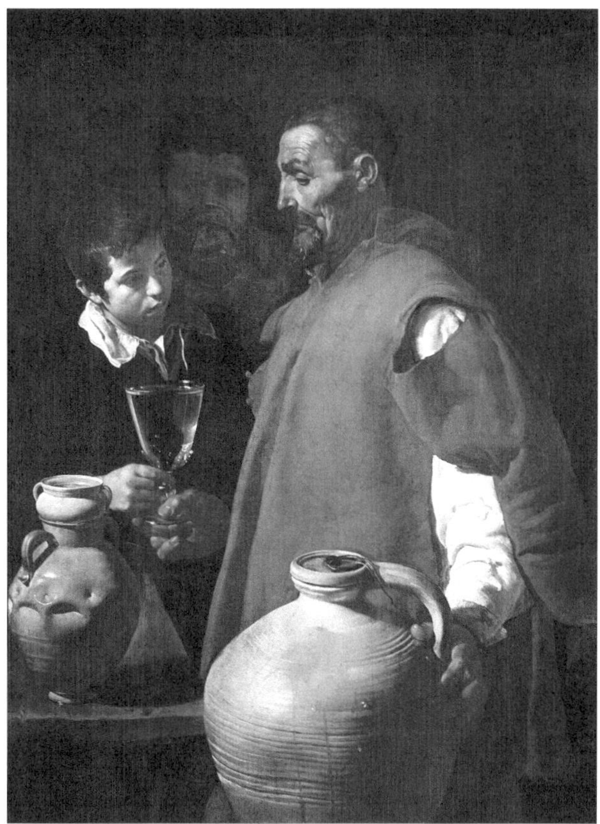

FIGURE 21 Diego Velázquez, *The Water Seller of Seville*, c. 1617–1623. Oil on canvas; 105 × 80 cm. London, Apsley House.

that has ascended on the picture's surface. This painting of Narcissus about the origin of painting apparently has it all: reflection, mirror image, realism, dewdrops, and even includes the trope of a trompe l'oeil insect that would become a Renaissance favorite in the motif of a fly.[28]

As if obsessed with his own his prized technique, Van Huysum scattered many—way too many—dewdrops over his composition, and he may have wittingly been "quoting" Philostratus. For in addition to his dewdrops, he places right next to it, on the tulip's petal, a bee, instead of the more traditional fly. He must have been acutely aware of the classical reference, and as a result the theoretical significance of the insect, whose presence entails an entire, centuries-old discourse on pictorial realism. As such, different degrees of separation from reality are now included within the contour of a petal,

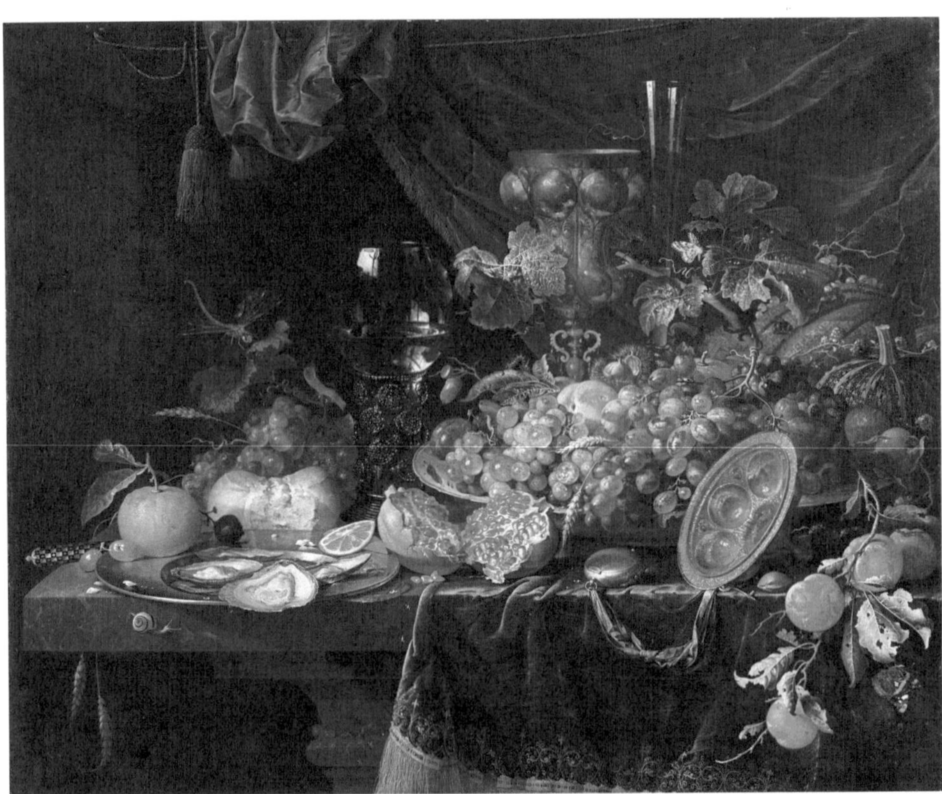

FIGURE 22 Abraham Mignon, *Still Life with Fruit and Oysters*, 1660–1679. Oil on canvas; 60.5 × 75 cm. Amsterdam, Rijksmuseum.

from "traditional" realism of the bouquet embedded in perspectival depth, to the dewdrop as laying on the petal, balancing between realism and illusionism, to the bee as breaking through the painting's realism by purporting to have been landed on its varnished surface. By juxtaposing the bee to the dewdrops, Van Huysum has created his own version of the often debated yet subtle difference between realism and illusionism, most prominently played out Pliny's account of the rivalry between Zeuxis and Parhassios. The still life painter may have attempted to appropriate the debate by adapting it to the genre's conventions: his dewdrops are to Zeuxis grapes, what his bee is to Parhassios' curtain. If Klee's blobs were an instance of "thickness" comprising of paint that was "ascending" from its support that turned out to be theoretically dense, the same theoretical density can be claimed for Van Huysum, and I think Damisch could not have agreed more.

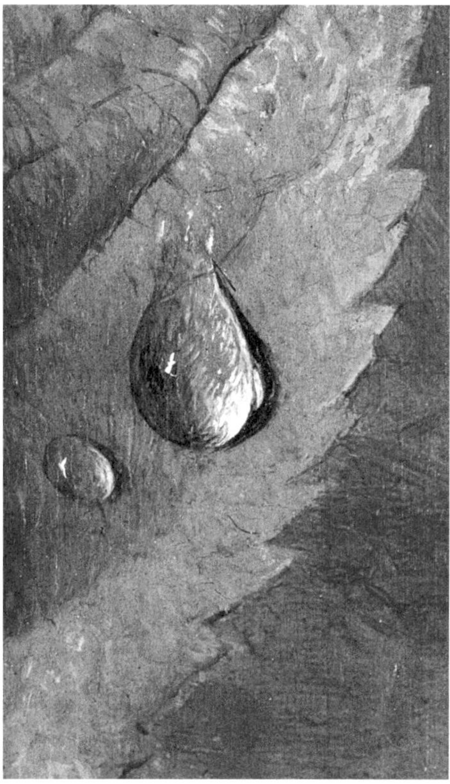

FIGURE 23 Jan van Huysum, *Basket of Flowers*, c. 1733. Oil on panel; 16 × 24 cm. Detail: leaf. Rotterdam, Museum Boijmans-Van Beuningen.

Van Huysum's exploration into various degrees of pictorial representation is taken even further by an additional "argument" in paint.[29] If we look again at a bead of moisture on a green leaf in *Basket of Flowers* (c. 1733; fig. 23) we see that the highlight showing reflecting light is paired with a weaker patch of white within the blob, marking its refraction. As a point, this tiny point of refraction is as ambiguous as a vanishing point, and as ambitious as Klee's color dots. Initially appearing as the ultimate pictorial touch of Van Huysum's brush, the water drop, in its invisible materiality, opens further outward, not so much marking the limit of transparency as, by widening its boundaries, *tending toward* it.

In rendering these tiny blobs of translucent liquid, Van Huysum could not have left a more superficial trace, and in many ways we could not be much farther from Deleuze and Guattari's exemplary abstract painting. Yet paradoxically, under a highlight indicating the drop's reflection, we suddenly "see" the thin layers of superimposed paint, often applied wet on a wet surface. How many invisible layers of paint are pushing this blob to the extreme? The same philosophical sophistication we find in Klee's *Equals Infinity* is apparent in Van Huysum's flower painting. In spite of their small size, these dewdrops blow up the notion of transparency to gigantic dimensions, raising the issue of the readability of pictorial transparency.[30] Placed midway between the petal and the bee, the dewdrop, like Klee's blob, is a reflection on the concept of a point, and it is equally a reflection on the extent to which, in paint, something can be vanishing, the appearance of a dewdrop, in this case. As we have seen, the transparency of the dewdrop *as concept* only becomes visible through its opposite: the opaque, ultimate highlight of impenetrable white; a little blob of white that gives the transparency direction and shape. I suggest that Van Huysum's dewdrops as the hallmarks of his virtuosity offer an attempt at thinking through the opposition of opacity to transparency, and the importance of the collapse of the latter in favor of the former. The dewdrop as such articulates some kind of a split on the level of the surface; it is at once visible—yet only by means of its highlight—and invisible in its extreme transparency. Where does the transparency of the painting under the highlight stop, and where does the panel begin?

Damisch has asserted that the "underneath" of painting has only been revealed in modernity, that has retained this "thickness" even though it continues to strive for surface effects.[31] In modern art, the split between the vanishing point and its mark becomes visible in paint, or rather "figured" as paint, while in early modern art it remains purely theoretical and invisible. Yet, and this is my main argument, early modern painting is as concerned with the "thinness" and transparency of painting as modernism is with the substance of paint. Through using different modes of application, Van Huysum and Klee are in agreement, in that their work attempt to think through issues of infinity, transparency and opaqueness. Van Huysum's still life with its undercoatings, glazes, and varnishes aims at surface effects, just as Klee's "seedbed" (his own term) does. Indeed, Van Huysum's dot seem to depart neither from the translucent ground of the water drop's surface nor from the background of the green leaf, but from the entire painting as such.

He continues to work on the surface of his painting, creating yet another statement in paint. If we look closely at a detail of the one of the tulip's petals in one of the previous flower arrangements (plate 11), we see that the extreme smoothness of the painting's surface is interrupted. The petal's fine veins have been marked by extremely thin incisions that give it a natural relief, as if an actual petal has left an imprint on the wet paint. The incisions, barely visible in reproduction, must have been slit by Van Huysum with a single brush-hair, slicing the wet paint so that the layers underneath would come to the surface through its grooves.[32]

Here, in the treatment of the petal—considered in light of the ultimate moment of transparency in the dewdrop that tends toward the mimetic limit—Van Huysum seems to have found another variation of such a limit, having pushed it away from transparency and toward the actual layer of paint as such. The purely optical invisibility of the dewdrop becoming visible only in its reflection has been complemented, to a certain extent, with the illusion of a petal's imprint in paint, which introduces a sense of touch in this otherwise diaphanous tableau. If there is a truth in painting, we may propose, on the basis of Van Huysum's flower still life, that if it cannot be told (as Cézanne famously suggested), it may be "thought" in paint. Was Klee trying to create an abstract painting while remaining within the realm of the figurative, as Damisch claims? Van Huysum makes essentially a modernist gesture—albeit very subtle—by letting the underside of painting come through without losing any of the extreme realism that he achieved. Ultimately, Klee and Van Huysum have made comparable statements in their work. They both raise the question as to what exactly is the status of a mark in paint on a surface. Even though Klee's visual statements can be backed up by his extensive pedagogical writings, Van Huysum is no less theoretical in his careful exploration of what precisely constitutes a mark left on surface in a painting. With both artists, it is the *work* as such that has the deepest theoretical dimension, and as such both cases serve as clear instances that painting is a form of thinking.

If "the eye thinks, even more than it listens,"[33] as Deleuze and Guattari write, paraphrasing Paul Claudel and Klee in one breath, we may wish to contemplate the possibility of painting as mute philosophy rather than mute poetry—to become aware that, according to Van Huysum's flower still life, there are plenty of issues still waiting to be visually thought or philosophically seen.

CHAPTER FIVE

Painting as a Space for Thought

Repetition changes nothing in the object repeated, but does change something in the mind which contemplates it.

DAVID HUME

Less than ever does the mere reflection of reality reveal anything about reality.

BERTOLT BRECHT

Not Yet Thought

When Hegel traveled to the Netherlands in 1822, he found it a wonderful country. The cities of Holland were among the finest he had seen, he wrote enthusiastically to his wife: exquisite, well cared for, and above all clean, as no rotting doors or broken windows could be found. "In The Hague and generally here, all the streets are filled with the finest shops, in the evening all the streets are lit up by their illuminations; endless assortments—gold, silver, porcelain, tobacco, bread, shoes—everything perfectly arranged in booths."[1] In the streets of The Hague Hegel found some of the neatly arranged, glimmering objects that he had observed in seventeenth-century Dutch paintings. What such paintings—whether tidy domestic interiors, busy street scenes, or still lifes—demonstrate for Hegel is not the subject matter of everyday life but the way they appear, the way they *shine*. In his writings on aesthetics, Hegel insists that the function of painting is not to imitate everyday life but to manifest the Spirit through external forms so as to elicit reflection. The transformation of a three-dimensional landscape into a two-dimensional picture enables us to reflect on it in ways we never would an actual landscape. Moreover, the colors and shapes that make up a painting are never meant to replace actual objects but to translate them into paint, which relieves them of their materiality: becoming mere appearances, they invite our contemplation. To denote such two-dimensional appearances,

Hegel uses the term *Scheinen*, which in German means both to appear and to shine and which has been translated as "pure appearance." In *Schein* (appearance and shine), the philosopher explains, the inwardness of the Spirit can fully express itself "in the reflection [*Widerschein*] of externality."[2] In his *Lectures on Fine Art*, Hegel is preoccupied with painting's capacity to "shine." He implies that painting, more than any other medium, can show this inwardness or essence of things—through their *appearance* rather than their being. His most prominent example in this regard is the corpus of seventeenth-century Dutch painting, in particular its representations of objects of daily life that, while uninteresting in themselves, let their subject matter be "outshone" by shine, as such. Especially in the chapter on romantic painting, he is fascinated by the luster of metal, the shimmer of a bunch of grapes in the candlelight, or a vanishing glimpse of sunlight through a window. "With what skill have the Dutch painted the lustre of satin gowns with all the manifold reflections and degrees of shadow in the folds, etc., and the sheen of silver, gold, copper, glass vessels, velvet, etc.," he writes with rising amazement. His close observations partly lead him to determine that painting's function is not to mirror the world but to "grasp this most transitory and fugitive material, and to give it permanence for our contemplation in the fullness of its life."[3] Even though paintings are packed with commodities and often present a feast for the eyes, Hegel insists that painting is not for consumption as it goes beyond sensuous apprehension and remains free to exist on its own account.[4] The Dutch had fixed the most transitory nature of reflections not as a means of recording or describing the world (as Svetlana Alpers would have it) but as a way of offering images for us to contemplate. Hegel sees the manifold reflections in Dutch paintings as a kind of "echo" of some kind of inner essence that *shines through*. Through the shine of things they make their "pure appearance," uncoupled from their materiality.

If we look, for instance, at a painting by Willem Kalf, we see how the artist has pushed his technique to produce this intense kind of "shine" to an extreme. *Still Life with an Oriental Rug* (c. 1660–1665; fig. 24) is a decadently messy arrangement of luxury items from the four corners of the world. We see an obviously expensive, heavy golden goblet surrounded by a delicate Wan-li porcelain bowl from China filled with exotic fruit from North Africa, a watch, a rug from the Middle East, and a heavy silver dish. A tall Venetian glass and a rummer glass, both half filled with wine, are placed behind this heap of costly objects. Compositions like this one are widespread among seventeenth-century still lifes; however, the deep black background that yawns behind his objects is characteristic of Kalf. Rather than giving us the empty wall that we usually see in such scenes, he chose this seemingly infinite

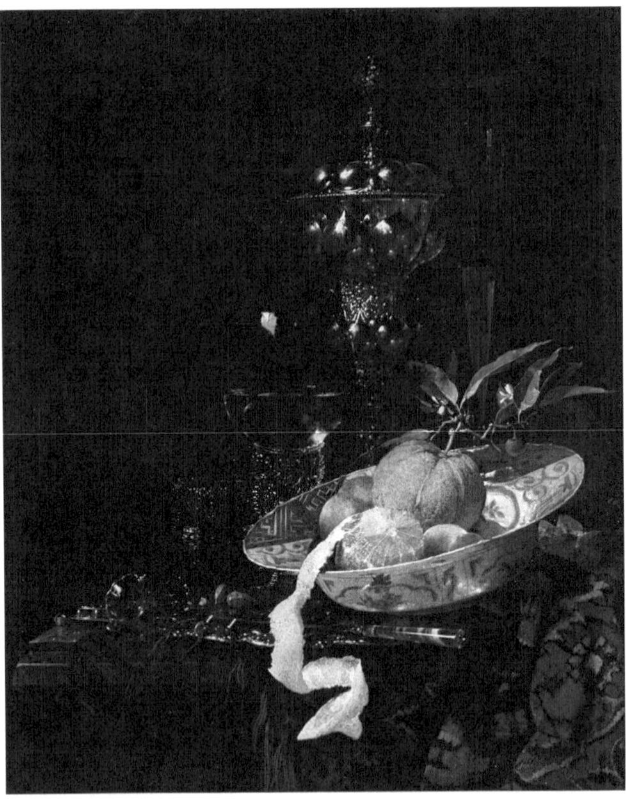

FIGURE 24 Willem Kalf, *Still Life with an Oriental Rug*, c. 1660–1665. Oil on canvas; 65 × 54 cm. Oxford, Ashmolean Museum, bequeathed by Daisy Linda Ward, inv. A563. Photo © Ashmolean Museum, University of Oxford.

darkness to maximize the effects of reflection. The objects in his paintings sparkle and glimmer like jewelry in a box, providing an absolute feast for the eyes, celebrating the virtuosity that lies in the creation of the *image* of the objects rather than the objects themselves. Indeed, Goethe, writing about one of Kalf's paintings, famously remarked that if he had to choose between the (highly valuable) objects or the painting, he would definitely select the painting.[5] But Kalf goes even further. Looking closely at the tall, barely visible Venetian glass, we see that it lacks an outline. Refraining from drawing the glass's contours, Kalf decided instead to suggest its appearance by painting *only* the reflection of light on its rims. Assuming that the whole glass is *there*, right in front of us, at first we fail to notice that we are actually seeing the specter of the glass emerging from darkness by its sparkle alone. Hegel would have approved of Kalf's technique, which enabled him to sacrifice materiality for pure appearance in paint, successfully transforming glass into *Schein*, in the double sense of seeming and shining.

Hegel must have had a similar work (and perhaps Goethe's declaration) in mind when he observed that realistic representation is capable of pressing on "to the extreme of pure appearance, i.e. to the point where the content does not matter and where the chief interest is in the artistic creation of that appearance."[6] Like no other medium, painting can fix the light that is bouncing off surfaces already bearing impressions of fleetingness—"the appearances and reflections of clouds, waves, lochs, streams; the shimmering and glittering of wine in a glass"—and thereby capture a particular liveliness. "Here painting leaves the ideal for the reality of life," he writes.[7] In the glittering in Kalf's glass, we see painting as lifting itself out of its materiality, of the glass as much as its paint, out of any essence, *only* to reflect that essence.

Through this pure appearance of a painted object (rather than an object itself), Hegel sees something greater "shining through," in this case, the inner spirit of the Dutch republic, the freedom it had achieved on its own terms. For the Protestant philosopher, Dutch painting was the example *par excellence* of a perfect match between the subjectivity of the increasing self-consciousness of the Dutch burgher ruling his own country and the spirit of freedom permeating the young republic, which had successfully thrown off the despotism of both the Spanish crown and the Catholic Church. The function of painting, or rather, of shine, is to evoke contemplation in the viewer so that the spirit can realize itself *through* him or her by way of the viewer's awareness of it. Painting, he writes, "opens the way for the first time to the principle of finite and inherently infinite subjectivity, the principle of our own life and existence, and *in painting we see what is effective and active in ourselves*."[8] Hegel's most daring passages in his *Lectures* occur when he argues for painting's major role as a site for contemplation, or rather, as a ground that "pictures" the subject's consciousness. The glittering of wine in the tall Venetian glass in Kalf's painting "sees" the consciousness of a contemplating viewer as much as the viewer sees the typically Dutch form of individualized republican freedom reflected in it. It is crucial for us to realize that this reflection of the subject does not occur "in" painting or result from it, but rather, that it happens on the level of pictorial reflection, or shine, the bouncing of light off glass. In that sense, shine is always on the move, somewhere in the middle between glass and its surrounding darkness, or between resonating the spirit and reflecting the activities of the mind.

Hegel must have had this ricochet structure of physical reflection in mind when he wrote, in the introduction to *Lectures on Fine Art*, that art stands in the middle between immediate sensuousness and ideal thought. He refers to a work by Gerard ter Borch (1617–1681) to demonstrate how the Spirit gets sensualized in art, not so much via colored shapes but through the play of different patches of colors, resulting in the effect of an overlay of shine on the entire image. Based in the city of Deventer in the Netherlands, Ter Borch became known for his exquisite small genre pictures featuring elegantly dressed ladies engaged in conversation or reading letters. He placed these female figures prominently in the foreground of his compositions so that the satin of their gowns nearly coincides with the surface of the painting. Typical for Ter Borch is the careful attention he pays to texture, which makes the satin of the dresses the very subject matter of his painting. Studying the satin closely, Hegel noticed how each spot of color is a different shade of gray, blue, white, or yellow; but seen from a distance, the effect produced is that of a soft sheen akin to actual satin. Unlike the highlights that we see, for instance, in Vermeer's interiors or Van Huysum's water drops, which maintain their materiality as little blobs of white paint shaped by the point of a brush, the sheen in Ter Borch's paintings results from the interplay of colors. Like music, Hegel writes, it produces this painterly effect from such an interconnection of hues: "[I]t is the juxtaposition *alone*," he insists, "which makes this glistening and gleaming."[9] As an effect rather than a quality of painting, sheen is completely dematerialized in Hegel's account. What emerges is an interweaving of various colors whose shine somehow starts to loom over the painting's surface. This begins to serve as a metaphor for his definition of thinking. It was probably when he was standing in front of one of Ter Borch's genre scenes that the philosopher recognized a similarity between philosophical and pictorial reflection. Just like the shine of Ter Borch's satin supersedes the painted surface, floating halfway between materiality and spirit, so too does an artwork occupy a middle position between sensible and ideal thought. An artwork, he writes, is "*not yet* pure thought, but, despite its sensuousness, is *no longer* a purely material existent either."[10] In the work of Ter Borch and Kalf, Hegel insists, we do not see consciousness "behind" the depicted objects as if it were the revelation of hidden meaning. Rather, consciousness "shines through," taking off from the very surface of the painting that it produced. This "taking off" is what Hegel defines as liveliness: the animated play of color that is like "objective music, a peal in colour" where the spirit manifests itself in thinking. "[T]he spirit reproduces itself in thinking, in comprehending the world," Hegel states.[11] We could say that in the work of Kalf and Ter Borch, we see painting on its way *to become* thought. This shiny route toward thought was to be continued, despite Hegel's proclaimed end of painting, and whether or not Hegel would have liked it, in what may seem an unlikely place: photorealist painting. In this chapter, I will look at the photorealist work of Richard Estes through a Hegelian framework to argue for the rise of a self-conscious form of painting that recognizes itself in another medium—photography—thereby "thinking" this transformation. Before examining Estes's work in detail, I will first say a few words about photorealism as emerging movement in the 1970s to demonstrate that photorealism is a lot more theoretically sophisticated than is generally assumed.

Photorealism as Pictorial Reflection

In 1975, Richard Estes painted *Central Savings* (plate 12). We see the front of a spick-and-span diner on a typical Manhattan street corner. It's bright midmorning—a quarter past ten, according to the clock in the center—yet the diner is completely empty. At first sight, this picture appears to demand little from us as viewers: no symbols to decipher, no clues about what exactly is being depicted here. Why have we paused here, in the middle of the sidewalk, whereas other passersby move on, their silhouettes briskly walking out of the frame? What *they* remain unaware of *we* can see: overlaid upon the shiny red counter and its empty stools is the dazzling spectacle of a reflected cityscape extending behind us. What strictly speaking should have remained outside our view is now contained within the diner. The dizzying doubling of reflections simultaneously bouncing off multiple shiny surfaces makes it difficult to determine what is inside and what is outside. Where, for instance, does the orange and red banner actually belong? And what about the silver strips running along the ceiling to the right? Something has entered this space that refuses to position itself, that refuses to take sides (in or out?) but seems suspended in the middle, stretched out, as it were, over both areas. For a moment we forget that while looking through the large glass window, we are also looking *at* it. The bright red letters spelling "BURGER" in reverse, projected at the window, are also projected *into* the space from outside. When we bend in to study them closely we note that they must be part of the diner's front that falls outside this painting's cropping. The backwards word has been projected into the space via its being doubly mirrored in the bank's windows opposite the diner, such that this reflection brings it back to the diner and into this picture. The term "reflection" comes from the Latin *re-flectere*, which literally means "to bend" and "to bring back." The reflections, brightly articulated and translucent, are nonetheless somewhat impenetrable despite the transparency of the window. The result is a jumble of mirror images bouncing off one another. Are we being invited to reflect on reflection?[12]

It seems as if we are not quite looking at a street corner in New York but staring into an abyss of transparent, superimposed images whose outlines dissolve in their mutual play. This kind of layered reflection is typical of Estes's urban landscapes in general, and his oeuvre as a whole. From his early-1970s shopfronts and wide-angled metropolitan vistas with deep perspectives plunging down the streets to his more recent iceberg and lake pictures, his oeuvre's declared subject matter is *shine*. We may even say that his paintings do not just show shine in all its aspects but also formulate a kind of theory about it. Clearly, in Estes's paintings, shine is presented as a property of light rather than of the smooth surface it touches. Following this line of thought, most of his work seems to make the argument—in pictorial terms—that in contrast to Hegel's argument about Dutch art, multilayered reflection is first and foremost the determining quality of photography. It has often been mentioned that Eugène Atget's early twentieth-century documentary photographs of Parisian shopfronts served as a starting point and inspiration for Estes's work.[13] However, Estes is not as interested in Atget's photographs as works that signal the fraudulence of capitalist consumer society and its urban alienation (as Walter Benjamin would have read them) as he is in the astonishing awareness that this type of layered reflection, so visible in photographs by Atget, had *never* been recorded in painting.

This observation has become the driving force behind his oeuvre. In 1968–1970, having completed his first photorealist painting, *Bus with Reflection of the Flatiron Building*, a young and daring Estes stated that "a thought . . . about reflection is that you're looking at what isn't there—the tactile and the visual reality do not coincide—they overlap. Since all objects reflect—glass and chrome only more so—perhaps you show the ways things look the less you show how they are or how we think they are."[14] This phenomenologically tinted statement made at the very start of his career has been significantly deepened and made sophisticated by the style that has become his hallmark. Not only has he aimed to explore the infinite potential of reflective surfaces to investigate the conditions of our perception of the world vis-à-vis those of photography, he has done so by recording their recording, by meticulously painting after a photographic model. The result is that his paintings reveal what previously only a camera had captured and our eyes never pause to see: the constant flux and flickering of reflected sunlight on (semi-)transparent surfaces while our bodies and eyes make their daily movements through the world.

Unlike what transpires in Dutch art, this shine in Estes acquires a "thickness" in the double sense of the term "reflection," as both surface quality and contemplative depth. I am interested in the extent to which Estes's reflections make his work not only photographic but also—following Hegel in this regard—philosophical. Following up on the potential theoretical significance of highlights in the previous chapter, I will examine the philosophical sophistication of Estes's thickness by bending back—one could say *re-flecting*—his visual form to its philosophical conceptualization. Before Hegel started to write on shine, the concept of reflection had a long history in philosophical discourse and has been celebrated as the "unifying principle of all philosophy," as the separation of the self from the immediacy of the world of objects gives the subject the space—and the freedom—to think. Since Descartes's *First Philosophy* reflection has become a principle *par excellence* of the act of thinking, as such, and has informed all philosophy of mind ever since.[15] Significantly, reflection as a philosophical concept necessitates that any action of reproduction be thrown back upon itself for further scrutiny. And this might well be what Estes visualizes so well: a throwing back of a mirror image onto a transparent surface, opening it up to be further investigated by whomever would like to pick up that challenge. What Estes's work reveals, however, is that the object of philosophical scrutiny does not present itself as a well-articulated entity. On the contrary, the very space of scrutiny between us as viewers and what we are offered is obscured and blurred, and two of the most persistent metaphors of painting—as mirror and as window—are superimposed. How can we think through these contradictions, even at the moment that both window and mirror start to crack?

The excessive use of reflection in Estes's *Central Savings* is an indication that this painting may "appear" in a Hegelian way, wittingly or unwittingly, as a reflection of a deeper consciousness. I am interested in the extent to which we see the reflection of consciousness at play in Estes's painting, which, very much like seventeenth-century Dutch painting, deals with the banality of daily life. In *Central Savings* this quotidian surface has superimposed upon it an excess of multiple reflections, fixed by Estes in the form of a deep glow. However, Estes's painting is fundamentally different from the works of seventeenth-century Dutch painting in one major aspect: it aspires to appear to be something else. Standing in front of *Central Savings*, we see a photograph, even as we know we are looking at a painting. Our disorientation reveals how Estes's picture has effortlessly overruled our authority as subject by managing to deceive our senses. What exactly does this image think it *is*?

Playing with the limitations of its medium, Estes's painting fits perfectly into a long art-historical tradition, represented most famously by such works as Diego Velázquez's *Las Meninas* (1656) and Jan van Eyck's *Arnolfini Portrait* (1434), of self-reflexive images that often pose conundrums for their viewer through ambiguous reflections. In both the Velázquez and the Van Eyck paintings, a mirror hanging on the back wall reflects figures occupying the space stretching out in front of the painting, where *we* are expected to stand. These paintings present an unsolvable paradox to us as viewers, who will forever be puzzled by the fact that the mirror cannot possibly reflect us, and our viewpoint is therefore denied by the very configuration that enables us to see the painting *from* that position. Victor Stoichita has called these paintings "self-aware," meta-images that offer witty commentaries on the nature and status of their own representation. Through their playfulness, they nonetheless seriously explore the possibilities and limitations of visual representation. While the overall argument of my book is inspired by Stoichita, I will attempt to go beyond him by using Hegel's notion of self-consciousness to argue that in the context of the rich history of self-reflexive imagery, Estes's work pushes this kind of self-awareness to an extreme. *Central Savings* goes way beyond its ostensible limitations when it radically presents itself as something it is not, namely a photograph, making obvious reference to the "killing" of painting by the invention of photography (as Paul Delaroche was said to have famously observed when seeing a daguerreotype for the first time). Photography is painting's negation, its other. Rather than being self-aware or self-reflexive, Estes's painting is self-conscious in a Hegelian way, as it tries to "think" itself as not-a-painting, to think how painting would *appear* (or rather shine) as photography.

If we consider the grand narrative of realistic representation, we see that photography, entering history in the late 1830s, was considered from the get go as painting's replacement, because it would patently put an end to the justification, aim, and function that painting had been understood to possess for centuries. Photography cast painting into a crisis from which it only slowly recovered through a long period of self-analysis called modernism. I am less interested in what painting may have lost in its transformation in the wake of photography (such as the aura of authenticity, as Benjamin would have it) than what it has gained in terms of consciousness. In particular, I am interested in understanding how Estes's *Central Savings* can assist us to better grasp Hegel's definition of thinking as a movement of a return to the self from otherness, which is a "merging" of thinking self and self-as-object that we also see in Estes's blending of painting and photography, a visual articulation of this movement as a return of painting from photography.

The premise of my argument about photorealism's philosophical potential is based in its young history. Proclaimed as a new evaluation of photography in the early 1970s—at Harald Szeemann's Documenta 5, among other venues—and rebuked as a failed artistic project only a few years later, the photorealism of Estes and his fellow painters Robert Bechtle, Ralph Goings, Audrey Flack, and Chuck Close made something visible that subsequently needed to be repressed. Its marginalization by art historians and critics (now yielding) who could barely hide their contempt, in combination with its commercial success and its ever-growing dynasty of new generations of photorealists deliberately imitating their predecessors, gives its emergence a certain urgency. Indeed, we should not forget that photorealism was where painting for the first time genuinely engaged with photography, not just as aid or inspiration for artists, as with Cézanne and Eakins, among others, but as a zone for negotiating a newfound realism in photography so all-encompassing that we have forgotten how much it has conditioned our vision. Compared to realistic painting, a photograph is to a certain extent frameless and intervenes freely with our imagination, memory, and perception like no other image. The question arises whether photography has been a rupture in the history of realistic representation or whether it effected a smooth transition of realism's project from painting to photography. Is photorealism a continuation of that process from painting to photography, extending it to achieve a kind of synthesis of both? In any case, from the moment of its appearance, photorealism filled a vacuum: it became one of the few sites where photography was adequately reflected on or *theorized*. At the beginning of the 1970s, debates on photography's theoretical potential were thin. Allan Sekula and Susan Sontag had yet to publish their revolutionary writings on the subject, and while occasionally there were some significant preliminary steps toward an analysis of photography, only sporadically would one encounter deep reflection on the subject. Considered as a response to abstract expressionism and minimalism, and showing themselves to be as serious about painting as pop art is ironic, photorealist paintings are surprisingly capable of philosophizing about the complicated nature of their own representation—and of the problematics of the photographic recording of the world as such.

This chapter will make the initial neglect of both photographic theory and photorealism at the beginning of the 1970s productive. I argue that it is through this marginalization that photorealism can be seen as a literal mode of reflection on photography at a time when no one really was giving it a proper thought. Estes's paintings will be presented as a theory on the way photography has added a dimension to the visible world that won't easily give itself up to scrutiny. Ultimately, photorealism as pictorial practice manages to offer us a point of view for reflection, and its attempt to *become* photography has made it a perfect argument against the prototypical model of photography that insists on being taken for granted. Photorealism of the 1970s demonstrates what the later explosion of photographic theory thirty years later would confirm: without reflection on photography, we won't notice how photography has in fact replaced our experience of the world, and moreover, how it has conditioned our modes of seeing to such an extent that any true reflection on its impact is very hard to carry out. I argue that in light of recent theories of photography by Vilém Flusser and others, photorealism can prove itself to be particularly useful as a form of non-photography that nonetheless identifies with photography's vision, and from which a proper critique on photography is possible.

In that context, photorealism's investment in reflection gains new relevance in light of the work of François Laruelle, in particular the affinity he sees between traditional philosophy, whereby the philosopher places him- or herself at a distance from the world in order to comment on it, and photography, which mimics this presumed objectivity through its camera position. But before I will present photorealism as fitting within this tradition as a philosophy expressed in visual terms—or as a so-called theoretical practice, as Laruelle would have it—I will first explain its emergence, initially alongside the work of Gerhard Richter, within the (short-lived) debate on hyperrealism. One of the questions I will answer is why Richter, with his blending of painting and photography, received critical acclaim as a "deep" thinker-painter (similarly, Jeff Wall's work has been considered theoretical), while Estes and his cohort were initially disregarded as superficial realists.[16]

Reflexive of What? Estes's Cityscapes

About fifteen years after *Bus with Reflection of the Flatiron Building*, Estes painted *Prescriptions Filled* on a wide, relatively large panel (1983; plate 13). As we stand in front of it, our gaze plunges deep into the sharp diagonal composition typical of Estes's cityscapes. Estes has been inspired by the typically baroque, often fictional views of Venice or Rome. In contrast to such bird's-eye views hovering over piazzas, Estes brings the viewpoint back into the body of the city dweller. In *Prescriptions Filled* we, as viewers, are walking down Barclay Street in lower Manhattan, having paused at the corner of West Broadway, where we are about to turn to look at an optician's display of glasses. Like most of his other cityscapes, this one encloses a wide-angled view that captures more visual information than our eye can process at once. Able to "look around" in his work, we are offered things twice: for instance, the white City Hall and the brownstone Potter buildings on our left are reflected in the shop window, drawing us into a playful verification process. The picture recalls a Rorschach blot, as the two sides would fold in on each other, but the reflection is not picture perfect: whereas the mail van and the black limousine on the far left have been doubled in their entirety, the orange

Beetle is cropped by a window sill, and the brownstone and its neighbor get "Prescriptions" and "Filled" written all over their façades.

Due to Estes's reliance on photographs, his work has been compared (by himself as much as others) to those early modern painters such as Canaletto (1697–1768) or even more so Bernardo Bellotto (1721–1780) who most likely employed a camera obscura, yet—despite their use of projective technology—it is precisely these earlier artists' handling of light and reflection that is fundamentally different from what Estes is doing. In Canaletto's *vedute*, the effect of brightness has been produced by the application of hundreds of small white highlights that we become aware of only when we study his canvases up close. In contrast, Estes's razor-sharp reflections are produced by an extreme smoothness and are carried out with much greater exactitude than Canaletto's and Bellotto's dots: every transparent surface is successfully transformed into a distorted mirror in a way only a photograph has been able to capture. By appropriating this essentially photographic quality as the very foundation of all his painting, Estes has given an interesting twist to the traditional metaphor of painting as a mirror of nature, or as a window onto the world. His paintings suggest that by taking photography rather than the world as his model, mirror and window are superimposed, canceling each other out and turning the work into something other than what the older paintings offered. Is this what photography looks like from the eye of a painting?

Moreover, in *Prescriptions Filled*, the display of glasses directs us to question what we see, not just between the urban view on the left and its distorted double on the right, but what the entire work makes us see: namely, that it is neither a window nor a mirror nor an image of the world, but the treatment that our vision of it has undergone since photography's intervention. What would Estes like us to see? What exactly is *Prescriptions Filled* reflective of? We get a better understanding by going back to one of the earliest exhibitions of Estes's work as interest was rising, around 1970, in what was then called new realism.

For his celebrated Documenta 5 in 1972, Harald Szeemann took the relation between reality and image as the thematic thread of his exhibition, dividing it into seventeen sections with titles such as "the trivial," "utopia," and "science fiction," which were organized by various curators. Section 15, entitled "realism," was curated by Jean-Christophe Ammann, the director of the Kunstmuseum Luzern. Departing from the 1960s' disregard for the figurative, Ammann decided to select a wide range of work that showed the current return to realistic representation; he was interested in how these works revealed tensions between the conceptualization of realism as representation and its appropriation as method. In his curatorial work just preceding the preparations for Documenta 5, Ammann worked from the idea that art is a form of self-exploration and is conscious of its materiality, as we see, for instance, in his 1970 exhibition in Lucerne, *Visualisierte Denkprozesse* (*Visualized Thought Processes*). For Documenta 5, Ammann selected the consumerist pictures of cakes and hotdogs made by Wayne Thiebaud, which for him explored realism *in* representation. He contrasted them with Gerhard Richter's painted photographs, instances of an artist playing with realism in a more methodical way. Richter's paintings were part of a group that also included Jasper Johns's *Flag*, in which we see a collapse of object and symbol, and the painted postcards of Malcolm Morley, which create a sense of distance from reality by distorting the transparency of a photograph and postcard. A third group comprised examples by photorealists, including Estes as well as Robert Bechtle, Robert Cottingham, and Ralph Goings. Ammann characterized their work as "extreme images" that resulted from a strong link between subject matter and method, which allowed these artists to take a critical stance toward both.[17]

Ammann's selection was intended to demonstrate the various ways that realism was conceptualized not so much through but "in" art, articulated in the materiality of the chosen photorealistic work. The radicalization he observed in photorealism resulted as much from the use of photography as a model as from the elimination of a stylistic "hand." These artists had taken up the challenge of painting an image of the world based on a mechanical recording and without wanting to change it, bypassing the world-as-object. Photorealism, according to Ammann, represented a genuinely self-conscious thought process that generated an image-world in which references were made only to other modes of image-making.

Ammann could not have envisioned, in 1972, how this self-referential image-world would expand. Each of the early photorealists began to develop a repetition-compulsion in both subject matter and practice that was repeated self-consciously by subsequent "generations" of photorealist artists. The Documenta pictures all embrace the boredom of everyday life by representing it just as it appears: Bechtle's *'61 Pontiac* (1968–1969) shows the artist's young, middle-class family uneasily posing in front of their car for a snapshot taken on what seems to be a typical Sunday afternoon. Cottingham's *Roxy* (1971–1972) is a close-up of unlit neon letters on the dilapidated tympanum of an arcade in bright sunlight; Estes's *Key Food* (1971) shows a desolate strip of New York shops; Goings's *Airstream* (1970) depicts a silver trailer in the Arizona desert casting a heavy shadow on the sun-blazed sand. Perhaps the most exciting contribution is John De Andrea's lovemaking couple *Arden Anderson and Norma Murphy* (1972): for all their nudity the figures lack any erotic spark, as if they were going through the motions out of habit. Such images picture a vulgar capitalist world of margarine and popcorn, of faded movie theaters and bleak parking lots, that somehow seems prefabricated and "canned." "Photorealists painted tastelessly a tasteless world," Jean-Claude Lebensztejn wrote in 1981. "If it had a taste, [it] had the flavor of disillusion."[18] This meticulously recorded "arsenal of mediocrity" lacks the joy and irony (or drama) of, for instance, pop art, which had demonstrated how a dull can of soup could be transformed into a compelling work of art. Sharing with pop art an investment in seriality, photorealism revealed its repetition-compulsion on a variety of levels, for instance, in its artists' commitment to (one could say obsession with) one particular subject matter: Audrey Flack specialized in modern still lifes, Cottingham replicated one movie marquee representing a bygone era after another, and year in year out Goings continued to paint salt-and-pepper sets from diners. Estes, for his part, created hundreds of street scenes, and Ben Schonzeit almost mechanically produced one gigantic blow-up of supermarket fruit and vegetable displays after another. For these artists, to produce copies after photographs was an accepted way of making art to such an extent that each repetition took the form of a reenactment of a previous painting's making. Their repetition-compulsion, expressed in subject matter and method, continued with the rise of subsequent generations of photorealists whose artists have deliberately styled themselves as followers of, say, Cottingham or Goings via their choice of subject matter and composition pattern.

Ammann was fascinated by the photorealists' repetition-compulsion. Most commenters, however, were less enthusiastic. In 1974, Robert Hughes fulminated against what he saw as the lazy, apolitical attitude of Bechtle, Schonzeit, and others. He was less concerned with everyday middle-class life as a subject and more agitated about what he regarded as their boringly simple dependence on photography to make paintings. "All that remains is technique," he wrote, "that elaborate, deadpan *verismo* which has propelled Photo-Realism into its popularity among those collectors who, wearied or intimidated by the ideological conflicts of the '60s, have no appetite left for 'difficult' art."[19] Like many art historians at the time, Hughes was not prepared to see the ideological potential inherent in the analogy made between deadpan realism and photorealism's zombielike middle-class subjects, who were desperately trying to "snapshot" their life into action. Neither could he predict the immense flight taken subsequently by photography, which would lead

Vilém Flusser to claim that we currently live in a photographic universe.[20] To that extent, we could say that photorealist painting anticipated the way photography would take over our perception of the world.

Hughes holds tight to a centuries-old bias favoring originality over copying. "To draw reality is still to examine thought itself," he insists, aligning himself with art historians' long denial of artists' use of the camera as an aid for their pictorial practices. The thoughtless nature of copying that Hughes, and many commentators after him, noted as characteristic of photorealism is diametrically opposed to Ammann's conviction that the self-reflexive thought process of the photorealist work of art as such is what made these artists interesting. Ammann was among the first to notice that the specific photorealist technique was developed not just to copy photography but to mimic photographic reproduction. If there is a "thought" in this kind of copying that Hughes was so quick to dismiss, this mimicking is ultimately a way to step back to observe realism and what photography has done to it. What does it mean for a painter to commit fully to following a medium that was said to have killed painting, or at least to replace it in terms of a truthful recording of reality, and which has changed our perception of the world forever? In the sense that it engages with this change in perception, photorealism is a form of reflection. Hughes's (widely shared) rejection of photorealism in fact signals a sense of unease toward its hybridity, which apparently is eroding the very foundation of Hughes's conception of art (or "difficult" art, as he would have it).

In recent years, the work of Bechtle and Estes in particular has become embedded—and rightly so—in histories of the use of photography as a drawing aid in painting, from Eakins and Degas to Hockney and Rosenquist. This "shared intelligence" of both media was further explored in the late 1980s and '90s in the growing debates on appropriation, the position of the copy versus the original, indexicality, and referentiality.[21] Stylistic discussions of photorealism usually home in on particular photographic qualities such as reflection, shine, brightness, exactitude, cropping, and camera viewpoint, explained by pointing to the artists' use of photographs as models. But few commentators have delved deeper into the significance of repetition as a vital element of photorealist practice, even though Estes and his fellow photorealists often remarked that they had little interest in the subject matter portrayed and, by contrast, were deeply invested in the very practice of painting as such.

Why, then, we are compelled to ask, did the photorealists initially evoke such negative responses, while, for instance, Richter's painted photographs (or for that matter Jeff Wall's photographed paintings) were embraced by art historians and critics alike, and now run the risk of being overdiscussed and overtheorized as meaningful images? The answer might be found in the photorealists' interest in a complete absence of originality or authorship, an idea celebrated in poststructuralism beginning in the 1980s but never really applied to the art that genuinely attempted to move away from Romanticism and the primacy of the artist's expression. Whereas Richter firmly held onto the notion of the singularity of the artist by developing a signature style, for instance, by adding to his paintings a photographic blur, any such assertion of originality was rejected by the photorealists via their obsession with translating—inch by inch—a photographic image into paint, which ultimately created an image of prefabricated life, but more importantly redefined a work of art as something wholly substitutable. In most literature discussing the use of photography, such as that on Thomas Eakins, the comparison between photography and painting never loses its fascination, for one thing because the distinction between original and referent is clear cut. What photorealism carefully negotiates is precisely the dissolution of the dualism of subject and object, world and picture, and even of photography and painting. The image is inauthentic, superfluous, desubjectified, an act of compulsion rather than inspiration. It is presented as a kind of merchandise that is not merely located in the objects we presume are these paintings' subjects (cars, shopping windows, food) but that has impregnated the world.

Photorealists' insistence that their works are substitutable clashes spectacularly with the model of unsubstitutability on which our understanding of an artwork is based (as it was, of course, in 1972 as much as today).[22] To that extent, Estes is quite an exception, as his obsession with reflection directed him to various types of scenery that contain different sorts of reflective surfaces, from those of the inner city to those of ferry routes and arctic seascapes. In addition to its commitments to copying and to subject matter devoted to a niche topic, there is another striking feature about photorealism's course over the past four decades. New generations of photorealists have stepped into their predecessors' footsteps—almost literally, one might say. They have developed kinships with earlier photorealists as if latter-day clones of the older painters, each duplicating the work of his or her hero: John Bader and David Finnigan worked "after" Ralph Goings and created pictures of diners and trailers that are almost identical to his; Clive Head has appropriated Estes's style and topics. Photorealism as a whole is uncannily self-referential toward its different levels of oeuvre, technique, methodology, and the movement's own history; as such, it has thrown fresh light on the notion of reflection. Even the prefix in the movement's name, whether it is called photo-, super-, or hyperrealism, suggests a critical distance. Having pushed physical reflection to an extreme by making it hyperreflective, Estes's work releases thoughts on the connection between photography and painting—even though few art historians or critics would care to see it.

There are exceptions. In the context of Lacan's theory of trauma, Hal Foster discusses photorealist examples in *The Return of the Real* as part of a group of works including Warhol's *Death and Disaster* series, Richter's blurry paintings, and Cindy Sherman's *Untitled Film Stills.*[23] He uses Estes's *Double Self-Portrait* (1976; plate 14) as an example of a contemporary model of pictorial reflexivity akin to *Las Meninas*. Given the near-total dismissal of substitutability as a model, and in light of the related concepts of the inauthentic and the lack of authorship, it is significant that Foster, to fit his larger art-historical paradigm of unsubstitutability, selects what is for Estes an atypical work. In *Double Self-Portrait* we see an empty diner similar to the one portrayed in *Central Savings*, in which various reflections and refractions are at the point of collapse or, as Foster writes, implosion. We may have been surprised to find in *Central Savings* only shadows of briskly walking passersby, but no photographer; in *Double Self-Portrait*, Estes includes a reflection of himself proudly standing next to his tripod while pressing the shutter. As we have seen with all of Estes's work, nothing is one-of-a-kind—everything carries its double with it. Further in, toward the back of the diner, a much smaller part of the torso of Estes's reflection is doubled in the mirror wall. Likening it (via Lacan's comments on trompe l'oeil) to the kind of superficiality developed in illusionistic painting as deceptive surfaces with nothing behind them, Foster presents Estes's painting as a visual conundrum deeply rooted in capitalist spectacle, whereby the lines and windows of Estes's shopfront flatten pictorial depth and thereby flatten psychic depth. For Foster, photorealism conceals reality rather than revealing it. In addition, Foster seems to forget that photorealism represents a conundrum less about the real than about realism, as such. If anything, it presents us with a reflection, not of reality but of the way we experience it through what we take to be its most reliable means of recording. In contrast to Foster's notion of the simultaneous flattening of pictorial and psychic depth in Estes's work, I suggest that Estes has deepened these depths through "shine." I agree with Foster that Estes's painting, like *Las Meninas*, can be considered a model of pictorial reflexivity. But I am not convinced by his linking of photorealism to trompe l'oeil, as so many critics have done to explain away photorealism's extreme resemblance to photography as a lazy twentieth-century version of baroque trompe l'oeil painting that aimed to fool the spectator. Rather, I would argue that the opposite is the case.

Early modern trompe l'oeil is two-dimensional painting that aspires to have its objects taken as three-dimensional things. Their illusionism is so effective that even though we as viewers know a given work to be merely a painting, our senses will conflict with our cognitive faculties, and almost automatically we feel the impulse to stretch the hand out to verify what must be a perceptive failure. Traditionally, early modern trompe l'oeils are self-aware images *par excellence*: they are ambitious artworks that seek to literally *become* the objects they represent. Their greatest wish is to overcome their limitations as two-dimensional images to participate in the world *as objects*. Probably the most perfect embodiment of this aspiration is *Reverse Side of a Painting* by Cornelius Gijsbrechts of 1670. This work was specifically made to be placed against the wall of a *kunstkammer* so that curious visitors would turn it around, only to be disappointed to find the same image—the reverse of a painting—but this time *not* an image, but reality. We could say, with Stoichita, that this is the ultimate self-aware image, which in the wake of iconoclasm had achieved full awareness of its being—and of its nothingness. Even if we would present photorealist paintings as contemporary trompe l'oeils, they possess everything Gijsbrechts's tour de force lacks: a sense of depth, any hint of spectacle, and, more importantly, reflections or shadows—no real light ever shines *in* trompe l'oeils or *from* them. After all, the objects in these paintings are meant to arise out of nowhere to fool us, outsmarting our perception and putting us in our place.

While Estes's work might deceive the eye in letting it think that it is a photograph, it is essentially very different from what a photograph is. First, its illusionism comes off spectacularly well in reproduction when the paintings are scaled down to the size of photographs as we generally know them, but when we see the actual paintings we marvel at how much they are *like* photographs, not identical to them. Recalcitrant and thought-provoking as *Reverse Side of a Painting* may be, its disguising itself as an object produces a self-awareness that, however fitting to early modern easel painting, is no longer relevant for paintings created after photography (and modernism, for that matter)—an invention that has resulted in as fundamental a shift in representation as in self-consciousness. (After all, what would our self-image be without photos?) The type of self-reflexivity at work in the photorealism of Estes possesses a different kind of complexity than Gijsbrechts's trompe l'oeil or Velázquez's *Las Meninas*. I argue that Estes effectively moves away from baroque self-awareness and toward Hegelian self-consciousness.

If, for Stoichita, the early modern baroque image was self-reflexive because it acknowledged, through the nature of its representation, its own being and its nothingness, Estes's painting goes further. He attempts to approximate a newfound essence of painting through a double gesture: he maintains painting's original aim of realism but does so by identifying it with the medium that has made it obsolete—photography. Whereas painting should not directly be compared to an operating mind, and Hegel's structure of self-consciousness does not allow for a straightforward translation into pictorial terms, *Central Savings* allows us to better understand his notion of speculative reflection as a "thinking through opposites" so as to come closest to the essence of self-identification. Here, reflecting surface and reflection (of the façade, of the street signs) overlap to the extent that some reflections stand out from their ground while remaining in it, as they won't show without the (transparent) surface. In his essay "The Image—the Distinct," Jean-Luc Nancy states that the figure/ground oscillation is distinctive of the image as such. A Hegelian philosopher, Nancy argues that the image, any image, is separated from its ground but is also cut out (like a silhouette or woodcut) within a ground. In this double operation of the image being within its ground and cut in it, standing out and impressed in, emerging from it and sinking into it, the ground disappears.[24] This operation is made visible in Estes's *Central Savings*, where the image of the façade is distinct from the façade and from its ground, all the while standing out from that ground. There is a distance between reflection and what is reflected, surface and figure, that I have referred to as a "thickness," where images seem to have split from their objects as much as from their reflection. What we see is not the thing itself but its sameness. This begs the question, what is the precise nature Estes's reflections within the history of philosophical reflection? To fully grasp Estes's *Central Savings* as a particular form of self-consciousness, we will look into Hegel's critique of Kant's philosophical reflection, from which the former's notion of self-consciousness springs.

Due to its optical connotations and its modeling after the physical properties of a light beam, philosophical reflection has often been obscured by the metaphors it has been given. It has been referred to as a "photology," a metaphysics of light that brings about a doubling of sorts: a setting apart of perceiving and thinking and of an awareness of the process of thinking as such. Photorealism is a photology, a mode of philosophical reflection in visual terms that can be considered a contribution to this branch of philosophy. Estes's work presents us with a complicated theory on reflection, whereby opposites not just mirror each other but also are superimposed and thus overcome the presumed distance between what is reflected and its reflection, the object and its reproduction—very much like Hegel's *aufheben*.

Photology in Painting

The concept of reflection is as old as philosophy itself. In both Greek and Latin philosophy the term distinguished between our sense experience of an object and the examination of this perception. In his *First Philosophy*, Aristotle pushed this distinction further via his theory of what he called *noesis noeseos*, the thought of thought. He observed that if we are to think about the conditions of all knowledge, we should study the foundations of philosophy itself. Reflection allowed for a distance between thinking as object and as process and, as such, it became a *medium* for understanding how thinking thinks itself. In his exploration of the history of philosophical reflection leading up to Derrida's deconstruction, *The Tain of the Mirror*, Rodolphe Gasché explains that for Aristotle, in the thinking of thinking, reflection thus was not only a medium that enabled him to think it but served at the same time as a ground of philosophy, as the basis on which this thinking of thinking could take place. At the same time, reflection is the very method by which the process of thinking about thought can occur. The notion of reflection as medium, foundation, and method was taken to an extreme by Descartes. In his work, the modern conception of reflection took shape. Take the example of his famous wax argument from his *Second Meditation*. Wondering about the distinction between himself as a "thinking thing" and the objects around him from which he is separated, the philosopher raises the question as to what extent he can know a piece of wax that he is holding in his hand. After all, even though his senses perceive its flowery smell, its consistency, and its color, he does not comprehend this piece of wax in its totality. Holding it in his hand, it starts to melt and change, and no matter how much information his senses give him, his imagination is unable to encompass in their totality the infinite forms this wax can take on. Therefore, his apprehension of the piece of wax cannot be possible without the actions of his mind, distinct from what it beholds. And to go even further: while he thinks he has tried to apprehend the piece of wax, the only thing he has gained knowledge about is not the wax as such, but the workings of his own mind: "with how much greater distinctness must I now know myself, since all the reasons that contribute to the knowledge of the nature of wax . . . manifest still better the nature of my mind."[25] For Descartes, reflection is the very foundation of philosophy: the only thing we can truly know is that we think.

Subsequently, John Locke arrives at a grammar of reflection when he defines reflection in his *Essay Concerning Human Understanding* as "that notice that the mind takes of its own operations."[26] Harking back to the original meaning of reflection as signifying the physical process of light as it is thrown back onto itself when it hits a polished surface, Locke explains how the mind's working can best be understood via optical metaphors: "The perception of the mind being most aptly explained by words relating to the sight, we shall best understand what is meant by *clear*, and *obscure*, in our *ideas*, by reflection on what we call *clear* and *obscure* in the objects of sight."[27] He contrasts the mind to an eye that, while it allows us to see, cannot perceive itself: "And it requires art and pains [paintings] to set it at a distance, and make it its own object."[28] For the mind, that kind of art is reflection that can put the mind's workings at a distance so that it can think itself. While the sense's understanding of external objects brings about sensations, Locke argues that the perception of the workings of the mind generates what he calls "an internal sense," which is reflection. For our discussion of reflection in Estes's painting, it is interesting to note that Locke considers reflection as combining a superficial, passive mirroring with a deep-seated activity that creates an image of the mind's operations.

Whereas for Locke reflection is in fact empirical, understood as it is in relation to the sensible, Kant takes a more radical standpoint. He rejects empirical reflection in favor of transcendental reflection, which he defines as that which "does not concern itself with objects themselves with a view to deriving concepts from them directly, but is that state of mind in which we first set ourselves to discover the subjective conditions under which [alone] we are able to arrive at concepts."[29] Kant descends even deeper into the mind's depths in seeking not only to understand its operations but to question the validity of cognition. His transcendental reflection inquires into the constitutive principles enabling a subject to conceptualize an (empirical) object. He wants to examine how a concept, let's say "dog," which can only exist in thought, is separated from its object as "four-footed barking animal" that the senses can perceive. Essential for Kant is the notion that reflection has become the *medium* by which the mind can separate itself from the object, thinking the synthetic unity between concept and object as well as examining the difference between them—all the while observing the unity of this process of reflection as a whole. As Hegel famously points out, this is a rather tight structure, whereby that which is being thought is forever separated from the thinking being, while the operation of reflection locks the whole construct into a synthetic unity.

The result is that the problem caused by reflection can be solved only by more reflection, effectively creating a mental abyss. We might better be able to picture this when a mirror is mirrored in another, the reflection of which in its turn is reflected, generating a bottomless pit of duplications. This is what Derrida calls a *mise-en-abîme* and what he tries to disentangle in deconstruction, which is essentially a reading method to bypass this process of repetition. *Mise-en-abîme* is a term going back to André Gide, who in a journal entry from 1893 remarked how much he enjoyed passages in novels where the work, as such, came to the surface, an operation he associates with the way that convex mirrors in early Netherlandish paintings such as Van Eyck's *Arnolfini Portrait* reflect a room featuring a crossed window stretching out in front of the figures where we as viewers are supposed to stand. Hoping to create the same structure in his novels, Gide mentions *Las Meninas* as an obvious example of this impossible overlap of pictorial and actual space, the awareness of which lifts us out of our viewer's position and up to a higher ground from which we reconsider the dualism in which we are embedded.

Within Kant's system, the only way to understand the nature of this dualism is to find a position outside the synthetic unity to further reflect on the problems caused by *this* reflection, which in turn will pose the same problem, thus setting in motion a series of reflections on reflections ad infinitum. Hegel notes that for Kant the understanding is an absolute and immovable finitude, which can reflect onto other things and onto reflection as such but cannot reflect onto *itself.* Within the Kantian system, the subject-object distinction is fixed. Consequently, Hegel reasons that Kant's notion of understanding is *unbending* in the literal sense of being irreflective, as it is incapable of moving beyond the fixed subject-object opposition. If we compare for a moment *Las Meninas* to Estes's *Prescriptions Filled,* we can see how Velázquez's painting presents us with a paradox in which the positions of viewer and painting are fixed. The discourse around this magnificent piece results from these positions being irreflexive. In Estes's painting, by contrast, they are not fixed but fluid.

Image and reflection, inside and outside, transparency and opacity are no longer identifiable in Estes's painting. Any attempt to disentangle the whirlpool of lines and color seems to throw us deeper into a space that is impossible to comprehend. However, Estes's work is highly useful for visualizing the Kantian oppositions of concept and appearance, thought and thinker, thinking and being, which are locked in a definite embrace that cannot be untangled without the opposites folding onto themselves. What Kant arrives at, and what is easier for us to understand when we look at *Central Savings,* is the problem inherent in the nature of reflection. The point for Kant is that the understanding is an absolute and immovable finitude, capable of reflecting onto other things as well as onto reflection as such—but it is absolutely unable to reflect *onto itself.*

And this is what Hegel, along with Fichte and Schelling, observes: Kant's "philosophical reflection" is incapable of recognizing this fixation. It can only deepen any reflection—just as we see in a *mise-en-abîme.* In a way, we see a visualization of this process in the groundless abyss of duplications of the diner's red counter in *Central Savings,* which reverberate to infinity. Therefore, within Kant's rigid structure, one is incapable of *overcoming* the separation between subject and object, or between a thinking being and its object of reflection.

There is only one way to avoid plummeting into the *mise-en-abîme* of endless reflection. What the process of mirroring already permits, and Estes's painting confirms, Hegel also fully realized: that a mirror reflecting an object also reflects itself *in* that object. What Estes's *Central Savings* overstates through its double reflections—and Kant forgot—is that reflection always "meets" itself in what it reflects. If we look at the left side of the diner, we see how over the red counter the reflection of the diner's front in the windows of the Central Savings bank literally "bends back" to itself when re-reflected onto both the main glass window and the silver paneling within the restaurant. The diner's reflected façade thus meets itself and "sees" this meeting reflected in the material off which it had originally bounced. This process also accurately mimicked in the neon sign reading "BURGER" and its fragmentary "echo": the letters "BURG" seem to be lifted off its earlier doubling as if bouncing off each other. If we assume, for the sake of the argument, that Estes's painting also doubles as a traditional mirror onto the world, we see it most dramatically start to crack here. In the moment of this "self-seeing," this painting becomes truly self-conscious by finding, in the whirlpool of reflections, not a picture of the world but an image of itself *in the process of reflecting itself.* What we see is a bouncing of sorts: a reflection of a reflection that gets reflected back into its mirror image. Any mirror reproduction in *Central Savings*, be it of the façade or of the neon letters, creates its "other": its negative, which is neither the subject nor the genuine object of reflection but their merging in a process of mediation that reflection has set in motion. We might better understand such mediation when we focus on the superimposition of the façade and its other: here is something that becomes so thick that, visually speaking, their appearances start to shine through each other, and here is the locus where the subject of reflection touches on its object so that they become double-sided. They become both.

For Kant, subject and object could never be both—it had to be either/or. Hegel's most profound criticism of Kant's system is that he had insisted on this rigidity, which ultimately led Hegel to state that it that nothing is always the other of something, nothing *is*, it exists. If, indeed, "just as little is seen in pure light as in pure darkness," Hegel says in *The Science of Logic*, and nothing "is not an intermediate state between being and nothing," then being and nothingness are both identical *and* contradictory.[30] What Hegel was ultimately looking for is a process of mediation that would cancel out the principle of opposition.[31] Distancing himself from Schelling and Fichte in this regard, Hegel read Kant closely and observed in his predecessor's monumental oeuvre moments of potential escape from this constricted either/or principle, germs that, while remaining true to Kant's system, signaled the possibility of more ambiguous zones between entities. By holding onto the principle of separation, Kant couldn't quite reach far enough. If Kant wanted man to understand being *through* reflection, Hegel aimed to demonstrate that, in Jean Hyppolite's words, "it is being that knows itself through man."[32] The only way to find out how being "knows itself," and how thought can think itself, Hegel asserts, is through what he calls *speculative reflection.*

The remainder of this chapter explores Hegel's notion of speculative reflection as a kind of thinking that can overcome opposites, in particular the subject-object opposition that was so stubbornly entrenched in Kant's work. Estes's photorealism strongly resonates with Hegel's speculative reflection and its ultimate result in sublation, or the *Aufhebung*, of opposites will be very helpful in articulating photorealism's commentary on the opposition of painting and photography, or, one might rather say, its rising above their separation.

The Self-Conscious Image

Hegel's model for the process of mediation that would cancel out opposites is, in fact, consciousness, or rather, self-consciousness. Via the *noesis noeseos*, the self-as-thinking-subject and the self-as-object become one, despite the antithesis of the distinction. Hegel is intrigued with how the subject experiences its inner self as most true when it observes itself as if it were an other, and with how there is, apparently, no greater sense of ownership of the self as when self-consciousness observes itself as that which it is not, all the while identifying with it. If we make "thinking" or the movement of knowing into a "concept," Hegel reasons, and call the entity that passively does the knowing an "I," then we see that the concept and the object are one and the same, not only for us, but also for knowing itself. In self-consciousness, being-in-itself and being-for-another is one and the same. "The 'I' is its own self, and at the same time it overarches this other which, for the 'I' is equally only the 'I' itself."[33] Going beyond the metaphor of the mirror image whereby the reflection is "the one of the one of the other, and the other is the other of the one," Hegel acknowledges the mirror's capacity to recognize itself and extends the metaphor when he lets self-consciousness see itself *as* seeing itself, reflect itself as reflecting itself.[34] He calls this absolute reflection or speculation. As Gasché points out, Hegel's absolute reflection expresses the boldness to *think* contradiction, to conceive of opposites in a unity, and this is exactly what happens when thought is not merely speculative.[35]

For Hegel, thinking is a *movement* whereby the self, in order to think about itself, needs to distance the thinking self from the self-as-object about which it thinks. "When thinking, I *am free* because I am not in another, rather, I remain utterly in my own sphere, and the object, which to me is the essence, is in undivided unity my being-for-myself; and my moving about in concepts is a movement within myself."[36] Thinking about the self is, then, a process of seeing the self as its negative, all the while identifying with it. The moment of the split between our thinking about the self and the self as different from itself is thus a movement from dividing the self to returning to the self: "But in point of fact self-consciousness is the reflection out of the being of the world of sense and perception, and is essentially the return from *otherness*. . . . As self-consciousness, it is movement; but since what it distinguishes from itself is *only itself* as itself, the difference, as an otherness, is *immediately superseded* for it."[37]

If we translate this situation to *Central Savings* we could say that the movement occurs on three levels: first, the letters have been projected onto the canvas before Estes traced them; second, we see in the process of reflection how the letters bounce off their surface, distancing from themselves in their mirror image; third, *they bend back* to the reflective surface, and this return from otherness is what is "seen" by the reflection, what makes it fully self-conscious in a Hegelian way. The self does not just do this on its own account. Rather, it senses its deepest sense of self when it recognizes itself most fully by superseding the difference between thinking being and object of thought. Thinking about ourselves thinking drives us forth as human beings, or as Hegel succinctly writes, "self-consciousness is *desire* itself."[38]

Estes's painting as a whole mimics this structure. While it is painting, it appears as its negative, photography, and its many reflections show a deep awareness of this distinction. Further adapting the structure of self-consciousness as a movement, this "reflectedness-into-self" (as Hegel writes), *Central Savings* allows us to see how in self-consciousness, photorealism's desire has been fulfilled: faced with another reflection, it first lost itself (as photography), then found itself (as painting). What happens next is that that the self, Hegel writes, "has superseded the other, for it does not see the other as an essential being, but in the other sees its own self." Folding onto itself, it "lets the other again go free."[39]

The question arises as to what exactly has freed itself in Estes's work. As we have seen, Estes engages with two partly intertwined metaphors for painting: a mirror of the world and a window onto the world. By letting the diner's window partly coincide with the picture frame, *Central Savings* attempts to unify these metaphors. However, it also tries to overcome the distinction between them by having the reflections of space extending behind the viewer, made visible "in" the window, overlay the diner's interior. The viewer seems caught up in between these two reflecting layers. Unlike in *Las Meninas*, where the viewpoint lying outside the pictorial space opposite the row of courtiers is hinted at by the reflection of the king and queen in the mirror, in *Central Savings* the viewer finds herself paradoxically between the diner's window and the reflections of the bank opposite it. And here the mirror cracks dramatically. If this were actually a photograph, the viewer would see her reflection the diner window. This what Estes denies us. In fact, we as viewing subjects do not take part in the spectacle that we see: the reflections we see occur solely between the painting and its appearance. Rather than placing us as viewers in a position to "reflect" and thus understand this painting, Estes shows us how painting understands itself, neither as window nor as mirror but as the ultimate self-reflection. For something has started to disappear in this process: painting as a medium.

Essence's Own Shining

Much has been written in recent years about art's post-medium condition. Artworks might still be driven by the modernist urge for flatness and purity (if that ever existed) but art forms have become conflated to such an extent that one can no longer make clear distinctions between media. Art's essence, therefore, must be found outside a specific medium. Estes's painting has conflated the media of photography and painting, yet it has done so based on another "medium," namely, philosophical reflection. Painting has recognized itself as photography in painting and as painting in photography, and all the while photography has equally emerged and appeared as painting. Both moments of reflection have been made possible by a third medium: reflection itself. This has enabled Estes—wittingly or unwittingly—to make a rather bold statement. He presents painting and photography not as opposites but as two sequential periods in the overall movement reproduction. Estes's work, and that of his followers, suggest that photography has continued painting's project within the larger history of realistic representation, within which it first alienated itself from painting as its negation, then ultimately merged with it in photorealism, all the while retaining its otherness in the process of identification. In Hegelian terms, Estes's statement belongs no longer to philosophical but to speculative reflection, which is characterized by the boldness to *think through* oppositions. Hegel defines speculative reflection as the movement of reflecting itself-into-itself, when it becomes the totality embracing both reflection-into-self and reflection-into-other.[40]

In this spectacularly ambiguous clash, something has been set free. What trompe l'oeil painting always confirms in its self-aware play with its being and its nothingness—its objecthood—is for photorealism no longer of any consequence, as the issue of its materiality or medium is vanishing. Attempting to define essence, Hegel writes in *The Science of Logic* that the negation of essence is shine, as it is nothing in and of itself.[41] However, as we have seen with Kalf's still life painting, shine is not something external to essence but is deeply linked to it. The shine we see (in Kalf's still life or in the appearance of objects) is essence's own shining. "This shining of essence within it is *reflection*," Hegel explains. In the immediacy of shine we see, in fact, being, or rather being's nothingness. Being is shine, Hegel writes, but he warns that "it is not that there is a shine of being *in* essence, or a shine of essence *in* being: the shine in the essence is not the shine of an other, but is rather *shine as such, the shine of essence itself*."[42] We could say that in the very shine of Estes's painting, we see the essence of painting, which is, according to photorealism, neither its materiality—despite Greenberg's lifelong argument—nor its subject matter but, as Hegel pointed out, its capacity to reflect, to think.

Darkened Light

Thirty-seven years after his famous *Double Self-Portrait*, Estes made another one, situated on what is probably the Staten Island Ferry in New York (2013; plate 15).[43] His silhouette's reflection in the ferry's bright blue framed window is flanked on the left by the words "NO SMOKING," while waves stretch out behind him. The pose of the silhouetted figure suggests that he is holding a camera in front of his face while pressing the shutter. Yet, in the place where the figure's face behind his camera should be, we find a hole shaped by the windows on the opposite site of the boat. Even though darkened, the silhouette remains transparent, allowing, for instance, for the benches inside the seating area to shine through. The benches in *Self-Portrait* provide the perspectival structure that leads up to the vanishing point, just as the street in *Prescriptions Filled* did; however, here this point is truly vanishing, as it disappears through the windows covering the figure's face in the direction of the vaguely visible Manhattan skyline behind it. It has been suggested that this self-portrait was inspired by Lee Friedlander's *New York City* (1966; fig. 25), in which we see Friedlander's looming shadow cast on the back of a woman walking in front of him, a gesture he repeats several times in his oeuvre. In Friedlander's photograph the shadow is unambiguous, while the question arises as to what Estes's silhouette, seeming to combine a reflection of the window and a shadow cast on it, actually is. In light of the history of

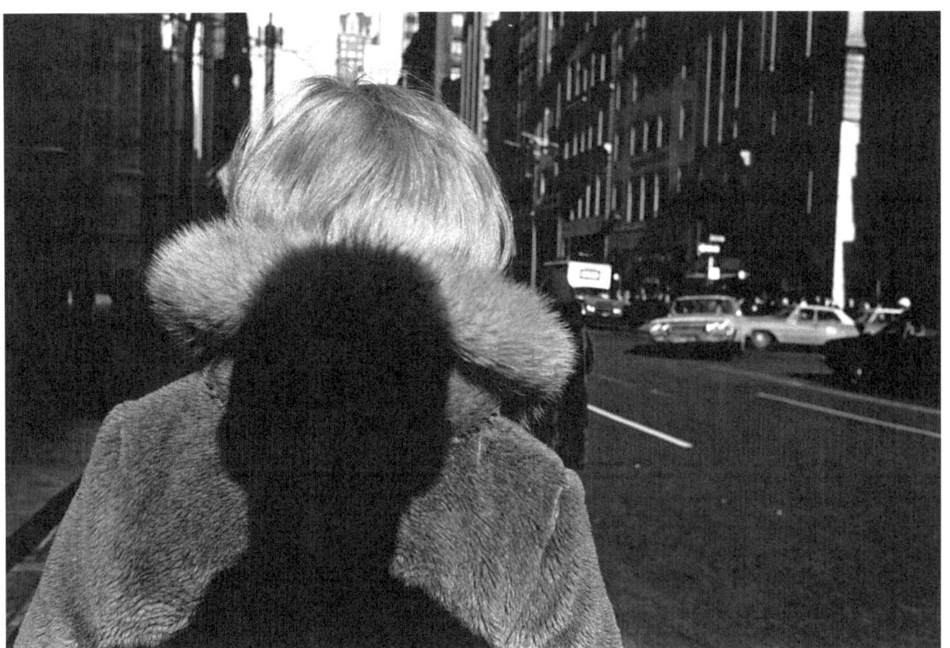

FIGURE 25 Lee Friedlander, *New York City*, 1966. Photograph. New York, MOMA. © Lee Friedlander, courtesy Fraenkel Gallery, San Francisco.

philosophical reflection, as well as the origins of painting, we may wonder what kind of statement Estes is trying to make here. In many respects, a shadow cast from an object onto a surface, which is in fact a part of the object, is in structural terms the opposite of a reflection (shadow is the obstruction of light; reflection shows light's pathways) which is a part neither of the object nor of the surface off which it bounces. We expect, in *Double Self-Portrait*, to see Estes's likeness, but what we get is the collapse of reflection and shadow, of image and semblance. These elements folding onto each other, the actual likeness disappears. Whereas in his cityscapes Estes lets the two most persistent metaphors of painting—window and mirror—coincide to such an extent that his canvases become simultaneously both and neither, in this *Self-Portrait* we witness the fusion of two other major art-historical concepts: shadow and reflection.

Shadow and reflection are concepts linked to the two predominant myths of art's origin: the legend of Narcissus, who fell in love with his specular image reflected in a pool and eventually drowned while trying to kiss it, and the tale of a Corinthian potter's daughter, who traced the shadow of her lover's profile on a wall while he was asleep on the eve of his departure. These two myths of origin correspond to different image categories developed by Plato in the *Republic*, where he writes that "by images [*eikona*] I mean first shadows [*skias*], then reflections in water [*phantasmata*] and other close-grained, polished surfaces, and all that sort of thing."[44] Within Plato's philosophy, reflections as well as paintings are pure appearance and, as a consequence, are one degree separate from the real or the true (*aletheia*). Shadows are even further removed. As such, the shadow has been charged with a fundamental negativity that, Stoichita writes in his *A Short History of the Shadow*, was never abandoned altogether in the history of Western representation: "It became for all time the poor relation of all reflection, the forgotten origin of all representation."[45] These two scenarios of art history's mythic genesis, and subsequently the positive and negative conceptualizations of the image, collide in Estes's painting, where his reflection seems to *become* a shadow while the shadow appears in reflection. Is he attempting to abolish Plato's distinction?

It was impossible for Plato to conceive of a fusion between the two different categories of reflection and its negative, the shadow. But such a conflation—or plasticity, as it is called—became central to Hegel's philosophy, as we have seen, in particular with regard to his essential concept of *aufheben*, often translated "to sublate." The form of *aufheben* Hegel uses is almost always a verb, indicating that he is dealing with a process, not a state, of sublation. As a consequence, the union of two extremes (for instance between self-as-subject and self-as-object or as other) is never a fully realized union but is rather a process of becoming, whereby the separate parts first come-into-being and cease-to-be before the sublation of becoming takes place. Sublation is a moment of passing that, Hegel insists, has always already come to pass; this is what he refers to as the dialectics of being, which is essentially a movement. The history of art has an excellent example of such coming-into-being that is simultaneously a ceasing-to-be in its representation of light, or, more precisely, where light ceases to be and darkness comes into being, which occurs most profoundly in chiaroscuro painting.[46] Or rather, chiaroscuro occurs as a moment of transition, when a shadow turns into an image, a shade into form, though the precise shift from one into the other cannot be drawn out. Such moments of chiaroscuro can be found most famously in the work of Rembrandt as well as in Kalf's still lifes, where the pitch-black background slowly turns into three-dimensional space, inhabited by drinking glasses whose outlines are only hinted at through subtle shades of light and darkness.

By projecting his shadow onto the reflecting ferry window, Estes has utilized a more complex version of chiaroscuro, whereby reflection and shadow fall upon each other even as they remain distinct all the while. In Estes's silhouette, reflected light and projected darkness find their own outlines as each other's in a near-perfect blending. They are no longer separate but are *becoming* the other: the cast shadow has become reflection in the moment the window bounces back its mirror image. On the other side of this clash stands Estes, photographing what he will soon turn into paint, while he disappears. What is happening is difficult to put into words: concepts and media merge, the protagonist of this work is at once its creator and model, its painter and its photographer, and art history's origins are brought back into the work. In light of the history of philosophical reflection, this silhouette is conceptually hybrid, as it combines a reflection bouncing off an object and a shadow of an object falling onto it.

It is as if this work is the perfect visual comment on Hegel's explanation of *aufheben*: "The *aufheben* stands out against the background of an impossible saying, of an unsayable difference, unsayable because one cannot *define* being and nothingness. One can at the most *picture* the one as 'pure light' and the other as 'pure night,'" but one will nevertheless be immediately forced to recognize that "in absolute darkness" and that, consequently, "something can be distinguished only in determinate light of darkness (light is determined by darkness and so is darkened light, and darkness is determined by light, is illuminated darkness), and for this reason, that it is only darkened light and illuminated darkness which have within themselves the moment of difference and are, therefore, *determinate* being."[47]

In his book on Hegel, Jean-Luc Nancy writes that *aufheben* is the articulation that rises within the chiaroscuro—"it is the very voice of philosophy," he writes.[48] If chiaroscuro is the voice of philosophy, we see in Estes's blending of shadow and reflection its visual equivalent: painting on its way to becoming thought.

Painting's Wonder

In 1739, Nicolas Spayement, an obscure painter of nature scenes and fish pieces, created a classical landscape populated with figures clad in early eighteenth-century worker's attire carrying out various tasks (plate 16).[1] Backed by a hilly landscape, men are preparing large slabs of stone that have been quarried from a stone pit. Various figures transport materials toward a city along a meandering pathway to the right, while women wash laundry in a small stream running diagonally through the composition, and a fisherman sitting nearby hopes for a good catch. Even the animals are appropriately diligent: on the left, cattle are duly grazing while chickens frantically pick at the ground. At the foot of the hillock, children bounce on a seesaw, not interfering with the toiling adults. The hilltop windmill seems to have been put there just to demonstrate that not only creatures but machines, too, contribute to the daily round of work.

Approaching this picture at the Musée des Arts décoratifs in Paris today, we immediately note the questionable quality of the painting. Roughly outlined, the figures do not blend very well into the poorly rendered landscape, and the picture has been mounted in a rather pompously sculpted gilded frame featuring a clock.[2] Doubling as a timepiece, this rather bizarre painting-object (I derive this term from Marcia Pointon's notion of portrait-object) hides an ingenious surprise: when wound up, on the hour a clockwork mechanism will cause the tableau to jump into action. The laboring figures, sixty in total, are all wooden cutouts that move within the picture in accordance with the particular activities they are doing. A hybrid object, neither a picture nor a real clock, and not quite an automaton in the common sense of the term, this is no doubt one of the most animated paintings of its period. Is this what painting looks like when time—literally—is added to it?

The subject of the tableau underscores this object's awareness as a clock-painting. The laboring figures do double duty, standing for different temporalities: the to-and-fro movements of the two sowing men in the foreground represent repetition, the cattle stand for the cycle of nature, the fisherman for patience, and the smoker for idleness. The river is a reference to Heraclitus's famous dictum that no one steps into the same river twice. In addition, the image aspires to be the emblem of progress, as men on the left have quarried large slabs of stone with which to erect a new city on the right. An artist finishing a large, reclining nude on the tympanum of the main building sums up this tale's closing chapter: the triumph of deserved, leisurely rest.

Resulting from a collaboration between a minor painter and a major clockmaker, this *tableau mécanique* was originally made in 1739 and became part of one of the most prestigious cabinets of curiosities of its time, that of the French aristocrat Joseph Bonnier de la Mosson (1702–1744). An extensive art collection made up part of Bonnier's curiosity cabinet; this tableau, however, was meant not to be hung on the wall as an artwork but to be placed among models of engineering devices, claude glasses, wax eyes, and other timepieces, as we can see in the detailed drawings of the cabinet's original layout by Jean Courtonne (1739–1740; fig. 26). Apparently, this *tableau mécanique* was considered to be an instrument, an example of mechanical ingenuity meant to inspire awe. It is also a typical instance of a philosophical tool or instrument that exemplifies a particular problem. Indeed, this clock-painting was likely an active participant in a lively debate on mechanical philosophy, initiated by Descartes and Boyle, among others, who assumed that the world is built not of organisms (as Aristotle had thought) but of discrete units of moving matter that operate together like a machine—like a clock. The idea of the world-as-picture has been taken up by the makers whose image of civilization—made up of nature and culture—is literally backed up by an enormous clock mechanism. Instead of *stating* that the world exists in different parts, it *shows* how these parts move individually, like a machine driven by an invisible engine. The clock is not a metaphor for a world-picture, it *is* a world-picture, as much as the picture is a clock, and as such it not only highlights various issues of the dispute but in retrospect can be said to predict where it may lead—from a celebration of a balanced world running like clockwork with perfect working conditions to a pronouncement with determinist implications that society is a puppet theater where humans without free will are captured in perpetual motion (as Kant would later characterize mechanical philosophy), to ultimately Marx's final reasoning that mechanical progress produced the monster of the Industrial Revolution. In that sense, this work enables such a debate to take its course beyond its course.

Drawing up an annotated catalog for the sale of the entire collection after Bonnier's early death in 1744, Edmé-François Gersaint could not hide his unbridled enthusiasm for what must have been—even in this remarkable

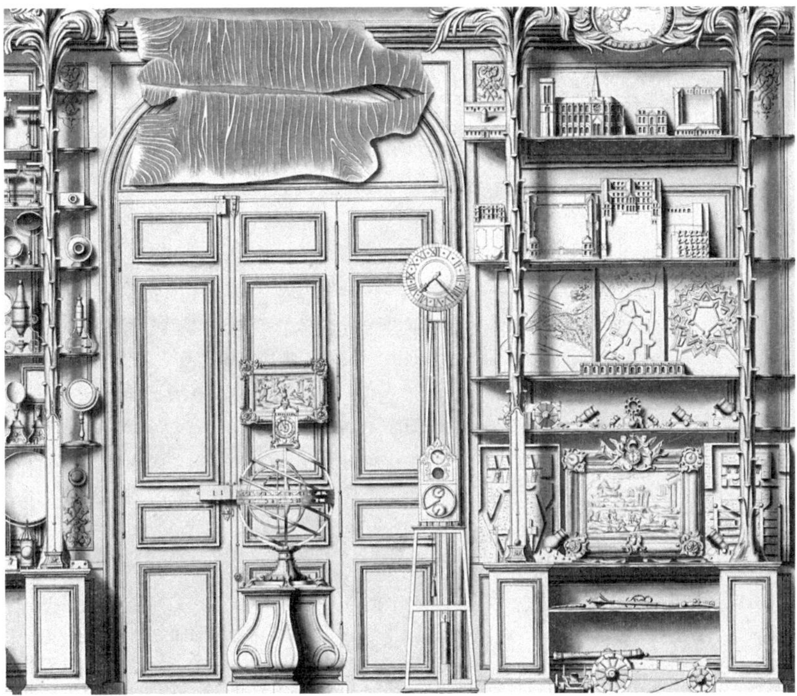

FIGURE 26 Jean Courtonne and Jean-Baptiste Courtonne, *Cabinet de Bonnier de la Mosson* (*The Physics and Mechanics Cabinet*), 1739–1740. Pen and ink on paper; 37 × 195 cm. Detail. Paris, Bibliothèque de l'Institut National d'Histoire de l'Art, Collections Jacques Doucet, OA 720 (1–8).

cabinet—an extraordinary object.[3] The ingenuity of this philosophical tool clearly filled him, and likely many others, with pure wonder—doing justice to the German term for such a cabinet as a wonder room, a *Wunderkammer*.

In *Theaetetus*, Plato lets Socrates say that the only beginning of philosophy is wonder. He uses *thaumazein*, meaning to marvel, to admire, or to venerate (the word is related to the verb *theaomai*, to look at, to gaze). One of the examples provoking wonder or *thaumazein* is a puppet show—the usual Greek word for puppet is *thauma*—in which the figures move and behave as though they were alive. Plato may be referring to the ritual automata used in religious practices, with which he was doubtless familiar.[4] Does our *tableau mécanique*, likewise consisting of moving figures, provoke a similar kind of *thaumazein* so as to begin a philosophical exploration? Plato's example of the puppet theater as a source of wonder continued to resonate in the history of philosophy, popping up in the writings first of Descartes, who wondered while staring out of his window whether his eye could tell the difference between actual passersby from dressed-up automata, and later of Freud, who found in the story of *The Sandman* a starting point for his theory of the *Unheimlich*.

In many ways, the amazement provoked by a puppet theater or automaton may not be quite the *thaumazein* that Socrates had in mind as the source of amazement that actually sets off a philosophical inquiry. Kant differentiated such amazement from the *Verwunderung* (marvel) that disappears when the sense of novelty diminishes. After all, once the operating mechanism behind an automaton or puppet theater—or Bonnier's clock-painting, for that matter—has been revealed, the object is bound to lose part of its magic. To indicate a more profound sense of wonder, leading to further inquiry, Kant uses the term *Bewunderung* (admiration). Insisting on an even more precise formulation as to what kind of amazement really initiates a process of thinking, Heidegger adds two more concepts: *Bestaunen*, amazement provoked by the awareness of something extraordinary occurring in our ordinary life, and *Er-staunen*—for him the most profound sense of wonder—when we are astonished at something most *ordinary* in our ordinary lives. This ultimately leads for Heidegger to the question I posed at the beginning of this book: "Why are there beings rather than nothing?" For Heidegger, this perplexity about the most basic elements of ordinary life is the actual *thaumazein* that serves as the drive behind philosophizing, and in essence, this may indeed be close to what Socrates had originally in mind.

Following Heidegger in this regard, I have presented pensive images as images that provoke wonder about the most ordinary of things. That is why realistic scenes from daily life, in particular in Dutch seventeenth-century art that raised the ordinary to the level of the monumental, have been the optimal sites to explore this Heideggerian version of *thaumazein*. The perplexity they evoke in us, as viewers, provokes a slow looking that transforms itself in thinking, or that moment of looking comes to see that thought itself has passed into visual form. And this is what pensive images do to us: raise questions about the existence of ordinary things that make us stop in our tracks. If asking this question is a "happening," as Heidegger suggests, it happened to us through the dangling ribbon of the satin jacket so carelessly thrown over a chair in Bisschop's *Interior*, in the little window at the end of the series of rooms past the sweeping maid in Emanuel de Witte's interior, in a dewdrop sliding off a waxy petal in one of Van Huysum's flower pieces, in the sparkle on a wine glass in Kalf's still lifes, and in the shining red counter in one of Estes's shop windows. These works served as stumbling blocks that, while arresting us in our tracks, gave us a sense of direction, an insight (as Benjamin would have it) that would take us inside the work, where our desire to see more has frequently been met by our staring into the abyss of infinity. Where are we located vis-à-vis the work of art? Is the work pushing us toward the depths of the unknown? "*Thaumazein* both opens our eyes wide and plunges us in the dark," writes John Llewelyn. "[I]t is both startled start and flinching in bewilderment."[5] Traditionally, for Aristotle and others, this sense of wonder has been generated by an *aporia*, an impasse, an irresolvable problem. Indeed, we as viewers and art historians know all too well how painting can pose an unsolvable paradox (*Las Meninas* or the *Arnolfini Portrait* are the most obvious examples) that continues to give us food for thought. Important as these works—and the debates they inspire—are, as I have demonstrated, pensive images confront us with an impasse as well as a way around it. As my discussions of various works have shown, pensive images are capable of "thinking through" opposites.

Even though our *tableau mécanique* is a philosophical instrument and, as such, is an incredibly clever object in the sense of Hunter and Lucchini's coinage, it may not retain our sense of wonder and thus would fall into Kant's category of *Verwunderung*. After all, when we turn it around to open its reverse to admire the secret of its clock mechanism, some of its initial wonder will weaken. As my analyses have indicated, pensive images cannot be opened up. They don't have secrets to be revealed or hidden meanings to be unveiled. Their doings *do something to us*: whether they hurt us (for Barthes), startle us (for Benjamin), or encounter us (for Deleuze), they enable some kind of breakthrough that sets off a train of thoughts by derailing our pattern of thinking. At the end of his book *The Honor of Thinking: Critique, Theory, Philosophy*, Rodolphe Gasché writes, "The wonder that causes thinking would thus be nothing less than an awareness of being overtaken by the resources of that in which one is caught."[6] Pensive images form a new category of immersive art. In contrast to trompe l'oeil, panorama, of other kinds of illusionism that overwhelm by enchantment and delight to lift us out of our ordinary experience, pensive images slowly overtake us, not to lift us out of the ordinary but to push us deeper into it, in order to guide us home.

Acknowledgments

This book's foundation is a seminar series entitled *The Pensive Image* that I ran from 2006 to 2008 at the Jan van Eyck Academy in Maastricht, the Netherlands, a postgraduate institute for research in the fine arts, design, and theory. The lively, stimulating, and thought-provoking research culture I found there shaped—or rather reshaped—my intellectual horizon forever. I am deeply grateful to the participants of the seminar for generously sharing their ideas with me, in particular Anthony Auerbach, Nikolaus Gansterer, Sönke Hallmann, Brenda Hofmeyer, Antony Hudek, Ils Huygens, Tom van Imschoot, Charlotte Mott, and Stephane Querrec, as well as my fellow advising researchers in the Theory Department, Katja Diefenbach and Dominiek Hoens. I also would like to thank then director Koen Brams, whose radical positioning I will always admire. I also want to warmly thank James Elkins for his involvement at the very start of this project and for his continuous support. I am grateful to Rineke Dijkstra for her presentation at the symposium launching the project.

The conceptualization of this book was brought to completion during my headship of the Ruskin School of Art at the University of Oxford from 2014 to 2016. The lively debates on artistic research within the school—of theory as practice, and practice as theory—gave a deeper dimension to my notion of art as a form of thinking. I am grateful to Malcolm Bull, Brian Catling, Justin Coombes, John Cussans, Daria Martin, Katrina Palmer, Corin Sworn, and Lynette Yiadom-Boakye for many inspiring conversations. In particular, I would like to thank Elizabeth Price, whose work and thought has sharpened my ideas in more ways than I can express. I also thank Anthony Gardner, with whom I organized the symposium *Art Out of Time* in 2014, which united academics, artists, and curators around the ongoing debate on the close links between early modern art and contemporary art practice. It is my hope that this book will inspire artists and thinkers as much as it has been inspired by them.

My year as an individual fellow at the Netherlands Institute for Advanced Study (NIAS) in Amsterdam was as inspiring as it was productive, and I want to thank the other fellows for many helpful suggestions during this last writing stage, in particular Karin Bijsterveld, Serena Ferente, Maartje Janse, Bert-Jaap Koops, Claartje Levelt, David Onnekink, Ulinka Rublack, Bert van der Berg, Niels van Doorn, and Olav Velthuis.

The Department of History of Art at the University of Oxford has been very supportive, and I thank my colleagues, especially Craig Clunas, Gervase Rosser, and Alastair Wright. St. Peter's College has been most accommodating in providing a great working environment—and I don't know what would have become of me without the friendship of Sondra Hauser, Abigail Williams, and Claire Williams. Many thanks also to Mieke Bal, Tim Barringer, Susanna Berger, Stijn Bussels, Jas Elsner, Briony Fer, Tamar Garb, Michael Ann Holly, Geert Janssen, Maria Loh, Lisa Milroy, Keith Moxey, Rose Marie San Juan, Paul Smith, Michael Squire, Ernst van Alphen, Caroline van Eck, and Thijs Weststeijn. I also wish to particularly thank Amy Powell, with whom I organized the 2017 CAA panel *Taking Stock: Early Modern Art Now*; Marisa Bass, Claudia Swann, and Anne Goldgar, who co-organized our 2018 RSA panel, *Conchophilia*; and my then graduate students, Lucy Whelan and Anita Paz, for co-organizing the 2015 AAH panel *Thinking Images*.

I am deeply grateful to the Leverhulme Trust and the Clark Art Institute, as well as to Oxford's History Faculty Research Committee and the O'Connor Fund at St. Peter's College, for generously providing financial support toward this project, and to the two anonymous readers at the University of Chicago Press for their wonderful and enormously helpful feedback.

Parts of chapter 4 have been published in different form in "The Pensive Image: On Thought in Jan van Huysum's Still Life Paintings," *Oxford Art Journal* 34, no. 1 (March 2011): 13–30, and in "Sublime Still Life: On Adriaen Coorte, Elias van den Broeck, and the *Je ne sais quoi* of Painting," in "The Sublime in the Seventeenth Century," edited by Stijn Bussels and Bram van Oostveldt, a special issue of the *Journal of the History of Netherlandish Art* 8, no. 2 (June 2016). A section of chapter 5 has appeared in different form in "Photorealism as Pictorial Reflection," in *The Art of Hegel's Aesthetics*, edited by Paul Kottman and Michael Squire (Munich: Wilhelm Fink Verlag, 2017). The *tableau mécanique* that opens my concluding chapter was the topic of my article "A Clock Picture as Philosophical Experiment: The *Tableau Mécanique* in the Physics Cabinet of Bonnier de la Mosson," *Art History* 39, no. 2 (April 2016): 340–55.

On the home front, I would like to warmly thank my parents and my siblings, Roel and Juul, and their families, for their ongoing support; as well as Viktor; Rosemarijn & Eric; Lucas; Pieternel; Natasha & Joachim; Hanneke; Susan; Michelle & Philip; Nicolien; and Thomas. Willy and Marjolein are deeply missed. Lastly, Yasco and Kees always tease me that images cannot think—this book won't change their minds, but I cannot but dedicate it to them anyway.

Notes

Art as a Form of Thinking

1. Balzac, *Louis Lambert*, 40.
2. Heidegger, *An Introduction to Metaphysics*, 29.
3. *Diderot on Art II*, 122.
4. Melion, "Introduction: Meditating on Pictures."
5. Falkenburg, "The Household of the Soul," 7.
6. For the nature and course of such trajectories in painting, see Falkenburg, "The Household of the Soul."
7. Aristotle, *De memoria et reminiscentia*, 449b 31. See for an English translation Aristotle, *On Memory*, ix–xiv and 2–8.
8. Van Hoogstraten, *Inleyding tot de hooge schoole der schilderkonst*, esp. chap. 2, and Weststeijn, "Excursus: Painting as a 'Sister of Philosophy,'" in *The Visible World*.
9. Proust, "Rembrandt," *Marcel Proust on Art and Literature*, 337.
10. "Je vous ai écrit que, pour votre respect, je servirais Monsieur de Lisle. Je lui ai trouvé la pensée, je vieux dire la conception de l'idée, et l'ouvrage de l'esprit est conclu. Ce subject est un Passage de la Mer Rouge par les Israélites fugitives. Le composé est de 27 figures principalement" (Du Colombier, *Lettres du Poussin*, 244).
11. Puttfarken, "Poussin's Thoughts on Invention and Disposition." According to Francis Junius, "Many who have a deeper insight in to these Arts, delight themselves as much in the contemplation of the first, second, and third draughts which great Masters made of their workes, as in the workes themselves [. . .] seeing [. . .] the very thoughts of the studious Artificer" (*The Painting of the Ancients*, quoted in Pace, "Nicolas Poussin," 84).
12. Van Gogh, *The Complete Letters*, 2:416.
13. See Shiff, *Cézanne and the End of Impressionism*, 175.
14. Gasquet, *Cézanne*, 152.
15. See Grootenboer, *Rhetoric of Perspective*, for more on Merleau-Ponty's use of art for his phenomenology of perception.
16. See Merjian, "Untimely Objects," 203.
17. Deleuze and Guattari, "Introduction: The Question Then . . . ," and "Percept, Affect, and Concept," in *What Is Philosophy?*, 1–14 and 163–200.

18. Adorno, *Aesthetic Theory*, 72.
19. Barthes, *Camera Lucida*, 38 (original emphasis and capitalization).
20. Rancière, "The Pensive Image," 120. This essay was first published in French in 2008, while my seminar at the Jan van Eyck with the same title started in January 2006. It is of no importance to determine who was first to have taken Barthes's notion as a title and I hold onto this title as an homage to both philosophers.
21. Rancière, "The Pensive Image," 55.
22. Richter, *Thought-Images*, 13.
23. See Grootenboer, *Rhetoric of Perspective*, for a detailed exploration of the implications of thought in painting for the history of art, in particular for seventeenth-century Dutch still life paintings.
24. Graw, Birnbaum, and Hirsch, ed., *Thinking through Painting*.
25. Nemerov, "The Boy in Bed."
26. Marin, *On Representation*, 174–96.
27. Annunciation paintings have provided wonderfully dense theoretical objects for both Marin and Didi-Huberman. It is no coincidence that Michael Baxandall developed his notion of "period eye" around Annunciations, while Daniel Arasse claimed that linear perspective unfolded within the theme of the Annunciation in *L'Annonciation italienne: une histoire the perspective*. For an exploration of Annunciation painting as theoretical objects, see Grootenboer, "Reading the Annunciation."
28. Recently the distinction separating theory, philosophy, and criticism has been well articulated by Rodolphe Gasché in *The Honor of Thinking*.
29. Westermann, *A Worldly Art*; Weststeijn, "Een Wereldse Kunst."
30. Wolf, *Vermeer and the Invention of Seeing*, 174; Snow, *A Study of Vermeer*.
31. Bernstein, "Wax, Brick, and Bread," 32.
32. Appadurai, *Globalization*, 10.
33. Ambrožič and Vettese, *Art as a Thinking Process*, 50, 75.
34. Deleuze and Guattari, *What Is Philosophy?*, 6.
35. Laruelle, *Photo-Fiction*; *The Concept of Non-Photography*.
36. Martin, "Bubbles and Skulls," 559.

Chapter One

1. Barthes, *Camera Lucida*, 55.
2. For a recent discussion of Barthes's *punctum* and *studium*, see Fried, "Barthes' *Punctum*"; James Elkins's response, "What Do We Want Photography to Be?"; and Diarmuid Costello's response to both, "On the Very Idea of the 'Specific' Medium."
3. Barthes, *S/Z*, 38.
4. Schor, "Pensive Texts and Thinking Statues."
5. Nancy, *The Muses*, 63.
6. Rancière, "The Pensive Image."

7. Ibid., 123.
8. Elsaesser, "Stop/Motion."
9. Bellour, "The Pensive Spectator."
10. Ibid.
11. Stewart, "Photogravure." See also his *Framed Time.*
12. Mulvey, *Death 24x a Second*, 195.
13. Quoted in Mulvey, *Death 24x a Second*, 181.
14. Dubois, "Photography Mise-en-Film."
15. See Elsaesser, "Stop/Motion," 116.
16. Ibid., 122 (emphasis added).
17. Bazin, "The Ontology of the Photographic Image," 8.
18. Ibid., 6.
19. See Friday, "Stillness Becoming," 45.
20. Notable exceptions includes Røssaak's *The Still/Moving Image*, and Victor Burgin's essays on film, in particular, "Possessive, Pensive and Possessed," in *Stillness and Time*, 165–78.
21. Beate Allert makes this point in "Goethe and the Visual Arts."
22. Peter Wollen makes a brilliant point about how Goethe intends to "cinematize" the sculpture group in "Time, Image and Terror."
23. Goethe, "Observations on the Laocoon," 8. For this essay, translator John Gage reprints an anonymous translation published in the *Monthly Magazine*, vol. vii, 1799, 349–52 and 399–401, retaining original spelling and punctuation.
24. Goethe, "Observations on the Laocoon," 81.
25. Ibid.
26. See also Hegel, quoted in Richter, *Laocoon's Body and the Aesthetics of Pain*, 177.
27. What I suggest here is different from Michael Fried's important distinction between absorption and theatricality, which delineates a perceptual dynamic that remains within the realm of the optical. Obviously, pensive images are absorptive, but in contrast to Fried, the trajectory they set out for their viewers is speculative. Rather than for the beholder to become absorbed in the image, the pensive image absorbs the beholder, in the sense of taking over the routine pathways of the mind and offering a different way of thinking (Fried, *Absorption and Theatricality*).
28. Goethe, "Observations on the Laocoon," 80.
29. Ibid., 81.
30. Quoted in Gombrich, "Moment and Movement in Art," 42.
31. Ibid.
32. Ibid.
33. "so ist es gewiss, dass jener einzige Augenblick und einzige Gesichtspunt deses einzigen Augenblickes, night fruchtbar genog gewahlet werden kann. Dasjenige aber nur allein is fruchtbar, was der Einbildungskraft freies spiel lasst. Je mehr wir sehen, desto mehr müssen wir hinzu denken können. Je mehr wir darzu denken, desto mehr müssen wir zusehen glauben" (Lessing, *Laocoön*, 19).
34. "'t Is niet genoeg, dat een beelt schoon is, maert daer moet een zeekere

beweeglijkheyt in zijn, die macht over d'aenschouwers heeft. . . . [Schilders] beroeren 't gemoed niet, zoo ze deeze beweeglijkheyt overslaen" (Van Hoogstraten, *Inleyding tot the hooge schoole der schilderkonst*, 292–93; English translation from Weststeijn, *The Visible World*, 185).

35. Wellbery, *Lessing's Laocoon*, 120.
36. Barthes, *Camera Lucida*, 57 (original emphasis).
37. Wellbery, *Lessing's Laocoon*, 119.
38. It-narratives or object-narratives are stories written from the point of view of an object, for example, a coin or shoe. Such stories were in vogue toward the end of the eighteenth century, particularly in England (Blackwell, *The Secret Life of Things*).
39. Claudel, "Introduction to Dutch Painting," 47–48.
40. Diderot, "From 'Disconnected Thoughts on Painting, Sculpture and Poetry,'" 669.
41. Jean-Luc Nancy has written extensively on the restlessness of thought in *Hegel: The Restlessness of the Negative*.
42. For more on the pensive images of Jacob Vrel, see my article "Arresting What Would Otherwise Slip Away."

Chapter Two

1. See Potts, *Flesh and the Ideal*, 1.
2. "Ruhe allein ist Trägheit, und eine Art [von Nichts] Tod," quoted in Richter, *Laocoon's Body and the Aesthetics of Pain*, 46. I have slightly amended Richter's English translation.
3. Richter, *Laocoon's Body*, 46.
4. Winckelmann, *History of the Art of Antiquity*, 313.
5. Quoted in Potts, "Introduction," 30.
6. Quoted in Potts, *Flesh and the Ideal*, 20.
7. Winckelmann, "Description of the Torso in the Belvedere in Rome," xiii.
8. Ibid., xiv.
9. Alex Potts, *Flesh and the Ideal*, 179.
10. Winckelmann, *History of the Art of Antiquity*, 204.
11. Winckelmann, "Description of the Torso in the Belvedere in Rome," xv.
12. Ibid., xvi.
13. Ibid.
14. Ibid., xiv.
15. Ibid., xvi.
16. Quoted in Potts, *Flesh and the Ideal*, 97.
17. Quoted in Wellbery, *Lessing's Laocoon*, 99.
18. Herder, "Critical Forests," 54. See, on Herder's critique of Lessing, Norton, "Towards an Ontology of the Arts."
19. Adler, "Herder's Style," 333.
20. Ibid., 344.

21. Ibid., 346.
22. Trabant, "Herder and Language," 121.
23. Müller-Michaels, "Herder: Denkbilder der Kulturen," 67.
24. Herder, "Nemesis."
25. Quoted in Stimilli, "Daimon and Nemesis," 102.
26. Adler, "Herder's Concept of *Humanität*," 112–13.
27. "In Bildern konnte gesagt werden, was sich durch mutternackte Abstraktion nimmer oder äusserst matt und elend sagen lässt" (Herder, *Sämmtliche Werke*, 360–61).
28. "Nemesis und die Hoffnunung verehr'ich auf Einem Altare" (quoted in Stimilli, "Daimon and Nemesis," 104).
29. Herder, "Nemesis," 575.
30. Quoted in Weststeijn, "From Hieroglyphs to Universal Characters," 257. Weststeijn's essay is an exquisite exposé of the interest in hieroglyphs and pictograph in the Netherlands in the seventeenth century.
31. Comenius, *The Way of Light of Comenius*, 186. See also Weststeijn, "From Hieroglyphs to Universal Characters," 265.
32. Cooper, earl of Shaftesbury, *Second Characters of the Language of Forms*, 91.
33. Vico, *The New Science of Giambattista Vico*, 139.
34. I have discussed Diderot's notion of the hieroglyph at length in my *Rhetoric of Perspective* (see esp. chap. 1).
35. Julie Chandler Hayes explains this in detail in her chapter on Diderot in *Reading the French Enlightenment*, 155ff. See also Connelly, "Poetic Monsters and Nature Hieroglyphics."
36. Weststeijn, "From Hieroglyphs to Universal Characters," 239; Van Hoogstraten, *Inleyding tot de hooge schoole der schilderkonst*, 90. See also Spaans, "Art, Science and Religion in Romeyn de Hooghe's *Hieroglyphica*."
37. Weststeijn, "From Hieroglyphs to Universal Characters," 252.
38. Eberhard Wilhelm Schutz, "Zum Wort 'Denkbild,'" 229nn35–36.
39. I have based this section on the studies by Gaier, "Metadisziplinäre Argumente und Verfahren Herders"; and Müller-Michaels, "Herder: Denkbilder der Kulturen."
40. Nisbet, *Herder and the Philosophy of Science*, 50.
41. Philipp Otto Runge's famous *Morning* of 1808 is a clear case in point. See also Stefan Greif, "'Wer kann Farben tönen?'"
42. "Das Denkbild war gleichsam die ganze Charakteristische, Historische, Philosophische under Poetische Sprache der Schöpfung" (Herder, "Aelteste Urkunde," 302–3).
43. Müller-Michaels, "Herder: Denkbilder der Kulturen," 68.
44. Herder, *Selected Writings on Aesthetics*, 358–59 (original emphasis).
45. "Thinking involves not only the flow of thoughts, but their arrest as well" (Benjamin, *Theses on the Philosophy of History*, 262).
46. Adorno, "Benjamin's *Einbahnstrasse*," 680.

47. Benjamin, *"One-Way Street" and Other Writings*, 61.
48. Richter, *Thought-Images*, 47.
49. Nijland-Verwey, "Denkbeeld-Denkbild."
50. Verwey, "Oorsprongen" (my translation), 115.
51. Winckelmann, "Geschichte der Kunst des Altertums," 45.
52. Goeree, *Inleyding tot de praktyk der algemeene schilderkonst. . .*, 34.
53. "Maar alsoo wy hier vooren niet sonder reden gezeid hebben, dat het vermogen der Schilderkonst algemeen is, om alles, behalven levende Zielen, in de Beelden voort te brengen, hebben sommige evenwel in twijffel getrokken, of men ook wel levenloose dingen, die in haar beweging zijn, kan uytbeelden? 't Geen wy (schoon by weynige in agt genomen,) hier rond uyt van Ja willen staande houden; want niemand sal konnen tegenspreken, dat de Konst de natuure in allen navolgt, voornametlijk in het gene welke in een verblijf van tijd, met na-denken kan gezien worden" (Goeree, *Inleyding*, 34).
54. Bal, *Travelling Concepts in the Humanities.*

Chapter Three

1. Already in the sixteenth century, Dutch art theorist Karel van Mander had used the Dutch word *ploegen* (to plow) to describe how the viewer's eye penetrates a landscape painting, a process he called *insien* (looking in) or *doorsien* (looking through). See also Martha Hollander's excellent *An Entrance for the Eyes*, 8, 46.
2. See for a detailed discussion of Diderot's "walk," see Grootenboer, *The Rhetoric of Perspective.*
3. *Diderot on Art II*, 122.
4. Montaigne, *Selected Essays*, 44.
5. I draw here on Susan Bernstein's brilliant *Housing Problems.*
6. Descartes, "Discourse on the Method," 116.
7. Rodis-Lewis, "Descartes' Life and the Development of His Philosophy," 31. For this section on Descartes, I draw on Melehy, *Writing Cogito*, in particular chapter 5, "The Method: The Writing of the Subject," and on Lyons, *Before Imagination.*
8. Rodis-Lewis, "Descartes' Life," 31.
9. Descartes, master of rhetoric, leaves us in no doubt about the significance of this first thought as he announces it: "Among the first that occurred to me was the thought that there is not usually so much perfection in works composed of several parts and produced by various different craftsmen as in the works of one man" ("Discourse on the Method," 116).
10. Descartes, "Discourse on the Method," 118.
11. Ibid., 112.
12. Ibid., 126.
13. Aristotle, *Poetics*, 1457 b7. Metaphors, he says, bring about learning (*Rhet.* III.10, 1410b14f.)

14. "Il est, pour aisie dire, dans une demeure empruntée. . . ." (Dumarsais, *Traités des Tropes*, 119).
15. The argument about the house metaphor preceding metaphor is made by Mark Wigley in "The Domestication of the House," 102.
16. Wigley, "The Domestication of the House," 97.
17. For an extensive discussion of relevance of this location for Heidegger's thinking, see Adam Sharr, *Heidegger's Hut*.
18. Heidegger explains this in *Being and Time*, in particular in chapters 5, "Being-in as Such," and 6, "Care as the Being of Da-Sein." See also Critchley and Schürmann, *On Heidegger's Being and Time*; and King, *A Guide to Heidegger's Being and Time*.
19. Heidegger, "Building Dwelling Thinking," 149.
20. Ibid., 157.
21. Ibid., 157.
22. Ibid., 156.
23. Heidegger, *Being and Time*, 179.
24. Heidegger, *What Is Called Thinking*, 28.
25. Heidegger, *What Is Called Thinking*, 9.
26. Heidegger, *Basic Writings*, 382.
27. Bernstein, *Housing Problems*, 18.
28. Heidegger, *What Is Called Thinking*, 45.
29. Ibid., 16. Heidegger claims the same in "The Origin of the Work of Art," in *Poetry, Language, Thought*, 18.
30. Husserl, "Psychological Studies in the Elements of Logic."
31. Though little studied in twentieth-century art history, the dollhouse has increasingly enjoyed the attention of scholars in recent years because of the rise of material-culture studies. My discussion here draws mainly on Broomhall and Spinks, "Imagining Domesticity in Early Modern Dutch Dolls' Houses"; and Pijzel-Dommisse's excellent *Het Hollandse Pronkpoppenhuis*.
32. Pijzel-Dommisse, *Het Hollandse Pronkpoppenhuis*, 284.
33. The account of Zacharias von Uffenbach, in sections per room, has been included in Pijzel-Dommisse, *Het Hollandse Pronkpoppenhuis*, 247ff.
34. Ibid., 258.
35. Sir William Temple and Peter Mundy are among the best-known instances of seventeenth-century foreign travelers who wrote accounts of domestic arrangements they witnessed on their visits to Holland. See Temple, *The Work of William Temple, bart*, esp. 1:39. Mundy remarked, "All in generall striving to adorne their houses, especially the outer or street roome, with costly peeces . . . wonderful Nett and cleane" (*The Travels of Peter Mundy in Europe and Asia, 1608–1667*, 70–71). See also Hollander, *An Entrance for the Eyes*; Franits, *Paragons of Virtue*; and Fock, "Semblance or Reality?"
36. This argument has been made by Bernstein, "Wax, Brick, and Bread."
37. Luyken, *Het leerzaam huisraad in vijftig figuuren*.

38. Adams, *Public Faces and Private Identities in Seventeenth-Century Holland*; Woodall, "Sovereign Bodies." See also my "How to Become a Picture."
39. Hollander, *An Entrance for the Eyes*; Fock, "Semblance or Reality?"
40. Alexander and Strauss, *The German Single-Leaf Woodcut 1600–1700*, 305–6 (English translation from Broomhall and Spinks, "Imagining Domesticity," 107).
41. To consider a dollhouse like Oortman's as an egodocument has been put forth by Broomhall and Spinks in "Imagining Domesticity," 122.
42. Stewart, *On Longing*; Bachelard, *The Poetics of Space*. On miniaturization and intimacy, see also Grootenboer, *Treasuring the Gaze*.
43. Heidegger, *Poetry, Language, Thought*, 17.
44. "Alles zeer kleyn en egt" (Pijzel-Dommisse, *Het Hollandse Pronkpoppenhuis*, 329).
45. Ibid.
46. Bryson, *Looking at the Overlooked*, 105–6.
47. See Grootenboer, "How to Become a Picture," 329–30.
48. Berman, *In Another Light*, 235. See also Rosenblum, "Vilhelm Hammershøi, at Home and Abroad."
49. Heidegger, "Art and Space," 44.
50. Ibid., 45.

Chapter Four

1. "O bloosend Fruitgewas, met zil'vren daeu beladen! Nachtdruppen die de blonde Apollo zomers zweet!" (Van Gool, *De Nieuwe Schouburg der Nederlandsche Kunstschilders en Schilderessen*, 26).
2. Philostratus the Elder, *Imagines*, 89. See also Segal et al., *De Verleiding van Flora*, 95.
3. De Man, *Allegories of Reading*, 289.
4. See, e.g., *Still Life with Apricots, Cherries and a Chestnut* (1685), *Still Life with Berries, Medlars, and Grapes* (1686), or *Still Life with Hanging Bunch of Grapes, Two Medlars, and a Butterfly* (1687).
5. Dibbets, "Aardbeien, abrikozen, kruisbessen en perziken: vier stillevens van Adriaen Coorte." See also Buvelot, "The Still Lifes of Adriaen Coorte."
6. This refers to the title of Schama's brilliant book on Dutch visual culture of the seventeenth century, *The Embarrassment of Riches* (1988).
7. De Lairesse, *Groot Schilderboek*, 268.
8. Bredius, "De Gildeboeken van St. Lucas te Middelburg," 6:229.
9. Harrison, Wood, and Gaiger, *Art in Theory 1648–1815*.
10. Damisch, "Egale infini." For an in-depth discussion of Damisch's ideas, see Bois, "Painting as Model," repr. in Bois, *Painting as Model*. See also his "Tough Love."
11. Klee, *The Thinking Eye*, 3. For more on Hegel's *aufheben*, see chapter 5.
12. Ibid., 112.

13. Ibid., 69.
14. Ibid.
15. Alberti, *On Painting*, 43; quoted in Damisch, *Origin*, 65. See also "Hubert Damisch and Stephen Bann: A Conversation," 177.
16. Damisch, *Origin*, 285.
17. Damisch, "Equals Infinity," 65.
18. Ibid., 67.
19. Deleuze and Guattari, *What Is Philosophy?*, 197; "no one needs philosophy," 6.
20. Ibid., 169.
21. De Bolla, "The Blush of the World."
22. I have elaborated on the significance of perspective's invisible structure in my *The Rhetoric of Perspective Realism and Illusionism in Seventeenth-Century Dutch Still Life Painting.*
23. Deleuze and Guattari, *What Is Philosophy?*, 194.
24. Kolfin, *Voor koningen en prinsen*, 74–75. See also Van Huysum's *A Basket with Flowers* (c. 1732–1733), Museum Boijmans Van Beuningen, Rotterdam (*De Verleiding van Flora*, cat. no. F26).
25. *The Diary of Samuel Pepys*, vol. 9, April 11 and 12, 1669.
26. Leonardo da Vinci, *Codex Leicester*, Folio 62: "A drop of dew with its perfect curvature affords us an opportunity to consider how the water sphere contains within itself the body of the earth without destruction of its sphericity of surface. If you take a cube of lead the size of a grain of millet, and by means of a very fine thread attached to it you submerge it in this drip, you will perceive that the drop will not lose any of its original roundness, although it has been increased by an amount equal to the size of a cube which has been sit within it."
27. Philostratus, "Narcissus," 89. On Philostratus's Narcissus, see also Stephen Bann, "Philostratus and the *Narcissus* of Caravaggio."
28. See *De Verleiding van Flora*, cat. no. 27 and 28. The bee mentioned in Philostratus's *Imagines* inspired the motif of the trompe l'oeil fly in early modern painting, mentioned by Vasari in the Life of Giotto, among other places. Interestingly, Van Huysum seems to rely on the original written source rather than the pictorial motif it has grown into by placing a bee rather than a fly on the tulip's petal.
29. I follow here Damisch's idea of truth in painting, as he most clearly formulated in "Eight Theses For (or Against?) A Semiology of Painting." This idea has been explored in a different way by Jacques Derrida in *The Truth in Painting.*
30. In John Raphael Smith's mezzotints after Jan van Huysum's still lifes (which were well known in eighteenth-century Britain) it is even more apparent how Van Huysum's dewdrops do not seem to have any outlines and are genuinely translucent. Smith engraves Van Huysum's flower pieces "to the letter" and has an eye for every small detail. He faithfully copies each of the far too numerous dewdrops, yet cannot possibly capture the level of their transparency (New Haven, Yale Center of British Art, B 1977.14.14217–8).

31. Damisch, "Underneaths of Painting," 205.
32. Segal and Dik, *De Verleiding van Flora*, ch. 6; Kolfin, *Voor koningen en prinsen*, 74–75.
33. Deleuze and Guattari, *What Is Philosophy?*, 195.

Chapter Five

1. Wiedmann, *Hegel*, trans. Joachim Neugroschel, 1968, 8; quoted in Michelson, "De Stijl, Its Other Face," 5.
2. *Hegel's Aesthetics*, 2:801–2. For an extensive discussion of "shine" and art, see Sallis, "Carnation and the Eccentricity of Painting." See also Angela Vanhaelen's excellent discussion of shine in Hegel and Barthes in relation to seventeenth-century Dutch painting in "Boredom's Threshold: Dutch Realism."
3. *Hegel's Aesthetics*, 2:599.
4. Ibid., 1:36.
5. Quoted in Norman Bryson, *Looking at the Overlooked*, 124–25.
6. *Hegel's Aesthetics*, 2:812.
7. Ibid.
8. Ibid., 1:797 (emphasis added).
9. Ibid., 1:600 (original emphasis).
10. Ibid., 1:38 (original emphasis).
11. Ibid., 1:599–600.
12. Only after I completed this chapter did I discover Aron Vinegar's exciting essay "Reluzenz: On Richard Estes," in which he links Estes's work, in particular his reflections, to Heideggerian thought.
13. See Wilmerding, *Richard Estes*, esp. chap. 3, "Artistic Precedents and Correlations." On Estes's use of photography in the creation of his realism, see Sims, "Richard Estes' Realism."
14. Sims, "Richard Estes' Realism," 11 (quote taken from the artist's statement in the exhibition catalog *Richard Estes—Recent Paintings*).
15. Wagner, *Philosophie und Reflexion*, i; Gasché, *The Tain of the Mirror*, 13–14.
16. Weinberg, "Introduction: Make it Real."
17. *Documenta 5: Befragung der Realität Bildwelten heute*, 15-1–15-3.
18. Lebensztejn and Cooper, "Photorealism, Kitsch and Venturi," 80.
19. Quoted in Weinberg, "Photographic Guilt," 51.
20. Flusser, *Towards a Philosophy of Photography*, 64.
21. Lynes and Weinberg, *Shared Intelligence*.
22. For a discussion of models of substitutability, see Wood, *Forgery Replica Fiction*, chap. 1.
23. Foster, *The Return of the Real*, 142ff.
24. Nancy, "The Image—the Distinct."
25. Descartes, *Discourse on Method and the Meditations*, 84–85.
26. Locke, *An Essay Concerning Human Understanding*, 105.

27. Ibid., 363 (original emphasis).
28. Ibid., 43.
29. Kant, *Critique of Pure Reason*, 267; quoted in Gasché, *The Tain of the Mirror*, 18.
30. Hegel, *The Science of Logic*, 344.
31. Hegel, "Aphorism from the Wastebook," 4.
32. Hyppolite, *Logic and Existence*, quoted in Gasché, *The Tain of the Mirror*, 34.
33. *The Hegel Reader*, 87.
34. Gadamer, quoted in Gasché, *The Tain of the Mirror*, 43.
35. Gasché, *The Tain of the Mirror*, 44.
36. Hegel, *Phenomenology of Spirit*, 119.
37. Ibid., 105 (original emphasis).
38. Ibid., 105. For a highly accessible explanation of Hegel's notion of self-consciousness, see Pippin, *Hegel and Self-Consciousness*.
39. Hegel, *Phenomenology of Spirit*, 111.
40. Gasché, *The Honor of Thinking*, 63.
41. Hegel, *The Science of Logic*, 344.
42. Ibid. (original emphasis).
43. For more on optic contradictions and a merging of media, see Stewart, *Transmedium*.
44. Quoted in Stoichita, *A Short History of the Shadow*, 24.
45. Ibid., 25.
46. For the history of the term *chiaroscuro*, see Verbraeken, *Clair-Obscur*.
47. Hegel, *Science of Logic*, 92–93.
48. Nancy, *The Speculative Remark*, 38.

Painting's Wonder

1. For an in-depth discussion of this item, see Grootenboer, "A Clock Picture as a Philosophical Experiment."
2. For a more detailed description of the workings of the clock mechanism, see Michel, "Le Cabinet de Bonnier de la Mosson et la participation de Lajoue," 211–21. Marcia Pointon briefly discusses this work in her unprecedented *Brilliant Effects*.
3. Gersaint, *Catalogue raisonné d'une collection considerable de deverses curiosités en tous genres*. For a detailed discussion of Bonnier's cabinet, see also Hill, "The Cabinet of Bonnier de la Mosson (1702–1744)."
4. Shershow, *Puppets and Popular Culture*, 17.
5. Llewelyn, "On the Saying That Philosophy Begins in *Thaumazein*."
6. Gasché, *The Honor of Thinking*, 362.

Bibliography

Adams, Ann Jensen. *Public Faces and Private Identities in Seventeenth-Century Holland: Portraiture and the Production of Community*. Cambridge: Cambridge University Press, 2009.

Adler, Hans. "Herder's Concept of *Humanität*." In Adler and Koepke, *A Companion to the Works of Johann Gottfried Herder*, 93–116.

———. "Herder's Style." In Adler and Koepke, *A Companion to the Works of Johann Gottfried Herder*, 331–50.

Adler, Hans, and Wulf Koepke, eds. *A Companion to the Works of Johann Gottfried Herder*. Rochester, SC: Camden House, 2009.

Adorno, Theodor W. *Aesthetic Theory*. Translated by Robert Hullot-Kentor. Minneapolis: University of Minnesota Press, 1997.

———. "Benjamin's *Einbahnstrasse*." In *Notes to Literature*, vol. 2, translated by Shierry Weber Nicholson, 322–27. New York: Columbia University Press, 1992.

Alberti, Leone Battista. *On Painting*. Translated by John R. Spencer. New Haven, CT: Yale University Press, 1971.

Alexander, Dorothy, and Walter L. Strauss. *The German Single-Leaf Woodcut 1600–1700*. 2 vols. New York: Abaris Books, 1977.

Allert, Beate. "Goethe and the Visual Arts." In *The Cambridge Companion to Goethe*, edited by Lesley Sharpe, 193–206. Cambridge: Cambridge University Press, 2002.

Alpers, Svetlana. *The Art of Describing: Dutch Art in the Seventeenth Century*. Chicago: University of Chicago Press, 1983.

Alpers, Svetlana, and Michael Baxandall. *Tiepolo and the Pictorial Intelligence*. New Haven, CT: Yale University Press, 1994.

Ambrožič, Mara, and Angela Vettese, eds. *Art as a Thinking Process: Visual Forms of Knowledge Production*. Berlin: Sternberg Press, 2013.

Appadurai, Arjun. *Globalization*. Durham, NC: Duke University Press, 2001.

Arasse, Daniel. *L'Annonciation italienne: une histoire the perspective*. Paris: Hazan, 1999.

———. *Take a Closer Look*. Princeton, NJ: Princeton University Press, 2013.

Aristotle. *On Memory*. Trans. with interpretative essays and commentary by R. Sorabji. Providence, RI: Brown University Press, 1972.

Bachelard, Gaston. *The Poetics of Space: The Classic Look at How We Experience Intimate Places*. London: Beacon Press, 1992. Orig.: Pr. Univ. de France, 1958.

Bal, Mieke. *Quoting Caravaggio: Contemporary Art, Preposterous History*. Chicago: University of Chicago Press, 1999.

———. *Reading Rembrandt: Beyond the Word-Image Opposition*. Cambridge: Cambridge University Press, 1991.

———. *Travelling Concepts in the Humanities: A Rough Guide*. Toronto: University of Toronto Press, 2002.

Balzac, Honoré de. *Louis Lambert*. Paris: Charpentier, 1842.

Bann, Stephen. "Philostratus and the Narcissus of Caravaggio." In *Philostratus*, edited by Ewen Bowie and Jas Elsner, 343–55. Cambridge: Cambridge University Press, 2009.

Barthes, Roland. *Camera Lucida*. New York: Hill and Wang, 1981.

———. *S/Z*. New York: Farrar, Strauss and Giroux, 1975.

Baudrillard, Jean. "The Trompe-l'Oeil." In *Calligram: Essays in New Art History from France*, edited by Norman Bryson, 53–62. Cambridge: Cambridge University Press, 1988.

Bazin, André. "The Ontology of the Photographic Image." *Film Quarterly* 13, no. 4 (Summer 1960): 4–9.

Bellour, Raymond. "The Pensive Spectator." In *Between-the-Images*, translated by Allyn Hardyck, 86–97. Zurich and Dijon: JRP/Ringier and Les press du réel, 2012.

Benjamin, Walter. *"One-Way Street" and Other Writings*. Translated by Edmund Jephcott and Kingsley Shorter. London: NLB/Verso, 1979.

———. *Theses on the Philosophy of History*, no. XVII. In *Illuminations: Essays and Reflections*, edited by Hannah Arendt, translated by Harry Zohn, 253–64. New York: Schocken Books, 1968.

Berger, Susanna. *The Art of Philosophy: Visual Thinking in Europe from the Late Renaissance to the Early Enlightenment*. Princeton, NJ: Princeton University Press, 2017.

Berman, Patricia G. *In Another Light: Danish Painting in the Nineteenth Century*. London: Thames & Hudson, 2007.

Bernstein, Jay. "Wax, Brick, and Bread: Apotheoses of Matter and Meaning in Seventeenth-Century Philosophy and Painting." In *Art and Thought*, edited by Dana Arnold and Margaret Iverson, 28–51. Oxford: Blackwell, 2003.

Bernstein, Susan. *Housing Problems: Writing and Architecture in Goethe, Walpole, Freud and Heidegger*. Stanford, CA: Stanford University Press, 2008.

Blackwell, Mark, ed. *The Secret Life of Things: Animals, Objects, and It-Narratives in Eighteenth-Century England*. Lewisburg, PA: Bucknell University Press, 2007.

Bois, Yve-Alain. *Painting as Model*. Cambridge, MA: MIT Press, 1990.

———. "Painting as Model," review of Hubert Damisch, *Fenêtre jaune cadmium, ou, les dessous de la peinture*. *October* 37 (Summer 1986): 125–37.

———. "Tough Love." *Oxford Art Journal* 28, no. 2 (2005): 245–55.

Bolla, Peter de. "The Blush of the World: Bonnard's Nude and the Disembodied Look." Public lecture, Department of History of Art, University of Oxford, 2012.

———. *The Education of the Eye: Painting, Landscape, and Architecture in Eighteenth-Century Britain.* Stanford, CA: Stanford University Press, 2003.

Bredius, Abraham. "De Gildeboeken van St. Lucas te Middelburg." In *Archief voor Nederlandsche kunstgeschiedenis,* by Fr. D. O. Obreen, 6:229. Rotterdam, 1884–1887.

Broomhall, Susan, and Jennifer Spinks. "Imagining Domesticity in Early Modern Dutch Dolls' Houses." In *Early Modern Women in the Low Countries: Feminizing Sources and Interpretations of the Past,* 99–122. Farnham, UK: Ashgate, 2011.

Bryson, Norman. *Looking at the Overlooked: Four Essays on Still Life Painting.* London: Reaktion Books, 1990.

Burgin, Victor. "Possessive, Pensive and Possessed." In *Stillness and Time: Photography and the Moving Image,* edited by David Green and Joanna Lowry, 165–78. Brighton: Photoworks, 2005.

Burke, Edmund. *A Philosophical Inquiry into the Origin of Our Ideas of the Sublime and the Beautiful* (1757). In Harrison, Wood, and Gaiger, *Art in Theory 1648–1815,* 516–26.

Buvelot, Quentin. *The Still Lifes of Adriaen Coorte: With Oeuvre Catalogue.* Zwolle: Waanders, 2008. Exhibition catalog.

Carruthers, Mary. *The Craft of Thought: Meditation, Rhetoric, and the Making of Images, 400–1200.* Cambridge: Cambridge University Press, 1998.

Clark, T. J. *The Sight of Death: Experiments in Art Writing.* New Haven, CT: Yale University Press, 2006.

Claudel, Paul. "Introduction to Dutch Painting." In *The Eye Listens,* 1–52. New York: Philosophical Library, 1950.

Comenius, J. A. *The Way of Light of Comenius.* Translated by E. T. Campagnac. Liverpool: University Press; London: Hodder and Stoughton, 1938.

Connelly, Frances S. "Poetic Monsters and Nature Hieroglyphics: The Precocious Primitivism of Philipp Otto Runge." *Art Journal* 52, no. 2 (Summer 1993): 31–39.

Cooper, Anthony Ashley, Earl of Shaftesbury. *Second Characters of the Language of Forms.* Edited by Benjamin Rand. Cambridge: Cambridge University Press, 1914.

Costello, Diarmuid. "On the Very Idea of the 'Specific' Medium: Michael Fried and Stanley Cavell on Painting and Photography as Arts." *Critical Inquiry* 34 (Winter 2008): 274–312.

Critchley, Simon, and Reiner Schürmann. *On Heidegger's Being and Time.* London: Routledge, 2008.

Damisch, Hubert. "Egale infini." In "Histoire/théorie de l'art." Special issue, *Critique* 315–16 (August–September 1973): 691–723.

———. "Eight Theses For (or Against?) A Semiology of Painting." *Oxford Art Journal* 28, no. 2 (2005): 257–67.

———. "Equals Infiniti." Translated by R. H. Olorenshaw. In "Visual Poetics." Special issue, *XXth Century Studies* 15–16 (1973): 56–81.

———. *The Origin of Perspective*. Translated by J. Goodman. Cambridge, MA: MIT Press, 1994.

———. "The Underneaths of Painting." *Word and Image* 1, no. 2 (1985): 197–209.

Damisch, Hubert, and Stephen Bann. "Hubert Damisch and Stephen Bann: A Conversation." *Oxford Art Journal* 28, no. 2 (2005): 157–81.

Deleuze, Gilles. "The Image of Thought." In *Difference and Repetition*, 229–62. New York: Columbia University Press, 1994.

Deleuze, Gilles, and Félix Guattari. *A Thousand Plateaus: Capitalism and Schizophrenia*. Translated by Brian Massumi. Minneapolis: University of Minnesota Press, 1987.

———. *What Is Philosophy?* London: Verso, 1994.

De Man, Paul. *Allegories of Reading: Figural Language in Rousseau, Nietzsche, Rilke and Proust*. New Haven, CT: Yale University Press, 1982.

Derrida, Jacques. *Memoirs of the Blind: The Self-Portrait and Other Ruins*. Chicago: University of Chicago Press, 1993.

———. *The Truth in Painting*. Chicago: University of Chicago Press, 1987.

Descartes, René. *Discourse on Method and the Meditations*. New York: Prometheus Books, 1989.

———. "Discourse on the Method." In *The Philosophical Writings of Descartes*. Vol. 1, translated by John Cottingham, Robert Stoothoff, and Dugald Murdoch, 20–56. Cambridge: Cambridge University Press, 1990.

Dibbets, Taco. "Aardbeien, abrikozen, kruisbessen en perziken: vier stillevens van Adriaen Coorte." *Bulletin van het Rijksmuseum* 52, no. 2 (2004): 52–65.

Diderot, Denis. *Diderot on Art II: The Salon of 1767*. Edited and translated by John Goodman. New Haven, CT: Yale University Press, 1995.

———. "From 'Disconnected Thoughts on Painting, Sculpture and Poetry.'" In Harrison, Wood, and Gaiger, *Art in Theory 1648–1815*, 668–73.

Documenta 5: Befragung der Realität Bildwelten heute. Edited by H. Szeemann, Marlis Grüterich, Katio von den Velden, and Jennifer Gough-Cooper. Kassel, June 30–October 8, 1972. Exhibition catalog.

Draaisma, Douwe. *Metaphors of Memory: A History of Ideas about the Mind*. Cambridge: Cambridge University Press, 2000.

Dubois, Phillip. "Photography Mise-en-Film: Autobiographical (Hi)stories and Psychic Apparatuses." In *Fugitive Images—From Photography to Video*, translated by Lynne Kirby, edited by Patrice Petro, 152–72 (Bloomington: Indiana University Press, 1995).

Du Colombier, Pierre. *Lettres du Poussin*. Paris: La Cité des Livres, 1929.

Dumarsais, César Chesneau. *Traités des Tropes*. Leipzig: Caspar Fritsch, 1757.

Elkins, James. "What Do We Want Photography to Be? A Response to Michael Fried." *Critical Inquiry* 31 (Summer 2005): 938–56.

Elsaesser, Thomas. "Stop/Motion." In *Between Stillness and Motion: Film, Photography, Algorithms*, 109–22 Amsterdam: Amsterdam University Press, 2011.
Falkenburg, Reindert. "The Household of the Soul: Conformity in the *Merode Triptych*." In *Early Netherlandish Painting at the Crossroads: A Critical Look at Current Methodologies*, edited by Maryan W. Ainsworth, 2–17. New Haven, CT: Yale University Press, 1998.
Fisher, Elizabeth, and Rebecca Fortnum, eds. *On Not Knowing: How Artists Think*. London: Black Dog Publishing, 2013.
Flusser, Vilém. *Towards a Philosophy of Photography*. London: Reaktion Books, 2006.
Fock, C. Willemijn. "Semblance or Reality: The Domestic Interior in Seventeenth-Century Dutch Genre Painting." In *Art and Home: Dutch Interiors in the Age of Rembrandt*, edited by Mariët Westermann. Zwolle: Waanders, 2001.
Foster, Hal. *The Return of the Real*. Cambridge, MA: MIT Press, 1996.
Foucault, Michel. *The Order of Things: An Archaeology of the Human Sciences*. London: Verso, 1992.
———. *This Is Not a Pipe*. Berkeley: University of California Press, 1984.
Franciscono, Marcel. *Paul Klee, His Work and Thought*. Chicago: University of Chicago Press, 1991.
Franits, Wayne E. *Paragons of Virtue: Women and Domesticity in Seventeenth-Century Dutch Art*. Cambridge: Cambridge University Press, 1995.
Friday, Jonathan. "Stillness Becoming: Reflections on Bazin, Barthes, and Photographic Stillness." In *Stillness and Time: Photography and the Moving Image*, edited by David Green and Joanna Lowry, 39–54. Brighton: Photoworks, 2005.
Fried, Michael. *Absorption and Theatricality: Painting and Beholder in the Age of Diderot*. Chicago: University of Chicago Press, 1988.
———. "Barthes' *Punctum*." *Critical Inquiry* 31, no. 3 (Spring 2005): 539–74.
———. *Why Photography Matters as Art as Never Before*. New Haven, CT: Yale University Press, 2008.
Gaier, Ulrich. "Metadisziplinäre Argumente und Verfahren Herders: Zum Beispiel: Die Erfindung der Soziologie." In *Herder Yearbook: Publication of the International Herder Society*, edited by Karl Menges, Wulf Koepke, and Wilfried Malsch, 59–79. Columbia, SC: Camden House, 1992.
Gasché, Rodolphe. *The Honor of Thinking: Critique, Theory, Philosophy*. Stanford, CA: Stanford University Press, 2007.
———. *The Tain of the Mirror: Derrida and the Philosophy of Reflection*. Cambridge, MA: Harvard University Press, 1986.
Gasquet, Joachim. *Cézanne: A Memoir with Conversations*. Translated by Christopher Pemberton. London: Thames & Hudson, 1991.
Gell, Alfred. *Art and Agency: An Anthropological Theory*. Oxford: Clarendon, 1998.
———. "The Technology of Enchantment and the Enchantment of Technology." In *Anthropology, Art and Aesthetics*, edited by J. Coote and A. Shelton, 40–66. Oxford: Clarendon, 1992.

Gersaint, Edmé-François. *Catalogue raisonné d'une collection considerable de diverses curiosités en tous genres, continuës dans les cabinets de feu Monsieur Bonnier de la Mosson*. Paris, 1744.

Gockel, Bettina, and Miriam Vomert, eds. *Vom Objekt zum Bild: piktorale Prozesse in Kunst und Wissenschaft, 1600–2000*. Berlin: Akademie Verlag, 2011.

Goeree, Willem. *Inleyding tot de praktyk der algemeene schilderkonst* . . . Amsterdam: Andries van Damme, 1704.

Goethe, Johann Wolfgang von. "Observations on the Laocoon." In *Goethe on Art*, edited and translated by John Gage, 78–88. London: Scholar Press, 1980.

Gombrich, Ernst. "Moment and Movement in Art." In *The Image and the Eye: Further Studies in the Psychology of Pictorial Representation*, 40–54. London: Phaidon, 1994.

Graw, Isabelle, Daniel Birnbaum, and Nikolaus Hirsch, eds. *Thinking through Painting: Reflexivity and Agency beyond the Canvas*. Berlin: Sternberg Press, 2012.

Greif, Stefan. "'Wer kann Farben tönen?' Schöpfung, Wahrnehmung und Landschaft in Herders Hieroglyphen-Ästhetik." In *Herder Yearbook* VII (2004), edited by Wulf Koepke and Karl Menges, 31–44. Heidelberg: Synchron Wissenschafts-verlag der Autoren, 2004.

Grootenboer, Hanneke. "Arresting What Would Otherwise Slip Away: The Waiting Images of Jacob Vrel." In *Time in the History of Art: Temporality, Chronology, and Anachrony*, edited by Dan Karlholm and Keith Moxey, 119–32. London: Routledge, 2018.

———. "A Clock Picture as a Philosophical Experiment: The Tableau Mécanique in the Physics Cabinet of Bonnier de la Mosson." *Art History* 39, no. 2 (April 2016): 340–55.

———. "How to Become a Picture: Theatricality as Strategy in Early Modern Portraiture." Caroline van Eck and Stijn Bussels, eds. In "Theatricality in Early Modern Visual Art and Architecture." Special issue, *Art History* 33, no. 2 (April 2010): 221–32.

———. "Reading the Annunciation." *Art History* 30, no. 3 (June 2007): 349–63.

———. *The Rhetoric of Perspective: Realism and Illusionism in Seventeenth-Century Dutch Still Life Painting*. Chicago: University of Chicago Press, 2005.

———. "Sublime Still Life: on Adriaen Coorte, Elias van den Broeck, and the *Je ne sais quoi* of Painting." *Journal of the Historians of Netherlandish Art* 8, no. 2 (Summer 2016), https://doi.org/10.5092/jhna.2016.8.2.10.

———. "The Substance of Wax." In "Theorizing Wax: On the Meaning of a Disappearing Medium," edited by Allison Goudie and Hanneke Grootenboer. Special issue, *Oxford Art Journal* 36, no. 1 (March 2013): 1–12.

———. *Treasuring the Gaze: Intimate Vision in Late Eighteenth-Century Eye Miniatures*. Chicago: University of Chicago Press, 2012.

Harrison, Charles, Paul Wood, and Jason Gaiger, eds. *Art in Theory 1648–1815: An Anthology of Changing Ideas*. Oxford: Blackwell, 2000.

Hayes, Julie Chandler. *Reading the French Enlightenment: System and Subversion.* Cambridge: Cambridge University Press, 2004.

Hegel, G. W. F. "Aphorism from the Wastebook." *Independent Journal of Philosophy* 3 (1979): 1–6.

———. *The Hegel Reader.* Edited by Stephen Houlgate. Oxford: Blackwell, 1998.

———. *Hegel's Aesthetics: Lectures on Fine Art.* 2 vols., translated by T. M. Knox. Oxford: Clarendon Press, 1988.

———. *The Phenomenology of Spirit.* Translated by A. V. Miller. Oxford: Oxford University Press, 1977.

———. *The Science of Logic.* Edited by Giovanni di George. Cambridge: Cambridge University Press, 2010.

Heidegger, Martin. "Art and Space." Translated by Charles Seibert. *Man and World* 1 (1973): 3–7. Originally published as *Die Kunst und der Raum*, with illustrations by Eduardo Chillida. St. Gallen: Erker, 1969.

———. *Basic Writings.* London: Routledge, 2011.

———. *Being and Time.* Translated by Joan Stambaugh. Albany: State University of New York Press, 1996.

———. "Building Dwelling Thinking." In *Poetry, Language, Thought*, translated by Albert Hofstadter, 143–62. New York: Harper & Row, 1975.

———. *An Introduction to Metaphysics.* New Haven, CT: Yale University Press, 1959.

———. "The Origin of the Work of Art." In *The Art of Art History: A Critical Anthology*, edited by Donald Preziosi, 413–26. Oxford: Oxford University Press, 1998.

———. *What Is Called Thinking.* Translated by J. Glenn Gray. New York: Harper & Row, 2004.

Herder, Johann Gottfried. "Aelteste Urkunde." In vol. 6 of *Sämmtliche Werke*, 33 vols., edited by B. Suphan et al., 302–3. Berlin, 1877–1913.

———. "Aphorism from the Wastebook." *Independent Journal of Philosophy* 3 (1979): 1–6.

———. "Critical Forests, or Reflections on the Art and Science of the Beautiful: First Grove, Dedicated to Mr Lessing's Laocoön." In *Selected Writings on Aesthetics*, translated and edited by Gregory Moore, 51–176. Princeton, NJ: Princeton University Press, 2006.

———. "Nemesis." In *Sämmtliche Werke.* Vol. 4, *Schriften zu Philosophie, Literatur, Kunst und Altertum 1774–1787*, edited by J. Brummack and M. Bollacher, 549–78. Frankfurt: Deutscher Klassiker Verlag, 1994.

———. *Sämmtliche Werke.* Vol. 8, edited by Bernhard Suphan, Carl Redlich, and Reinhold Steig. Berlin, 1892; repr., Hildesheim: Olms, 1967.

———. *Selected Writings on Aesthetics.* Translated and edited by Gregory Moore. Princeton, NJ: Princeton University Press, 2006.

Hill, C. R. "The Cabinet of Bonnier de la Mosson (1702–1744)." *Annals of Science* 43, no. 2 (1986): 147–74.

Ho, Angela. "Gerrit Dou's Enchanting Trompe l'Oeil: Virtuosity and Agency in Early

Modern Collections." *Journal of Historians of Netherlandish Art* 7, no. 1 (2015), https://doi.org/10.5092/jhna.205.7.1.1.

Hollander, Martha. *An Entrance for the Eyes: Space and Meaning in Seventeenth-Century Dutch Art*. Berkeley: University of California Press, 2002.

Holly, Michael Ann. "Witnessing and Annunciation." In *Past Looking: Historical Imagination and the Rhetoric of the Image*, 149–69. Ithaca, NY: Cornell University Press, 1996.

Hunter, Matthew, and Francesco Lucchini, eds. *The Clever Object*. Chichester: Wiley-Blackwell, 2013.

Husserl, Edmund. "Psychological Studies in the Elements of Logic." In *Husserl: Shorter Works*, edited by P. McCormick and F. Elliston, 126–42. South Bend, IN: Notre Dame University Press, 1981.

Hyppolite, Jean. *Logic and Existence*. Albany: State of New York University Press, 1997.

Joselit, David. "Painting Beside Itself." *October* 130 (Fall 2009): 125–34.

Junius, Francis. *The Painting of the Ancients*. n.p., 1638.

Kant, Immanuel. *Critique of Pure Reason*. Translated by N. K. Smith. New York: MacMillan, 1968.

———. "Observations on the Feeling of the Beautiful and the Sublime." In *Observations on the Feeling of the Beautiful and the Sublime and Other Writings*, edited by Patrick Frierson and Paul Guyer, 13–62. Cambridge: Cambridge University Press, 2011.

King, Magda. *A Guide to Heidegger's Being and Time*. Edited by John Llewelyn. Albany: State University of New York Press, 2001.

Klee, Paul. *The Thinking Eye*. Vol. 1 of *The Notebooks of Paul Klee*, edited by Jürg Spiller, translated by Ralph Manheim. San Francisco: Wittenborn Art Books, 2013.

Kleist, Heinrich von. "Emotions before Friedrich's Seascape." In Harrison, Wood, and Gaiger, *Art in Theory 1648–1815*, 1031–32.

Koerner, Joseph. *Casper David Friedrich and the Subject of Landscape*. London: Reaktion Books, 2009.

Kolfin, Elmer. *Voor Koningen en Prinsen: De Stillevens en Landschappen van Jan van Huysum (1682–1749)*. Delft: Museum Het Prinsenhof, 2006.

Lairesse, Gerard de. *Groot Schilderboek*. 2 vols. Amsterdam, 1712.

Lang, Karen. "The Dialectics of Decay: Rereading the Kantian Subject." *Art Bulletin* 79, no. 3 (September 1997): 413–39.

Laruelle, François. *The Concept of Non-Photography*. Falmouth and New York: Urbanomic and Sequence, 2011.

———. *Photo-Fiction: A Non-Standard Aesthetics*. Minneapolis, MN: Univocal, 2012.

Latour, Bruno. *Reassembling the Social: An Introduction to Actor-Network-Theory*. Oxford: Oxford University Press, 2005.

Law, Jules David. *The Rhetoric of Empiricism: Language and Perception from Locke to I. A. Richards*. Ithaca, NY: Cornell University Press, 1993.

Lebensztejn, Jean-Claude, and Kate Cooper. "Photorealism, Kitsch and Venturi." *SubStance* 10, no. 2 (1981): 75–104.

Leonardo da Vinci's Codex Leicester. Vol. 1, *The Codex*, edited by Domenico Laurenza and Martin Kemp. Oxford: Oxford University Press, 2019.

Lessing, Gotthold Ephraim. *Laocoön: An Essay on the Limits of Painting and Poetry*. Edited by E. A. McCormick. Baltimore, MD: Johns Hopkins University Press, 1984.

Llewelyn, John. "On the Saying That Philosophy Begins in *Thaumazein*." *Afterall: A Journal of Art, Context and Enquiry* 4 (Winter 2001): 48–57.

Locke, John. *An Essay Concerning Human Understanding*. Oxford: Oxford University Press, 1975.

Luyken, Jan. *Het leerzaam huisraad in vijftig figuuren*. Amsterdam: Wed. P. Arentz en K. vander Sys, 1711.

Lynes, Barbara Buhler, and Jonathan Weinberg. *Shared Intelligence: American Painting and the Photograph*. Berkeley: University of California Press, 2011.

Lyons, John D. *Before Imagination: Embodied Thought from Montaigne to Rousseau*. Stanford, CA: Stanford University Press, 2005.

Lyotard, Jean-François. "The Sublime and the Avant-Garde." In *The Continental Aesthetics Reader*, edited by Clive Cazeaux, 453–64. London: Routledge, 2000.

Magritte, René. "Letter to Michel Foucault." In *This Is Not a Pipe*, translated by James Harkness. Berkeley: University of California Press, 2008.

Marin, Louis. "The Classical Sublime: 'Tempests' in Some Landscapes by Poussin." In *Sublime Poussin*, 120–42. Stanford, CA: Stanford University Press, 1999.

———. *On Representation*. Translated by Catherine Porter. Stanford, CA: Stanford University Press, 2001.

———. "The Sublime in the 1670s: Something Indefinable, a 'Je Ne Sais Quoi'?" In *Sublime Poussin*, 209–23. Stanford, CA: Stanford University Press, 1999.

Martin, Wayne. "Bubbles and Skulls: The Phenomenology of Self-Consciousness in Dutch Still Life Painting." In *A Companion to Phenomenology and Existentialism*, edited by Hubert L. Dreyfus and Mark A. Wrathall, 559–84. London: Blackwell, 2006.

Melehy, Hasson. *Writing Cogito: Montaigne, Descartes, and the Institution of the Modern Subject*. Albany: State University of New York Press, 1997.

Melion, Walter. "Introduction: Meditating on Pictures." In *Ut Pictura Meditation: The Meditative Image in Northern Art, 1500–1700*, edited by Walter Melion, Ralph Dekoninck, and Agnes Duiderdoni-Bruselé, 1–60. Turnhout: Brepolis, 2012.

Merjian, Ara H. *Giorgio de Chirico and the Metaphysical City: Nietzsche, Modernism, Paris*. New Haven, CT: Yale University Press, 2014.

———. "Untimely Objects: Giorgio de Chirico's 'The Evil Genius of a King' (1914) between the Antediluvian and the Posthuman." *Res* 57/58 (Spring/Autumn 2010): 186–208.

Merleau-Ponty, Maurice. "Cézanne's Doubt." In *Sense and Non-Sense*, 9–25. Evanston, IL: Northwestern University Press, 1964.

———. "Eye and Mind." In *The Primacy of Perception*, 159–90. Evanston, IL: Northwestern University Press, 1964.

Michelson, Annette. “De Stijl, Its Other Face: Abstraction and Cacaphony, or What Was the Matter with Hegel?” *October* 22 (Autumn 1982).

Miller, Jonathan. *On Reflection*. London: National Gallery, 1998.

Mitchell, W. J. T. “What Do Pictures Want?” *October* 77 (Summer 1996): 71–82.

Montaigne, Michel de. *Essays*. Translated and edited with an introduction and notes by M. A. Screech. London: Penguin, 1991.

Müller-Michaels, Harro. “Herder: Denkbilder der Kulturen. Herders poetisches und didaktisches Konzept der Denkbilder.” In *Nationen und Kulturen. Zum 250. Geburtstag Johann Gottfried Herders*, edited by R. Otto, 65–76. Würzburg: Königshausen & Neumann, 1996.

Mulvey, Laura. *Death 24x a Second: Stillness and the Moving Image*. London: Reaktion Books, 2006.

Mundy, Peter. *The Travels of Peter Mundy in Europe and Asia, 1608–1667*. 4 vols. Edited by Richard Carnac Temple. London, 1925.

Nancy, Jean-Luc. *Hegel: The Restlessness of the Negative*. Minneapolis: University of Minnesota Press, 2002.

———. “The Image—the Distinct.” In *The Ground of the Image*, 1–15. New York: Fordham University Press, 2005.

———. *The Muses*. Stanford, CA: Stanford University Press, 1996.

———. *The Speculative Remark: On One of Hegel’s Bon Mots*. Stanford, CA: Stanford University Press, 2002.

Nemerov, Alexander. “The Boy in Bed: The Scene of Reading in N. C. Wyeth’s *Wreck of the ‘Covenant.’*” *Art Bulletin* 88 (March 2006): 7–27.

Nijland-Verwey, Mea. “Denkbeeld-Denkbild.” *Duitse Kroniek* 14, no. 1 (1962): 31–37.

Nisbet, Hugh. *Herder and the Philosophy of Science*. Cambridge: Cambridge University Press, 1970.

Norton, Robert E. “Towards an Ontology of the Arts: The First *Kritisches Wäldchen*.” In *Herder’s Aesthetics and the European Enlightenment*. Ithaca, NY: Cornell University Press, 1991.

Pace, Claire. “Nicolas Poussin: ‘Peintre-Poete’?” In *Commemorating Poussin: Reception and Interpretation of the Artist*, edited by Katie Scott and Genevieve Warwick, 76–113. Cambridge: Cambridge University Press, 1999.

Panofsky, Erwin. *Perspective as Symbolic Form*. Translated by Christopher Wood. New York: Zone Books, 1997.

Pepys, Samuel. *The Diary of Samuel Pepys: A Selection*. London: Penguin, 2003.

Philostratus the Elder. “Narcissus.” In *Elder Philostratus, Younger Philostratus, Callistratus*, trans. Arthur Fairbanks, 89–92. Cambridge, MA: Harvard University Press, 1931.

Pijzel-Dommisse, Jet. *Het Hollandse Pronkpoppenhuis: Interieur en Huishouden in de 17e en 18e eeuw*. Amsterdam: Waanders, 2000.

Pippin, Robert. *Hegel and Self-Consciousness: Desire and Death in the Phenomenology of Spirit*. Princeton, NJ: Princeton University Press, 2014.

Plato. *The Republic*. In *Aesthetics: A Comprehensive Anthology*, edited by Steven M. Cahn and Aaron Meskin, 24–33. Oxford: Blackwell, 2008.

Pointon, Marcia. *Brilliant Effects: A Cultural History of Gemstones and Jewellery*. New Haven, CT: Yale University Press, 2009.

Potts, Alex. Introduction to *History of the Art of Antiquity*, by Johann Joachim Winckelmann, translated by Harry Francis Mallgrave, 1–53. Los Angeles: Getty Research Institute.

———. *Flesh and the Ideal: Winckelmann and the Origins of Art History*. New Haven, CT: Yale University Press, 2000.

Proust, Marcel. "Rembrandt." In *Marcel Proust on Art and Literature*, edited and translated by Sylvia Townsend Warner, 37–44. New York: Carroll & Graf, 1984.

Puttfarken, Thomas. "Poussin's Thoughts on Invention and Disposition." In *The Discovery of Pictorial Composition: Theories of Visual Order in Painting 1400–1800*. New Haven, CT: Yale University Press, 1999.

Rancière, Jacques. "The Pensive Image." In *The Emancipated Spectator*, 107–32. London: Verso, 2009.

Richard Estes—Recent Paintings. New York: Allan Stone Gallery, 1968. Exhibition catalog.

Richter, Gerhard. *Thought-Images: Frankfurt School Writers' Reflections from Damaged Life*. Stanford, CA: Stanford University Press, 2007.

Richter, Simon. *Laocoon's Body and the Aesthetics of Pain: Winckelmann, Lessing, Herder, Moritz, Goethe*. Detroit, MI: Wayne State University Press, 1992.

Rodis-Lewis, Geneviève. "Descartes' Life and the Development of His Philosophy." In *The Cambridge Companion to Descartes*, edited by John Cottingham, 21–57. Cambridge: Cambridge University Press, 1992.

Roland, Michel M. "Le Cabinet de Bonnier de la Mosson et la participation de Lajoue." *Bulletin de la société de l'histoire de l'art français* 1975 (1976): 211–21.

Rosenblum, Robert. "Vilhelm Hammershøi, at Home and Abroad." In *Vilhelm Hammershøi 1864–1916: Danish Painter of Solitude and Light*, 31–48. Copenhagen: Ordrupgaard; New York: Guggenheim Museum, 1998.

Røssaak, Eivind. *The Still/Moving Image: Cinema and the Arts*. Lap Lambert Academic Publishing, 2010.

Rush, Fred. "Still Life and the End of Painting." In *The Art of Hegel's Aesthetics: Hegelian Philosophy and the Perspectives of Art History*, edited by Paul Kottman and Michael Squire, 159–88. Leiden: Wilhelm Vink, 2017.

Sallis, John. "Carnation and the Eccentricity of Painting." In *Hegel and the Arts*, edited by Stephen Houlgate, 90–118. Evanston, IL: Northwestern University Press, 2007.

Schapiro, Meyer. "The Still Life as a Personal Object—A Note on Heidegger and van Gogh." In *The Art of Art History: A Critical Anthology*, edited by Donald Preziosi, 427–31. Oxford: Oxford University Press, 1998.

Schor, Naomi. "Pensive Texts and Thinking Statues: Balzac with Rodin." *Critical Inquiry* 27, no. 2 (Winter 2001): 239–65.

Schutz, Eberhard Wilhelm. "Zum Wort 'Denkbild.'" In *Wort und Zeit. Aufsätze und Vorträge zur Literaturgeschichte*. Kieler Studien zur deutschen Literaturgeschichte 6. Neumünster: Wachholtz, 1968.

Segal, S., M. Ellens, and J. Dik, eds. *De Verleiding van Flora: Jan van Huysum 1682–1749*. Zwolle: Waanders Uitgevers, 2006.

Sharr, Adam. *Heidegger's Hut*. Cambridge, MA: MIT Press, 2006.

Shershow, Scott Cutler. *Puppets and Popular Culture*. Ithaca, NY: Cornell University Press, 1995.

Shiff, Richard. *Cézanne and the End of Impressionism*. Chicago: University of Chicago Press, 1984.

Sims, Patterson. "Richard Estes' Realism." In *Richard Estes' Realism*. Portland, ME: Portland Museum of Art, 2014.

Smith, Paul. "Cézanne's 'Primitive' Perspective, or the 'View from Everywhere.'" *Art Bulletin* 95, no. 1 (March 2013): 102–19.

Spaans, Joke. "Art, Science and Religion in Romeyn de Hooghe's *Hieroglyphica*." *Nederlands Kunsthistorisch Jaarboek* 61 (2011): 283–307.

Stewart, Garrett. *Framed Time: Toward a Postfilmic Cinema*. Chicago: University of Chicago Press, 2007.

———. "Photogravure: Death, Photography and Film Narrative." *Wide Angle* 9, no. 6 (1987): 11–31.

———. *Transmedium: Conceptualism 2.0 and the New Object Art*. Chicago: University of Chicago Press, 2017.

Stewart, Susan. *On Longing: Narratives of the Miniature, the Gigantic, the Souvenir, the Collection*. Durham, NC: Duke University Press, 1993.

Stimilli, Davide. "Daimon and Nemesis." *RES: Anthropology and Aesthetics* 44 (Autumn 2003): 99–112.

Stoichita, Victor. *The Self-Aware Image: An Insight into Early Modern Meta-Painting*. Cambridge: Cambridge University Press, 1997.

———. *A Short History of the Shadow*. London: Reaktion Books, 1997.

Taminiaux, Jacques. "The Thinker and the Painter." In *Poetics, Speculation and Judgment: The Shadow of the Work of Art from Kant to Phenomenology*, translated by Michael Gendre, 171–85. Albany: State University of New York Press, 1993.

Temple, William. *The Work of William Temple, bart*. 2 vols. London: F. C. and J. Rivington, 1815.

Trabant, Jürgen. "Herder and Language." In Adler and Koepke, *A Companion to the Works of Johann Gottfried Herder*, 119–21.

Van Alphen, Ernst. *Art and Mind: How Contemporary Images Shape Thought*. Chicago: University of Chicago Press, 2005.

Van Eck, Caroline. Introduction to *Art, Agency and Living Presence: From the Animated Image to the Excessive Object*, 11–28. Boston: De Gruyter, 2015.

Van Gogh, Vincent. *The Complete Letters of Vincent van Gogh*, vol. 2. London: Thames & Hudson, 1958.

Van Gool, Johan. *De Nieuwe Schouburg der Nederlantsche Kunstschilders en Schilderessen*, vol. 2. The Hague, 1751.

Vanhaelen, Angela. "Boredom's Threshold: Dutch Realism." In "The Erotics of Looking: Materiality, Solicitation and Netherlandish Visual Culture," edited by Angela Vanhaelen and Bronwen Wilson. Special issue, *Art History* 35, no. 5 (2012): 1004–23.

Van Hoogstraten, Samuel. *Inleyding tot de hooge schoole der schilderkonst; anders de zichtbaere werelt*. Rotterdam, 1678.

Van Oostveldt, Bram, and Stijn Bussels. "Introduction: The Sublime and Seventeenth-Century Netherlandish Art." *Journal of the Historians of Netherlandish Art* 8, no. 2 (Summer 2016).

Verbraeken, René. *Clair-Obscur: Histoire d'un Mot*. Nogent-le-Roi: Jacques Laget, 1979.

Verwey, Albert. "Oorsprongen." *Tweemaandelijksch Tijdschrift* 4 (1897–98): 115.

Vico, Giambattista. *The New Science of Giambattista Vico*. Translated by T. G. Bergin and M. H. Fisch. Ithaca, NY: Cornell University Press, 1986.

Vinegar, Aron. "Reluzenz: On Richard Estes." In *Heidegger and the Work of Art History*, by Aron Vinegar and Amanda Boetzkes, 249–65. London: Ashgate, 2014.

Wagner, Hans. *Philosophie und Reflexion*. Wurzburg: Ernst Reinhardt, 1959.

Weigel, Sigrid. "Thought-Images: A Re-reading of the Angel of History." In *Body- and Image-Space: Re-reading Walter Benjamin*. London: Routledge, 1996.

Weinberg, Jonathan. "Introduction: Making It Real." In *Shared Intelligence: American Painting and the Photograph*, edited by Barbara Buhler Lynes and Jonathan Weinbert, 2–27. Berkeley: University of California Press, 2011.

———. "Photographic Guilt: The Painter and the Camera." In *Robert Bechtle: A Retrospective*, edited by Janet Bishop et al., 46–61. Berkeley: University of California Press, 2005.

Wellbery, David E. *Lessing's Laocoon: Semiotics and Aesthetics in the Age of Reason*. Cambridge: Cambridge University Press, 1984.

Westermann, Mariët. *Art and Home: Dutch Interiors in the Age of Rembrandt*. Zwolle: Waanders Publishers, 2001.

———. *A Worldly Art: The Dutch Republic, 1585–1718*. New Haven, CT: Yale University Press, 2005.

Weststeijn, Thijs. "Een Wereldse Kunst." Inaugural lecture, Utrecht University, October 2017.

———. "From Hieroglyphs to Universal Characters: Pictography in the Early Modern Netherlands." *Nederlands Kunsthistorisch Jaarboek* 61 (2011): 23981.

———. *The Visible World: Samuel van Hoogstraten's Art Theory and the Legitimation of Painting in the Dutch Golden Age*. Amsterdam: Amsterdam University Press, 2008.

Wiedmann, Franz. *Hegel: An Illustrated Biography*. Translated by Joachim Neugroschel. New York: Pegasus, 1968.

Wigley, Mark. "The Domestication of the House." In *The Architecture of Deconstruction: Derrida's Haunt*, 97–121. Cambridge, MA: MIT Press, 1995.

Wilmerding, John. *Richard Estes*. New York: Rizzoli, 2006.

Winckelmann, Johann Joachim. "Description of the Torso in the Belvedere in Rome" (1759). In *Essays on the Philosophy and History of Art*, edited and translated by Curtis Bowman. Bristol: Thoemmes Press, 2001.

———. "Geschichte der Kunst des Altertums." In *Werke*, vol. 3, edited by Heinrich Mener and Johann Schulze, 64–73. Dresden, 1807.

———. *History of the Art of Antiquity*. Translated by Harry Francis Mallgrave. Los Angeles: Getty Publications, 2006.

Wolf, Bryan Jay. *Vermeer and the Invention of Seeing*. Chicago: University of Chicago Press, 2001.

Wollen, Peter. "Time, Image and Terror." In *Time and the Image*, edited by Carolyn Bailey Gill, 149–60. Manchester: Manchester University Press, 2000.

Wood, Christopher. *Forgery Replica Fiction: Temporalities of German Renaissance Art*. Chicago: University of Chicago Press, 2008.

———. Introduction to *Perspective as Symbolic Form*, by Erwin Panofsky, 7–26. New York: Zone Books, 1997.

Woodall, Joanna. "Laying the Table. The Procedures of Still Life." In "The Erotics of Looking: Materiality, Solicitation and Netherlandish Visual Culture," edited by Angela Vanhaelen and Bronwen Wilson. Special issue, *Art History* 35, no. 5 (2012): 976–1003.

———. "Sovereign Bodies: The Reality of Status in Seventeenth-Century Dutch Portraiture." In *Portraiture: Facing the Subject*, edited by Joanna Woodall, 75–100. Manchester: Manchester University Press, 1997.

Yates, Frances A. *The Art of Memory*. London: Routledge, 2012.

Index

Page numbers in **bold** indicate images of artworks.